My Self
My Family
My Friends

26 Experts Explore
Young Children's
Self-esteem

edited by
Betty Farber, M.Ed.

Preschool
Publications, Inc.

Preschool Publications, Inc.
Cutchogue, New York, U.S.A.

My Self   My Family   My Friends
26 Experts Explore Young Children's Self-esteem
Edited by: Betty Farber, M.Ed.

Cover Design: Lester Feldman
Book Illustrations: Susan Eaddy
Book Design: Arthur Farber

Material adapted from articles that appeared in
Parent and preschooler Newsletter issues prior to 1997.

© 2000 Betty Farber
ISBN 1-881425-07-X   printed in the United States of America

For ordering information please contact:
Betty Farber, President, Preschool Publications, Inc.
P.O. Box 1167, Cutchogue, NY 11935-0888, U.S.A.
Voice: U.S.A. 1.800.726.1708 • International 631.765.5450
Fax: 631.765.4927 • E-mail: preschoolpub@hamptons.com
Web site: www.preschoolpublications.com

Library of Congress Cataloging-in-Publication Data

My self, my family, my friends: 26 experts explore young children's
self-esteem / edited by Betty Farber.
    p. cm.
   Includes bibliographical references.
   ISBN 1-881425-07-X (pbk.)
   1. Self-esteem in children. 2. Child rearing. I. Farber, Betty.

BF723.S3 F37 2000
155.42'382—dc21

                      99-089706

Other Books
about Young Children
Published by
Preschool Publications, Inc.

The Parents' & Teachers' Guide
to Helping Young Children Learn:
Creative Ideas from 35 Experts

Guiding Young Children's Behavior:
Helpful Ideas for Parents & Teachers
from 28 Early Childhood Experts

CONTENTS

SECTION FOUR
BALANCING ACTIVITIES AND RELAXATION

SECTION FIVE
FEELINGS

SECTION SIX
ENCOURAGING YOUNG CHILDREN'S
POSITIVE VIEWS OF FAMILY

vi

Foreword

We all want what's best for our children. We want them to grow up strong and healthy. We want them to have the skills and confidence to face obstacles, to believe in themselves and their abilities. There is nothing that encourages achievement and protects against failure as effectively as children's certainty that they can, through work and effort, meet all challenges.

How can we help our children do this? That's where *My Self, My Family, My Friends* comes in. Twenty-six early childhood experts combine their wisdom and experience to help you guide your child to a strong, enduring sense of self-esteem and competence.

Section One describes the building blocks of the process: how to encourage young children's positive view of themselves. It talks about the importance of cherishing children, of meeting their basic needs so they can go on to reach higher and go further.

Of course, each child is unique. Sections Two through Four focus on children as individuals, and explores the influences on their growth and development. It answers questions such as: What do children need at different ages? Are boys really different from girls, or is it that we treat them differently? It also reminds us that children need balance in their lives and offers wonderful suggestions for ways to unwind. You may want to try some of these for yourself!

How do children come to understand their emotions and their power? How do children learn to manage their feelings? Section Five comes to the rescue with the perfect combination of advice, activities, and solutions.

Section Six focuses on the situations families face: siblings' issues, the joys of grandparents, heritage and traditions — it's all here.

Finally, children's relationships extend beyond family, so Sections Seven and Eight take you through the other side of children's lives: making and keeping friends, and learning how to get along with others in the world.

And so, here's the complete guide to children's self-esteem and its relationship to the people in your child's environment in one wonderful package. But this book does more than that. Not only is there background and theory, the how and why of children's development, there are also ways to put this knowledge into action with practical down-to-earth suggestions and ideas. Even more, each section offers information on books and resource materials for you and your child. Perhaps it should be called, *How to become a wiser and more confident parent.*

Neala S. Schwartzberg, Ph.D.
Developmental Psychologist,
Editor, Parent and preschooler Newsletter,
and regular contributor to health and parenting publications.

ix

Section One

Encouraging Young Children's Positive Views of Self

Section One
Encouraging
Young Children's
Positive Views of Self

Introduction

With fingers flying, a child unwraps a package. Inside is a gift she wants and needs. As you watch, you take pleasure in her delight. What could be more satisfying than a gift that brings joy to both the giver and the receiver?

 The contributors to this section describe a gift that every parent, teacher, and caregiver can afford, and that every child yearns for — the gift of self-esteem.

What does a child need in order to emerge as an individual with a feeling of self-worth? Children need to believe they are lovable and capable. They need to feel that they have a secure base, provided by parents and other caregivers. From the security provided by others, children can develop their own security.

What can parents do to encourage young children's self-esteem? They can give their children time, attention, and loving words. What can they avoid doing? They can avoid labeling their youngster, or talking about their child's weaknesses in front of others.

According to the authors in this section, birthdays are not the only days to celebrate your child. With the help offered in these chapters, you can celebrate your child all year.

SECTION ONE
ENCOURAGING YOUNG CHILDREN'S
POSITIVE VIEWS OF SELF

Chapter 1
A Celebration
of Self

Betty Farber

*Her self-concept, the total picture
she has of herself, includes how she feels
about her body, her mental abilities
and her interactions with others.*

The Self-Concept

Emily enjoys trying out new tricks on the jungle gym, likes to make new friends, and begins school with the expectation that all will go well. She knows that she **matters** to the important people in her life and sees herself as likeable. Her self-concept, the total picture she has of herself, includes how she feels about her body, her mental abilities and her interactions with others. Emily has a positive self-concept.

A child with a positive self-concept has high self-esteem: she values herself as a person of worth. She can accept her failures, because she knows that she can continue to learn and improve.

How the Self-concept is Formed

Young children's self-image is formed mainly by family members, teachers, and caregivers. Of these significant persons, parents are the most influential. Youngsters receive messages from parents and others, both verbally (what is said to them) and nonverbally (gesture and facial expression). From these messages, children evaluate how these significant persons feel about them. If the messages are mainly positive, youngsters are more likely to feel good about themselves.

Helping Children Develop a Positive Self-Concept

Set Reasonable Limits

Young children need parental guidelines for behavior. Parents can show that they have the confidence in their children to give them freedom within the limits that have been set.

Offer Choices

When parents offer choices to children at appropriate times it indicates that they are trusted to make decisions. This helps children to have confidence in themselves. Even very young children can make simple choices. Parents can ask, "Do you want to wear your red overalls or your blue ones?" If children start making choices at an early age, they will have had some practice to make really important decisions when they get old enough. (Hint: Only give choices when you will be able to accept your child's decision. For example: don't ask, "Do you want to eat now?" when the lunch is all ready on the table and getting cold.)

Set Realistic Expectations

Young children want to feel important and competent, but, in truth, they are limited in their abilities. There are many things that they cannot do very well as yet. Parents can keep their expectations realistic and praise their preschoolers' efforts toward competence. If your preschooler can't run as fast as her friend, tell her, "You sure tried hard, and that's the important thing." If your three-year-old shows you a picture he has drawn, you need not judge it as good or bad. Instead, look at his face, read his expression, and say, "You feel awfully proud of that picture, don't you?"

Birthday Celebrations

Give Children a Chance to Participate
Another way of raising children's self-esteem is to allow your youngsters to participate in planning family celebrations. For example, they can help to plan their own birthday parties. Even a two-year-old can decide if he wants apple juice or orange juice at his party. And as they grow older, preschoolers can help to shop for candy, make invitations, decide on games and choose their favorite cake. All of these activities help children to have feelings of self-confidence.

Birthdays are times when children can celebrate themselves. Make it their very special day. The following activities help to do honor to the occasion:

1. Birthday hat. Materials: construction paper, round edged scissors, glue, crayons, tape. Let your child help you cut strips of construction paper 2 inches wide as a headband. Cut out rectangles in the shape of candles, 4 inches long and about 1 1/4 inches wide. The number of rectangles corresponds to the age of the birthday child. Glue the "candles" to the inside of the headband. Write the child's name on the front. Tape the headband in the back, to fit the child's head.

2. Birthday throne. Materials: chair, crepe paper, construction paper, crayons. Decorate the chair for the birthday child with different colored crepe paper streamers. Attach a "Happy Birthday" sign to the chair back (behind the chair so that the child will not lean against it.)

3. Birthday badge. <u>Materials:</u> cardboard, scissors, felt, construction paper, glitter, sequins, glue, safety pin, tape. Cut a three inch cardboard circle. Cut a felt circle to match. Glue the felt on to the cardboard. Cut the number of the child's age out of construction paper. Have the birthday child glue the number, along with sequins and glitter, on to the circle. Let the glue dry. Tape the safety pin on to the back of the badge and pin it on.

4. Invitations. <u>Materials:</u> construction paper, scissors, watercolor markers. Pick a theme for the party and make the invitations fit the theme. For example: a teddy bear party, a pirate party, a dinosaur party. Trace a picture from a coloring book for the outline of a teddy bear, etc. on to the construction paper and cut it out. Write the information as to time and place. Younger preschoolers can help you put the invitations into envelopes, stick on the stamps and mail them. Older children can help to cut out and write the invitations and sign their name.

Party Activities

1. Place mat souvenir. Give the children something to do until all the guests arrive. Distribute construction paper and crayons. Ask the children to draw a picture that they will use as a place mat and keep as a souvenir to remember the birthday party. When the drawings are finished, cover each picture with clear contact paper, for protection from spills. (For children who don't want to draw, give out stickers in various designs to make the picture.)

2. Pin the eyepatch on the pirate, (or the tail on the teddy bear, etc.) Play "Pin the Tail on the Donkey" a new way. For fun, use the theme of your party. For a " pirate" party, trace or draw a large pirate face and hang it on the wall. Cut out enough eye patches from construction paper to fit the number of children. Write each guest's name on an eyepatch, so you will remember whose patch it was. For safety, use tape instead of pins. Blindfold the children, one at a time, and see how close they get to the pirate's eye.

3. Plan more games than you think you'll need. See *Resources* on page 46 for lists of books describing party games and ideas.

4. Don't give prizes to those who win the games. Young children do not understand competition. They may become upset when another child gets a prize, while they do not. Instead, give each guest an inexpensive gift when it's time to go home.

Finger Plays

Finger plays are poems that combine words and gestures. Here are some that are appropriate for birthday parties.   (The gestures are described in parenthesis).

<u>The New Balloon</u>

Once I had a new balloon,
Big and red and round, (Make a circle with your fingers.)
But I didn't have it very long
For it made a funny sound. Pop! (Clap your hands once, loudly.)

<u>Baking a Cake</u>

Today is <u>Johnny's</u> birthday.
Let's bake him a cake.
Stir and mix; and stir, (Stir imaginary cake.)
Then put it in the oven to bake. (Place in oven.)
Out it comes so nice and round, (Make a circle with your fingers.)
Let's frost it pink and white. (Spread frosting.)
And put <u>4</u> candles on it (Hold up 4 fingers.)
To make a birthday light.
Wow! What a sight. (Blow out the candles).

Helpful Hints to Enhance Children's Self-esteem All Year

• Tape your preschooler's art work to the wall.

• Write a note to your child and mail it to him.

• Use adding machine tape to measure your youngster's height. Let her color the tape as this will give her an idea of how tall she is. Write the date on it and keep it to see how tall she grows.

• Sing a song using your child's name. This is useful when you and your child are cleaning his room together. You can sing, to the tune of "Here We Go 'Round the Mulberry Bush" "Johnny is a helper, a helper a helper, Johnny is a helper, picking up the toys."

• Take your child to your office for a visit, when you don't have to stay all day.

• Place a piece of plain wrapping paper on the floor. Have the child lie down on it and trace her outline. Let her draw in the face and the clothing with crayons. Cut it out and hang it up — a life-sized portrait.

Chapter 2
Encouraging Your Child's Positive Self-concept

Lee Jackson

*Children's self-image
is a reflection of
what their parents
or significant others
have told them.*

Janie's grandmother said, "I'm so glad you came to see us today!" Janie asked, "Why?" but then answered her own question with, "Because you like me?" "Of course," grandmother said, "Because we love you and you make us feel happy when you visit." You could almost see the warm glow rush through Janie's four-year-old body. Her eyes sparkled and a smile lit up her face. Janie was getting positive reinforcement that she was wanted, accepted, and loved, which made her feel extra special.

Children's self-image is a reflection of what their parents or significant others have told them. What you say to your child creates a mirror that shows your child: *this is who you are.* If you tell a child that she is pretty or helpful or well behaved, she will believe this. Just as children believe it if you tell them they are terrible, can't do anything right, or that they are dumb or stupid. Words of praise or criticism create in the child's mind a picture of how they think they appear and the kind of person they are. You want them to have a good picture of themselves.

Three-year-old Sammy was helping his daddy carry a pail of water. His father commented, "You really are strong. You must have big muscles." Later that day, his friend asked him to help pull a wagon filled with blocks. Sammy said, "I can pull anything because I have big muscles." He believed this because his daddy said so.

The way children are held, cuddled, and talked to during their early days and years has a powerful effect on the way they will feel about themselves and those around them. For the nurturing of their whole self, they need the closeness as much as they need food.

How Does a Self-concept Develop?
Children's feelings about their own self-worth are influenced by how they have been treated by others. When a child feels good about himself, those feelings of worthiness carry over into adulthood. They care about themselves and others. They see themselves as worthwhile, contributing individuals.

All children have their own personalities and their own unique abilities. Every child has special talents and good qualities. Praising and encouraging these traits will help children develop self-esteem. Every child needs, and is entitled to, these feelings of self-worth.

Building Blocks to a Child's Self-esteem
<u>Communicate</u> <u>your</u> <u>love</u> <u>and acceptance</u>. First, children need to know that their parents *love them absolutely, without question.* It is parental love and acceptance above all else that children seek.

Communicate your love to your child by touching, holding and listening. Put your arm around your child, touch his shoulder, hug him, let him know you care and that he is important to you. Look at your child when she is talking to you. Children want you to "listen with your eyes." They want you to look at them and to pay attention to what they are saying. The events in your young child's life, trivial as they may appear, are important to them.

Be with your child mentally as well as physically. When you read a story with your child, forget about doing the dishes and the bills. Spend that time completely involved with your child. Let her know that you enjoy being with her. When she comes home from preschool, tell her how glad you are to see her. This lets her know that she's important in your life.

Respect the person that is your child. Use phrases such as "please" and "thank you" as you do with other people. If you need to criticize something about your child's behavior, wait until his friends or others have gone, rather than doing it in front of them.

Offer positive feedback for what your child is doing well. "You did a good job," is an important message, whether for a baby grasping a toy or a child singing a song she has memorized. Let your youngster know that she is *capable*. Complimenting her for putting her toys away, or for matching her socks are messages that say, "You are doing things well."

Recognize your preschooler's achievements. As your young child becomes more successful in each area of his growth, he builds confidence and a sense of self-worth. As parents, we need to be aware of our children's many successes and to help them when they are not so successful. Children need encouraging words and a proud recognition of their accomplishments. They need you to be involved with them and appreciate their unique qualities.

Look for ways to praise your child. "You helped your sister find her book today. She really liked that." You cannot praise your child too much if it is appropriate and sincere.

Avoid comparing your child with another. Sometimes this is difficult, especially when a sibling is particularly talented. When a child has a low level of self-esteem because of this, you can say, "Yes, your brother can run fast. But you have many gifts too. Look how well you can stack the blocks," or cut out pictures, or whatever is appropriate. Recognize the many unique talents of each child. Look for your child's strengths and then let him know you feel these are important.

If you must criticize, criticize the act, but not the child. It wounds a child's self-esteem to be told, "You are a bad girl." If you did not like what she did, you could say, "I felt really angry when you wrote with your crayon on the tablecloth. Tablecloths are for eating on, not for writing on." In this way, she learns that her actions have been inappropriate, but she still feels that as a person she is trusted and loved. She has not been shamed.

Avoid putting labels on your child. Even labels such as, "Johnny's the brightest boy in his class," places a huge burden on Johnny. Now he must always live up to these expectations. He will be under a great deal of stress in maintaining these high ideals you have set up for him. Set realistic expectations for your child.

If your child feels good about his accomplishments, respond positively to those feelings. "You feel proud of that birthday card you made for grandma. I can tell from your big smile."

If uncomplimentary labels are used by others, help your child to deal with them. Sometimes cruel comments or thoughtless words by other children about your youngster can cause anguish and heartache. If a child labels your preschooler with an uncomplimentary name, you can be supportive and understanding. You can say something like, "It sounds as if you were really upset when he said that." Allow your child to get it "off his chest." Offer hugs and security, but also try to help in dealing with the problem. Discuss what brought the matter up, what the other children did, and ask what he sees as possible solutions to this situation. Help him to develop a reasonable set of responses if such a situation occurs again.

Encourage your child's self-esteem. By using these "Building Blocks", parents can help children build their courage and self-image, and learn to have faith in themselves. These are the indicators that distinguish successful "can-do" adults who do not need to rely on others for their measure of self-esteem. By loving, respecting, praising, and supporting your preschoolers, their self-concept will continue to grow as they grow older, so that eventually their feelings of self-esteem will not be totally dependent on your approval and the opinion of others. They will have achieved self-esteem that will last all their lives.

Activities You Can Do with Your Child to Help Develop a Positive Self-concept

1. Put photographs of your child on the refrigerator or other viewing area at child's height.

2. Keep a photo album of your child's early years. Sit together and talk about how the child has grown and how important she has been to your family.

3. Have a sketch or actual layout of your family tree. Explain how your child fits into the picture.

4. Measure your child's height on a chart. Write the date and keep a running tally of her growth.

5. Share with your child the successes each of you have experienced during the day. Help your child understand that he is learning and succeeding every day.

6. Examine the kind of "warm fuzzies" you have exchanged during the week. <u>Warm fuzzies</u> are things done or said to make a person feel good.

Example of warm fuzzy: "You picked up all your toys. Good for you!"

Cut out small squares of fuzzy material and place in a box. Each person reaches into the box and pulls out a fuzzy. Exchange warm fuzzies with each other by telling something good about the other as you give away a fuzzy.

7. Play the sentence completion game. Let your child dictate to you his thoughts and ideas on:

I am happiest when...
I am good at...
I am getting better at...
I wish I could...
My friends like me because I...

Read his words back to him.

8. While singing a song or reading a story, insert your child's name.

9. Read books aloud to your child about ways of handling feelings and emotions. Your child will be more apt to accept himself when he hears about others having similar problems, worries, and conflicts. Discuss the situations with your child.

10. Spend regular, special time with each child. This could be a certain time each day, or regularly scheduled during the weekend. It is important for each child to know that he can count on specific time set aside for him alone.

Chapter 3
The Best Gift
You Can Give
Your Child

Stephanie Marston

*Only if children's basic
emotional needs are filled,
can they learn to like
and value themselves.*

Steven is four years old and lives in a very busy family. He has a younger sister who has just turned two. If you could peek into Steven's life, this is what you would see: Steven's father wakes him up and says, "Come on slowpoke, get a move on, or you'll be late for school." Steven gets dressed, walks into the kitchen, and sits down at the table, and begins chattering away, "Did you see Sesame Street yesterday? Big Bird was taking all the kids to the firehouse. I love Big Bird..." Steven continues babbling, trying to gets his parents' attention, until his father finally yells, "Steven, please! I don't care about Big Bird! Just eat your breakfast, or you'll be late for school." Steven grows quiet and finishes only part of his food.

When Steven gets to preschool, the following events occur:
 • He proceeds to ram his car into Larry's city of blocks. Larry glares at Steven and screams, "You wrecked my city — I hate you."
• At circle time a teacher asks, "Steven, would you like to tell us what you did over the weekend?" "No," Steven answers angrily. "I didn't do anything. You can't make me talk."
• At story time the teacher notices that Steven is pushing and pinching the kids on either side of him. When she has him sit next to her, he starts sticking out his tongue and making faces at the other kids, distracting their attention away from the story.

It is clear that Steven is crying out for several things. He wants attention and to feel connected. But because he doesn't feel good about himself, he continually finds aggressive, disruptive ways of getting these needs met.

A child's self-esteem affects every area of his existence, from the friends he chooses, to how well he does academically in school, to what kind of job he gets, to even the person he chooses to marry. But what exactly is this elusive, intangible thing called self-esteem?

What is self-esteem?
Defined simply, self-esteem is the sense of being *lovable and capable. When these two qualities* go together, a child has high self-esteem. Children need first to know that they are loved and accepted for who they are. Then, with this as a basis, their natural impulse is to take that love and learn to contribute it to the world in constructive ways. As you work to give your child this marvelous gift of self-esteem, the most important thing to understand is this: self-esteem evolves in kids *primarily through the quality of our relationships with them.* For the first several years of their lives, parents are their major influence. Later on, teachers and friends come into the picture. But especially at the beginning, you're <u>It</u> with a capital I.

Parents are, in effect, mirrors: what we reflect back to our kids becomes the basis for their self-image, which in turn influences all areas of their lives. To put it another way, who our children are is not nearly as important as who they think they are.

Your child's own VCR
Imagine that between your child's eyes and ears is a videocassette recorder. Everything our children hear, see, and feel is recorded onto a cassette. Guess who is the big star in their movie? You are. What you say and, more important, what you do, is recorded there for them to replay over and over again. We all have videocassettes. Adults just have larger libraries of tapes available.

You can create positive images on these cassettes, and learn how to enhance your children's feelings of being lovable and capable. The first of those steps is to gain a greater understanding of the nature of self-esteem itself.

On top of the world
Take a moment and recall a time when you felt really good about yourself. What were you doing? Whom were you with? Remember the experience in as much detail as possible. Think about what contributed to your feeling so good. Most likely it can be described by one or more of the following feelings:

• You felt that you were important to someone you respected and whose opinion you valued.
• You felt you did something that only you could have done in that particular way. You felt special and had a sense of your own unique gifts.
• You felt you were in charge and getting the things done that you set out to do. You felt confident that you could handle whatever you were faced with.
• You shared a difficult-to-express thought, feeling, or opinion with someone, and in doing so, you connected with that person on a deeper level than ever before.

Each of the above feelings represents one of the four primary aspects of high self-esteem described below.

Four factors for high self-esteem
Only if children's basic emotional needs are filled, can they learn to like and value themselves. For this reason understanding our children's needs is the first step in creating the proper climate for healthy growth and development. Our kids have lots and lots of individual needs, but they can all be grouped into four main categories:

Belonging
Uniqueness
Power
Freedom of Expression

Belonging

Belonging is first on the list simply because children are social beings, and their most fundamental need is to feel connected. They develop a sense of security through feeling that they belong within a group. The most obvious group is, of course, your family. As kids get older, they expand their need to belong to include outside groups as well, such as clubs, teams, their class, and the like. Most of what our kids do is geared toward finding "their place" in their families and in the world. In broad terms, a sense of belonging is developed through their relationships to people, places, and things.

The primary way kids develop a sense of belonging is when they feel loved by someone who regards them as special. Moreover, they need to know that this someone will protect and guide them. Children also require a sense of history. They need to have a sense of their roots and heritage. Have you ever noticed that kids are fascinated by stories about what they were like when they were babies and what they said and did as they grew? This sense of history and connectedness increases your children's feelings of security and safety, and helps them build the ability to make healthy connections in the world at large.

Uniqueness

All human beings have some basic similarities with the rest of humanity, yet all of our kids are unique unto themselves. Very early on, our children discover that they are different from you and others in their lives. It is important to recognize, accept, and appreciate these differences. Each child has his own individual expression to offer to the world. That expression can take many forms, from artistic interests, a way of thinking, athletic activities, a particular style of dressing, musical talents, different hobbies, etc. Our job is to join our children in discovering who they are.

Power

A sense of power is essential for every human being. For our children to have a strong sense of power, they need to feel that they can influence their environment and have some control over their lives. In order to accomplish this, they require our help in learning how to use their skills and abilities in positive ways. They also need to know that they can make good decisions and solve problems. By allowing our kids to make decisions for themselves and solve their own problems, we help them to develop a sense of independence and personal power.

It is additionally empowering for children to feel that they can make meaningful contributions to their families. When we give them responsibility, it is a vote of confidence in their developing sense of competence. There is a tremendous power in mastering any new task. But mastery is a learned process, so our kids need our support and encouragement in learning new skills and achieving their goals.

Freedom of Expression
Children must be able openly to express their feelings, and ask for what they want and need if they are ever to develop an integrated sense of self. They must be able to think their own thoughts, even if they differ from ours. They need to have the opportunity to ask us questions when they don't understand what we mean.

Needless to say, although kids blossom in a home atmosphere in which they can ask for what they want, they must also recognize that they may not always get what they've asked for. But they should never be blamed for asking.

There are two guiding principles to help you understand your kids — their actions and their motivations:
1. Get to know your kids' needs, and examine how they are currently being met in the four areas discussed above.
2. *Our kids are always trying to get their needs met.* Consequently, if one of these four basic needs is unfulfilled, the child will focus a great deal of his attention on that area in order to fill the emotional hole the best way he can.

How does all this apply to Steven?
If you could listen to Steven's internal dialogue about himself, it would probably sound something like this; "I'm not very important. Nobody really likes me. Nobody wants to play with me. No one will pay attention to me. Even my parents don't like me." In short, he lacks several of the four factors for self-esteem. He certainly doesn't feel powerful. He doesn't feel his parents listen to <u>and</u> respect him, and his sense of belonging to his family is badly eroded. So he attempts to fill in these emotional voids in the only way he knows how. For example, when Steven ruined Larry's block city, he was begging his friends to <u>notice him</u> and to act scared of him so that he could think of himself as powerful.

All children strive to see themselves as strong and capable. But if they cannot, they will match their behavior to their self-images. A child who believes that he is bad shapes his actions to fit his view of himself. A lack in one or more of the four factors that make up self-esteem is the real cause of misbehavior. What usually happens is that the more a child misbehaves,

the more he is punished, scolded, and rejected. And as his needs are not met, he becomes more firmly convinced that he is bad. It's a vicious, destructive cycle.

At the suggestion of Steven's preschool director, his parents came to see me for counseling. Nancy and Bob were caring parents who were overwhelmed with the job of raising two small children and working full time.

They both agreed that they never thought that raising kids would be this hard. I explained that once they were more in charge of the situation and felt better about themselves as parents, they would be able to relate with Steven in a way that was more satisfying for everyone. As we began to work together, I explained what happens when a child feels like a "bad kid" and attempts to get his need for attention met. Because this need is so fundamental, Steven would rather have negative attention than no attention at all.

We discussed Steven wanting to be treated like a baby. I explained to them that frequently when a new brother or sister arrives on the scene, children regress to more infantile behaviors, asking for a bottle or wetting the bed. This is a reaction to being dethroned and losing their place at the center of attention. Once Nancy and Bob understood the situation from Steven's perspective, they began to feel more compassionate toward their son, seeing him more as *a child with needs* rather than *a child with problems*.

I coached Nancy and Bob in how to acknowledge Steven's feelings while limiting his actions. I told them to use phrases like, "I bet you sometimes wish that you were still a baby;" "You're my special big boy, and no one can ever take your place;" "I know your little sister makes you mad sometimes. It's okay to feel mad, but it's not okay to hit her." I suggested that Nancy not be overly concerned with Steven's desire to regress, but that both she and Bob should concentrate on spending time alone with him on a regular basis.

After several weeks Nancy and Bob started to feel more in charge, and Steven's behavior began to change. Nancy established a regular Tuesday afternoon date with her son, and Bob scheduled a couple of uninterrupted hours with him on the weekends. "He seems to eat it up." reported Nancy. Bob added, "When I come home in the evening, I make a point of giving Steve a big hug and talking to him for a few minutes before I sit down to unwind. I can't believe it, but those few minutes seem to make such a difference. He's not so demanding after that. We've also started taking turns doing the bedtime ritual with each of the kids. This way they each get our focused time and attention. It seems to be working." To help Steven feel more important and in charge of himself, Bob and Nancy agreed to encourage him to do small chores, such as folding napkins or helping put away the laundry. Also, Nancy taught Steven how to use words when he felt angry or upset, and his teachers reinforced this.

After several months Steven had progressed dramatically. He now used his energy to build rather than to destroy. He was willing to try new things, confident of his ability to meet new challenges. He volunteered to do chores both at school and at home. He played cooperatively with other kids, and was frequently invited to play at their houses. At home he was more amenable and relaxed. His chattering and hitting had stopped completely. In short, he was becoming a child with self-esteem.

Chapter 4
Falling in Love
with Your Kids

Stephanie Marston

*To build your children's self-esteem,
you have to fall in love with them.*

To build your children's self-esteem, you have to fall in love with them. How do you do that? Well, you fall in love with them just as you would with anyone else. Here are nine basic ingredients for falling in love with your kids:

1. Spend time together.
2. Develop common interests.
3. Play together.
4. Talk together.
5. Touch each other.
6. Tell your children often that you love them.
7. Treat your kids as if they are the most important people in the world.
8. Create lasting memories.
9. Celebrate their uniqueness.

Let's explore those ingredients in detail.

1. Spend time together

Could you fall in love with someone if you spent an hour a day together, and during that time you were fixing dinner, folding the laundry, or reading the newspaper? Of course not. But we are busy people, and often that's all the time we feel we have to spare for our kids. The plain truth is, however, nothing takes the place of spending *focused* time with your child. When you set aside special time for your child, he says to himself, "If my parents take this time to be just with me, I must be important." This kind of special time is critical in building your child's self-esteem.

With your demanding schedule it sometimes seems impossible to take this special time out of your day. The key is to balance your own valid needs with those of your children. This may require a reordering of priorities. It is far too easy to lose sight of the wonder of your children amid the daily routines of running a household and/or often holding a job; we forget the preciousness of the present moment. There are numerous ways of spending effective time with your children.

• **Take Your Kids to a Special Place.** Take them somewhere out of the ordinary, so that they will have a memory of sharing a special place with you. When you share a special place with your kids, you include them in your world in a unique way. You say to them, "I enjoy you and want to share a special part of me with you." As a result they feel valued and respected.

• **Make a Date.** It's a good idea to have a regular date with your child to spend time with him/her alone. When you have several children, the need for one-to-one time is even greater. By making a date for focused time, you give your child a break from the constant competition for your attention, plus you promote greater cooperation between your kids.

One of the toughest things your child has to learn is to share you. By making a "date," your children will know that they can count on being with you on a regular basis. It adds to their sense of security and satisfies their need to feel special.

• **"The Spotlight's on Me!"** Children thrive on being the center of attention. We give our kids the spotlight when it's their birthday or special occasion. However, it's wonderful to do this more regularly. Try an activity called "Star for the Evening." On a specific night each child gets to be the star. The star receives the family's undivided attention at a show-and-tell session. The special child has an opportunity to talk about anything that is really interesting to him or her. At the end, the child receives a standing ovation.

2. Develop common interests

One day when my daughter, Ama, was six, I sat down with her and said, "Tomorrow's Sunday—let's spend the day together. What would you like to do?" Rather than giving her specific choices, I intentionally left the question general, because I was curious to see what her interests were. She thought for a moment. "I want to plant a garden." I was surprised. I had no idea that she even liked gardening!

So we went to the store and picked out some seeds and planted a garden. Then she went over and lay down on the grass, and I joined her. We looked up at the clouds and made up stories about what we saw in the cloud formations. We had a great time together. I learned that she and I loved to garden and to make up stories, two interests that we share to this day.

3. Play together

"Why do the elephants paint their toes red?"
"I don't know. Why?"
"So they can hide in cherry trees."
"I never saw an elephant in a cherry tree."
"See, it works!"

One of the essential ingredients for falling in love with your children is to have fun together. "Will you come play with me?" is something you hear over and over from children. Having fun comes naturally to children, but most of us have to rekindle our playful inner child.

Children appreciate it immensely when we lighten up and become playful. This play can take many forms, from roughhousing, to playing catch, to jumping in a pile of freshly raked leaves, finger painting, playing hide-and-seek, etc. Use your imagination.

4. Talk together

Most parent interactions with children are made up of talk such as, "Did you brush your teeth?" "Is your bed made?" "Did you pick up your toys?" You may ask, "What else do I find to talk to them about?"

The answer is simple: Something real. Tell them about your childhood, and what it was like for you. Tell them about the street where you lived, how mad you used to get at your mom, and how much you loved your best friend. Children are fascinated to learn about their parents, especially stories when you were the same age they are now. Let your kids know you. Talking about your past or your kids' past has special dividends, because children benefit immensely by having a sense of their roots and heritage.

They also love to hear stories about what they were like when they were babies, and what they did and said as they grew. Listening to these tales, they are not only able to see how they have grown and changed, they also feel important and reassured by our fascination with them and the incidents of their lives. When you give your kids the gift of these oral histories, you'll find that they will ask to hear the same stories over and over again.

• Listening Equals Love

Things happen to your children that may seem trivial and unimportant to you, but are of major importance to them. Put yourself in their shoes and show them that you genuinely value what they share with you. Every day, ask them about what happened in preschool, their friends, and their interests. Become an interested listener in their lives.

5. Touch each other

When you fall in love with someone, you hug and touch constantly. Children also need to be touched and hugged on a more regular basis. Family therapist Virginia Satir developed a prescription for touching: Four hugs a day for survival, eight for maintenance, and sixteen for growth. If you want your kids to thrive, make sure that they get hugged a lot.

We may prepare food for our children, chauffeur them around, take them to the movies, buy them toys and ice cream, but nothing registers as deeply as a simple squeeze, cuddle, or pat on the back. There is no greater reassurance of their lovability and worth than to be affectionately touched and held. By giving our kids appropriate physical contact, we send them into the world with renewed inner strength to cope with the multitude of challenges they face daily.

You need to combine both verbal and nonverbal messages in communicating your good feelings and love for your children. Holding your son's hand,

gently stroking your daughter's face, hugging and kissing, often speak louder than words.

6. Tell your children often that you love them

Your children don't automatically feel loved simply because they are your children. They need tangible demonstrations of your loving. We can use affirming statements to express our love to our children, such as "I love you just the way you are. I'm so glad you're my daughter!" These kinds of affirming messages need to be given to your children day in and day out for the rest of their lives. Researchers were surprised to find in repeated studies that these reassuring messages have a measurably calming and nurturing effect even on infants. By continually affirming our children's lovableness and capableness, we foster the development of a strong sense of self.

• Terms of Endearment

If you are uncomfortable saying "I love you" directly, or if you'd like an alternative way of expressing affection, use humor. Tell your four-year-old you love him bigger than the ocean and higher than the sky. You can also make up terms of endearment or pet names. Or use the familiar ones, such as sugarplum, honey pie, sweetie. Have fun in the process.

7. Treat your children as if they are the most important people in the world.

We need to treat our children with love, respect, and understanding if that's how we want them to treat us, others, and most important, themselves. Although our children deserve the same kind of consideration that we would give to an adult friend, we often treat our kids like second-class citizens. We talk down to them, embarrass them, order them around, and generally treat them disrespectfully. Even when we don't intend to, we build walls between ourselves and our children instead of bridges. Every time we criticize, embarrass, or order them around, we cement another brick into the wall. If we continue to treat them in this way, they will eventually shut us out because they have experienced too much hurt.

• Give your unconditional love

Our kids shouldn't have to earn our love, acceptance, or respect. These are your child's birthright and should be given freely. If children are only accepted and loved when they do what we expect or what we want, they feel insecure and never really feel that they are genuinely loved and valued. Respect and acceptance don't mean you accept or like everything they do, but that you love them no matter what. Unconditional love is loving your kids for who they *are*, not for what they *do*.

8. Create lasting memories

The most basic need that children have is to feel that they belong. In infancy a child's very existence and survival is based on belonging. As children develop and grow, their sense of belonging to a group enhances their emotional and psychological health.

• All together now

Take a few minutes and drift back through your childhood, and recall the happiest times you spent with your family. What were your happiest memories? Was it having your mom and dad tuck you in at night and reading stories? Or was it having a family gathering of all the relatives at your grandparents' house for a big dinner?

What these happy memories have in common is the warmth of a family doing something special together. As a family, take time to discuss the family traditions you already have and what new ones you would like to start.

9. Celebrate uniqueness

Did you know that with all the millions of people on this earth, there is no one exactly like you? There is no one with the same combination of eyes, hair, facial features; with the same hopes, fears, concerns, dreams; with the same genes and chromosomes — and with billions of people yet to be born, there will never be anyone just like you. You're unique, special, and one-of-a-kind. This is also true for each of your children. Children thrive when they know that the important people in their lives recognize their uniqueness. Here are five projects you can do with your children to help them realize that they are unique.

Making a Commercial

Ask your children to write a TV commercial about themselves that has pictures and words. What we know about commercials is that they never say anything bad about the product. They only sing its praises and tell you its good points. Your children will also focus solely on the positive in their commercials. Let them draw the pictures any way they like (have them describe to you what the pictures represent) and then have them dictate the dialogue for each picture.

An "I Am Special and Loved" Poster
Take an 8 1/2" by 11" piece of paper and attach a photo of your child at the top. Beneath the heading "I am special and loved" have your children dictate a description of their bodies, such as, "I have brown curly hair with long bangs." Have each child include special experiences (I've been to a circus) and accomplishments (I can build with my blocks). When you finish the poster, read the words back to your child. They will come to the marvelous realization that they really are special.

Scrapbooks
Scrapbooks are great. Kids love to save photos, birthday cards, letters, and anything they feel proud of. It gives them a way to look back on their history and see where they came from.

"My Special Box"
The Special Box can be a cardboard box or a shoe box that will hold your child's treasures: baby teeth, birthday cards, interesting stamps or coins, seashells, etc.

Photos
Your child should have two pictures next to his or her bed. One should show him or her happy while doing something: riding a bike, painting, or baking. The other photo should show your family together. Why put them next to their beds? Research has shown that there is a thirty-minute time period each day when your children will listen to you and absorb more than at any other time. That thirty minutes is the period just before your children go to bed. If you put photos of your kids being capable and loved next to their beds, these positive visual images are likely to be the last thing they see before they sleep and the first thing they see when they awaken. Consequently the message "I am lovable and capable," the two keys to high self-esteem, will be strengthened even while your children are asleep. Why does this work?

Here's the amazing thing: Studies show that during sleep the subconscious will review what has been recorded all day, between three to five times. But it will replay what has been recorded in the last thirty minutes before we go to sleep at least ten times. Those two pictures next to the bed are one way of making sure that "I am lovable and capable" gets reinforced ten times over.

Chapter 5
How Children Gain Confidence Through Child-directed Play

Pegine Echevarria

*Because children
have very little power,
they need opportunities in which
they are the leaders
and adults are the followers.*

Andrea, 3 years old, was playing quietly by herself. As the daughter of working parents, she often played alone. One weekend, her mother, Sue, was folding laundry and watching Andrea play. On impulse she sat on the floor next to Andrea. Andrea began to make believe Sue was in the beauty parlor getting her hair done. First Andrea brushed her mother's hair and then pretended she was painting her nails. The two spent the afternoon playing dress-up and party time. Andrea directed the activities by painting her mother's face with play makeup and dressing her up in party hats. Sue was surprised at how inventive and creative her daughter was. Instinctively, she had let Andrea direct the play.

As parents and professionals, we have a responsibility to help develop our children's self-esteem, confidence and pride. Yet we often miss a very important part of a child's world — his or her creative play.

How children gain confidence
Children's self-image is formed mainly by parents and other adults that are important to them. When parents acknowledge that their preschoolers have ideas and thoughts that they have developed on their own, the youngsters' self-esteem grows.

Adults gain confidence when their ideas are used to get new business, or when a dinner they cooked is praised. Children gain confidence when their ideas are followed in a play experience, and they can be in control of what the participants say or do.

Kenneth was building with blocks and was very involved in the project. "Put the block this way," his father said, "it'll look better!" "But that's not how it goes!" Kenneth, 4 1/2, repeated for the second time. He was becoming very frustrated and annoyed because his father was interrupting him with instructions.

While watching children play, adults often offer opinions or try to make the play into a learning experience by talking about the color or shape of a particular piece. "Katie, what a beautiful building you are making! Do you know what color the top block is?" Although parental intrusions into the child's world are well-meaning, continual interruptions end up disrupting a child's creative process. The child may get the message that her ideas are not good enough.

Think about trying a complicated new recipe. What would your reaction be to these two situations?
1. As you are measuring the ingredients and concentrating on the process, your husband wants you to describe what you are doing in detail. Would you appreciate the intrusion? How would you feel . . . ?

2. As you begin your cooking project, your husband puts on an apron and offers to help with the preparation. Wouldn't you feel loved and supported, knowing that he is interested in your activities?

Participate on the child's level

We can help build our children's self-esteem by <u>letting them lead in the activity</u> — even getting down on the floor with them. At playtime, children often find pleasure in just sitting next to their playmates. They may not even talk to each other. The sense that they are with someone is all they need. During this activity you are their playmate. Take their lead. If they don't want to talk, don't talk. When you participate on their level and do it <u>their</u> way, their self-esteem will begin to grow.

Some activities that you can participate in are: block building, kick ball, molding dough clay, drawing, painting, and pretending. This will allow your child to interact on his own level.

Because children have very little power, they need opportunities in which they are the leaders and adults are the followers. This builds confidence and self-esteem.

It is important for parents to acknowledge the capabilities of their young children. There is no better way to observe, learn, and acknowledge the strengths of children than by playing together.

Suggested Activities
for Playing with
Your Preschooler

When playing with your child, you don't need to think about teaching him anything or producing a beautiful finished product. Just enjoy your "playdate" with your child. Your preschooler may suggest what he wants to play with. Or, if he doesn't know what he wants to do, you may introduce one of the following activities. Then step back and let your child take the lead. That way both you and your child are involved. You will enjoy the play experience and your preschooler will enjoy the process of leading.

Playing with soft dough clay
Prepare for this activity by providing: smocks, a comfortable working area (kitchen table) and utensils (plastic knives-without sharp edges, cookie cutters, rollers). Have at least one can of soft dough clay per participant (or the equivalent if you've made your own. See recipe below). Just roll it, pound it, flatten it and squish it. No need to make a sculpture; stay with simple shapes.

Soft Dough Clay
1 cup salt
1 cup cooking oil
2 cups flour
water as needed
food color (optional)

Mix the dry ingredients in a bowl. Mix food color with about one cup of water. Add the water gradually, mixing and kneading until the dough is the desired texture. Keep dough in the refrigerator in a plastic bag after use.

Block building
Someone has to be the foreman when you build with blocks. In this activity your child is the foreman. You can make suggestions, but she gets the last word. Don't get offended if she doesn't accept your ideas. The purpose is to build her self-esteem, through listening to her ideas and accepting them.

Remember there may be little or no talking during these activities. Just build to your heart's content, but be prepared to remove the offending piece if the foreman so dictates. While you still set limits where safety is involved, this is one area where the preschooler gets to use her independence, power, and leadership capabilities. As foreman, she can sharpen these skills. This play experience is more meaningful because you are involved.

Coloring

There is nothing quite like a box of colorful crayons, blank pieces of paper, and imagination. Preparation is a key here. It is very important that you have a lot of coloring paper on hand — not coloring books where you must stay within the lines. Have enough space for everyone to color and make sure that the crayons are accessible to everyone. If you hate to color with broken crayons, have separate crayons for yourself, but remember to share!

You may ask your youngster to suggest a topic to draw. If he does not have a topic in mind, draw anything you want to, and enjoy the relaxing experience. Your drawing will be *your* masterpiece just as what your child draws is perfect for him.

Kick ball, or any ball playing

Playing ball can be a great self-esteem builder, as long as you play by your preschooler's rules. Children of this age group are not yet mature enough to play games with the prearranged rules that are accepted by older children and adults. In order for this to be a positive experience, play by your child's rules. Fair warning though, a preschooler's rules can change in the middle of play. Fair is whatever the leader, in this case your child, says is fair. Make sure you are in good shape because the energy level grows each minute.

Pretending with your child

Your preschooler may want you to join him in imaginative play, such as acting out an adventure with dinosaurs, or playing house. Again, take your cues from your child, and remember to speak to him as the character he is pretending to be. For example, if you are both dinosaurs, you can say, "I hear Tyrannosaurus Rex coming. I hope he's eaten enough for today." Or if you are playing house, you can say, "How is your baby feeling?" If your child answers, you can continue the conversation. If not, wait for him to start talking.

In this fantasy world your preschooler can express his ideas and exercise his imagination. When he directs the play, he feels in control of what is happening. This gives him a feeling of competence and helps build his self-esteem.

Have fun!

Chapter 6
Talking About
Your Children
in Front of Them

Lawrence Balter

*...what parent hasn't blurted out
something not meant for
a child's ears,
something the parent
would do anything
to take back.*

- "She is just like my sister—clumsy as an elephant."
- "This is my artistic son, and this is my smart one."
- "You're just like your father. Your temper is atrocious."

As children we heard our parents do it, and so as parents ourselves, we often make the same mistake. You say something to, or about, your child within his earshot. Though you intend it as an innocent remark, your child interprets it very differently. To him, it may sound like a judgment you have passed on him. And whether you realize it or not, you may be passing a lot of these judgments about your children in front of them.

Whether you say it to the child directly, or she hears you say it to others, what you say about a child communicates reams about what you think of her, and thereby contributes substantially to the child's own definition of herself.

The reason these parental evaluations take up such a prominent place in the child's self-image is that at the core of a child's identity is how he believes his parents view him. At times this can work to a child's advantage. A woman I know remembers her father always telling her what a tough kid she was. "She can handle anything," he'd brag to others. "You're tough," he'd tell her, "just like your old man." To this day, whenever things get rough, and she wonders if she'll get through some trying times, she recalls her father's characterization of her: "Dad always said I'm tough. I can do it!"

But even such positive evaluations of a child's capabilities can work against her. If you believe that your choice is either to tough it out on your own or disappoint your parent, you may end up unable to ask for help when you really need it. It goes almost without saying that when parental evaluations are pointedly negative, the effects can be devastating. Tell a child he's clumsy often enough, and he may never try out for any athletic teams. Complain that he never does anything right, and he may begin to grow into a ne'er-do-well.

As parents, we sometimes forget that kids often take negative comments more seriously than we do.

First, adults learn to make small talk, just to be sociable, and often fill this small talk with what they believe to be amusing but innocuous characterizations about others. Children hear these characterizations as well-thought-out ideas.

Second, adults learn to evaluate a criticism made of them in the context of all their strengths and weaknesses. But young kids frequently see things from an all-or-nothing point of view. You mention that his room is dirty and offhandedly call him a slob. You may mean it for that moment only, but he incorporates it into his sense of himself.

To some extent, talking about your child in front of him can be a no-win proposition. Will your positive comments bring too much pressure to bear, or will a negative comment be taken too much to heart? And what parent hasn't blurted out something not meant for a child's ears, something the parent would do anything to take back?

The Child's-Eye View

Toddlers

Though toddlers are somewhat less able than older children to interpret the words used to address or describe them, they will pick up on your tone of voice, your body language, and your impatience. You may never express the thought that you're a little concerned about your toddler's slow progress in developing manual dexterity, but when you grab the shoe she's trying to put on out of her hands and shove it on her foot quickly, she gets the message. Of course, every parent has moments when time constraints almost force such reactions. But a toddler whose parents regularly show respect and admiration for her efforts at independence will really blossom.

Preschool-Age Children

A preschool-age child is more verbal and has a greater understanding of what you're saying about him. He's also become aware of social situations where an adult may be evaluating him. If an adult walks into a preschool classroom, for example, every child will begin to put on a show, because this is the age at which children start to care about what adults think of them, and each child assumes himself to be the center of attention. As a result of these new concerns about adult recognition, the preschooler is starting to be quite sensitive to what he hears you say about him to others. He may not always understand all the words, especially because parents often talk in code in front of children this age, but he may understand he's being talked about and dislike it.

Parents sometimes make the mistake of telling others about a preschooler's needs and wants — before the child has had a chance to speak up for himself. The preschooler may need a few seconds to respond to questions. If a parent is always rushing in to fill any silent moment, the child does not get a chance to gain mastery over her communication skills — indeed, she may learn that it does not pay to think before you speak. Your child may also be offended that you are presuming to know how she feels or what she wants to say to others.

Another factor that comes into play here is that a preschooler can be quite sensitive to your telling others about his strengths and weaknesses. He's already started to become aware that he isn't good at everything, and it frustrates him to hear you point that out. Besides, kids should never hear you make judgments about them because such remarks can limit even further their own sense of what they can and can't do.

Preschoolers will also begin to feel embarrassed about stories you tell others about their babyish ways, such as having a security blanket or sucking a thumb. Your preschooler may now be even more sensitive to gestures of nonconfidence than when she was a toddler. You grab the orange juice away before she has a chance to try pouring it. Or you say impatiently, "Let me do it; I'll take care of it," as though you don't have any trust in her abilities. A preschooler may also be more sensitive than you realize about out-loud comparisons you make to his older siblings.

In fact, all it may take to hit a sensitive nerve is encouraging him to do something an older sibling did at that age. One mother I know, whose older child learned his letters at a very young age, began talking about letters with her second child at that same young age. But he just wasn't that interested. "Gee," she said innocently, "Matthew loved doing his letters when he was your age!" To which her preschooler replied loudly: "Me not Matthew! "

Missteps Parents Make

• *Labeling a child negatively.* Any negative label, regularly applied, can become a self-fulfilling prophecy. Calling a child a slob, a klutz, a trouble-maker, or a goof-off, either to her or in angry complaint to your spouse, relatives, or friends, can almost guarantee that the child will come to think of herself that way. This is especially true if you preface your labels with "You're always such a . . ."

• *Overpraising or bragging about your child.* I remember one youngster I knew, whose parents overgenerously praised a poem he wrote. They talked about it for days, made copies to send to friends and relatives, and even mailed it to the local newspaper. The child never wrote another poem, apparently convinced he could never again meet the extraordinary standards implied by his parents' gushing enthusiasm.

• *Talking about a child's problems or weaknesses as though she or he were not in the room.* You're having a conversation with a friend or a relative about some problem your son is having. You're fretting and you really need to tell someone, but you forget that your child is probably fretting about it, too. Whether his teacher says he never pays attention, or he's still wetting the bed, you divulge some secret, and he suddenly sits bolt upright. "Mom!" he remonstrates, before running from the room in tears.

You've exposed your child in a very painful way. We all deserve to have private matters kept private, and he may begin to feel panicked that he can't trust you to keep his secrets.

• *Comparing siblings in front of them.* Nothing can be more enraging to a child of almost any age than hearing "Your brother would never do such a thing" or, "Why can't you be more like your sister?" Sometimes parents mean well and try to find nice things to say about each sibling but still wind up in trouble. For example, the child who repeatedly hears that he's artistic, while his older brother is the intellectual one, may believe he can't achieve academically and therefore shouldn't bother trying. You should be especially careful not to make comparisons while both siblings are in the room. The one suffering in the comparison will feel doubly humiliated that his or her sibling was allowed to hear it. And the one being praised may feel a mixture of glee and guilt for getting accolades at a sibling's expense.

• *Telling cute stories about or laughing at a child.* You can't expect children to accept jokes at their expense in a good-natured way, or to understand that adults do not intend to mock children when they make jokes at their expense. Saying to a child, "I'm not laughing at you; it's just that you're so cute," doesn't comfort the child or assure him that you're really on his side.

• *Ranting about the difficulties of parenting.* "She's driving me crazy, I can't wait for school to start," said an exasperated mother recently, while her daughter stared up at her. All of us joke good-humoredly about the challenges of parenting. But if you're doing it in front of your child, you may cause her to feel that she really is a burden that you'd rather not have around. You certainly never want your child to hear you wish her away.

• *Telling kids that they've inherited your own or your spouse's traits.* "*You* are just like your father. Your temper is atrocious." Especially in families where the parents are fighting or are divorced, it's hard to avoid blurting out comments such as these. For recently divorced parents, the children may serve as haunting reminders of the person who has brought so much grief to the other. But you have to be careful that your children don't bear the brunt of anger that's not really intended for them.

New Moves

The underlying theme of each of the new moves described below is that you ought to treat your child with respect and attempt to see things from her point of view. In doing this, you convey to her that she is worthy of your regard for her as her own person.

• *New Move 1: Give your child affirmations.* Affirmations are statements that declare to a child that you believe in him. One man remembered that his father once said to him, "Son, you have a good head on your shoulders. You're going to amount to something." Over the years, his father's words often gave him confidence when he most needed it. Affirmations don't suggest that you expect perfection from your child. They simply tell him that you think he's capable and competent just because of who he is.

• *New Move 2; Tell your children that you accept them as valuable and unique members of your family.* Tell each child, "I'm really glad you're part of this family." Make clear that your acceptance isn't based on performance in school or at the piano, but that you appreciate the child's unique personality traits, talents, and abilities—even if they aren't the same as yours or those of his or her siblings.

• *New Move 3: Praise children appropriately.* The key to reasonable praise is to do it only when it is deserved and appropriate. Discerning and praising a child's true gifts, even if they don't fit in with your view of success, is the key to helping kids feel good about themselves.

• *New Move 4: Criticize children with sensitivity.* When you must express disappointment because of something a child has done, be critical without being heavy-handed.

• *New Move 5: Rather than labeling kids, analyze the behavior behind the label.* Instead of calling a child a slob, express your anger at the mess he made. If you roll up your sleeves and work with him as he cleans it up, he won't feel that you're attacking him, and your participation in solving the problem tells him you're still on his side.

When you start with these new moves, you'll find it much easier not to talk about your children in front of them in a way that will hurt or trouble them.

Chapter 7
The Building Blocks
for Self-esteem

Louise M. Ward & Elizabeth J. Webster

*...from earliest infancy
the child needs to feel
that he has a secure base...
[which is] provided by
parents and other caregivers.*

As early as 1950, Erik H. Erickson, well-known psychologist, put forth his theories about the crucial nature of early childhood experiences in providing the building blocks for self-esteem. Erickson saw human beings developing through 8 stages in their lifetime —from infancy to old age.

The first 4 stages focus on the following:
• infancy — basic trust vs. mistrust
• 1 $^1/_2$ - 3 years (approximately) — autonomy vs. shame & doubt
• 3 - 5 $^1/_2$ years (approximately) — initiative vs. guilt
• 5 $^1/_2$ - 12 years (approximately) — industry vs. inferiority
He considered each stage to be the foundation for the next stage; that is, how successfully a child was prepared at the first stage would determine how well he completed the next one, and so on through all those remaining.

Trust vs. mistrust
Erickson considered the issue of trust vs. mistrust to be the developmental task of the first year of life. How well the child's needs are met gives the child a sense of trust or mistrust in himself and his environment. At this stage the needs are largely physiological: to be fed when hungry and to be physically comfortable. When parents provide the environment where the child is protected from danger, is warm and dry, and is well fed, they are also helping the child build trust. They are providing an important base for many of the child's later accomplishments.

Moving on to the other stages
Erickson viewed trust of self and others, which begins to be developed from birth, as the basic element in self-esteem. Trust is so important because the preschool child must move on to believe the environment will not punish her for developing autonomy which is the ability to function independently. The young child must also dare to try new things without feeling guilty if some efforts are unsuccessful.

Current theories about trust
Authors more recently use slightly different language yet share the same ideas. Alicia Lieberman in *The Emotional Life of the Toddler* (The Free Press, 1993) stated that from earliest infancy the child needs to feel that he has a secure base. Such a base is provided by parents and other caregivers. They hold newborns so that they will not fall, and later stay close, as babies start to move around. As toddlers learn to walk, caring adults are there to see that they are permitted to move without hurting themselves badly. *Lieberman believes this secure base is essential at every stage of a young child's life so that she will trust in herself and the environment.* Lieberman makes the point that from the security provided by others the child can develop her own security. Lieberman calls this sense of security "inner balance." As a result of this inner balance children dare to try new things.

However, it can be observed that children vary in the ease with which they learn to trust and develop this inner balance — even when provided a secure base. What follows are two examples. One is about a child who had complete trust in his environment, while the other illustrates a parent's attempt to help her young son who did not trust the environment easily to feel more trusting and secure.

Three-year-old Tom, a child who did develop trust, was observed on his first visit to an Atlantic Ocean beachfront motel. He could hardly wait to get into the water. He ran ahead of his father until the water was chest high. There he laughed and squealed while he and his father played.

Tim, who was the same age as Tom, was a very different kind of child. As he walked across the sand he clung to his mother's hand. Twice he tried to get into the water, but jumped back each time a wave approached. He seemed terrified. His mother said," No hurry, you don't even have to go in now if you don't want to." Tim muttered that he wanted to. On the third try he made it, still clinging to his mother. They stayed about 10 minutes and returned, hand in hand, to play on the beach. They went in again later and this time went farther out and stayed longer. The next afternoon both boys were observed in the water, with Tim still staying very close to his mother.

Loving the child for what he is
Another way adults help a child develop self-esteem is to give him evidence that he is cared about for who he is, not for what he can do. Adults can help a child feel valued by refraining from comparing him to another child. Parents often do so with the idea that it provides a model or standard of behavior or performance. So often this backfires when the child interprets the message as, "I'm not good enough." Tim's mother never pointed out to him that the other boy was not afraid of the water. She valued Tim for what he could do, however long it took him to feel comfortable in this new environment.

Importance of communication
Much of what the child builds self-esteem on depends upon how well the adults around him communicate. Children, from infancy, want to talk. When they gurgle and make unintelligible noises, usually, at that stage, adults make noises in response. While later on, adults may ignore their preschooler's chattering — this is also a form of communication and should be listened to.

Each evening Sara's mother asked her, "Tell me what happened at preschool today." After about a week of discussing preschool events Sara sighed and said don't want to talk about that. I want to tell you why I'm mad at Freddie." Her mother wisely listened and heard about Sara's hurt feelings and her wish that she

could "punch him right out." Thus their conversation took on greater depth than it had previously. In addition, Sara learned an important lesson: that her mother did not reprimand her for being angry or feeling hurt. This was part of Sara's lesson in trust.

Love in the midst of discipline

Parents and other caregivers can make loving and valuing comments to the child in whatever state he is in. This holds true even in the midst of discipline. "I love you, but I must make you stop that," or "I don't like what you are doing right now," are two examples.

With life so hectic and demanding, parents may feel stressed and show anger at the child. Sometimes they feel guilty about their anger. However, this is the way children learn about anger, learn to acknowledge their own anger, and hopefully how to express it constructively. Thomas Gordon, author of *Parent Effectiveness Training*, wrote about the use of "I" messages when angry. For example, "I am very angry with you right now," is very different from "You are a bad, bad girl." The point is to express the anger without attacking the personhood of the child with statements such as "Why can't you do anything right," or, " That was a dumb thing to do." When parents use constructive expressions of anger, children have a model of a way to deal with their own as well as other people's anger.

Praise should be warm and genuine

It is amazing how sensitive young children are to insincerity. Adults will do well to think carefully about what they can genuinely praise in the child, keep a list of these things, and review the list often. They will see that the number of things which are praiseworthy will continue to grow.

Various authors in the book, *Parental Development* (edited by Jack Demick, Krisanne Bursik, & Rosemarie Dibiase. Lawrence Erlbaum & Associates, 1993.) make the point that parents can grow and change even as their children do. The fact that one is raising a child does not guarantee that the person will instantly know how to be a parent.

If parents observe carefully their children's patterns they will learn how to nurture them. For example, they will learn that talking very simply to children brings out new speech and language. In fact, parents will not use sentences that are longer than children can follow.

When parents follow the guidelines outlined for developing self-esteem in children, they will do well to pay attention to changes in their own behavior. In this way they will continue to develop their own self-esteem as parents.

Resources for Section One: Encouraging Young Children's Positive Views of Self

FOR ADULTS

"Not in Front of the Children..." How to Talk to Your Child About Tough *Family Matters,* by Dr. Lawrence Balter, with Peggy Jo Donahue. Viking, 1993. In this valuable parenting guide, Dr. Balter explains how to approach such topics as divorce, sex, illness, and death, with children of different ages. He gives practical suggestions about appropriate ways to talk to toddlers, preschoolers, and older children about these and other difficult subjects. Dr. Balter is also the coauthor of *Who's in Control? Dr. Balter's Guide to Discipline Without Combat,* Simon & Schuster, 1989, and other books for parents and children.

Annie Stories: A Special Kind of Storytelling, by Doris Brett. Workman, 1988. Parents use storytelling to help their children resolve problems when dealing with stressful events in their young lives.

I Saw a Purple Cow, by Ann Cole, Carolyn Haas, Faith Bushnell, & Betty Weinberger. Little, Brown, 1972. For more than 25 years, this book of creative activities has been helping parents and teachers to design party themes and everyday experiences using items found around the house.

The Disney Party Handbook, by Alison Boteler. Disney, 1998. Whether your child loves *The Lion King, Winnie the Pooh,* or *The Little Mermaid,* this book offers party decorations, games, and a menu to match these themes and many others.

Childhood and Society, by Erik Erickson. W.W. Norton, 1993. In this landmark work, Erickson put forth his theories about psychological development. He saw human beings developing through eight stages in their lifetime. Each stage was considered to be the foundation for the next stage, and the psychological conflicts presented at each stage must be resolved before the person can move successfully to the next stage.

PET [Parent Effectiveness Training], by Thomas Gordon. McKay, 1970. This book has become a classic, offering parents step-by-step guidelines for raising responsible children.

Parent & Child: Getting Through to Each Other, by Lawrence Kutner, Ph.D. Avon Books, 1992. This practical book on childrearing covers many relevant issues, including a chapter on *Self-concept.*

They're Never Too Young for Books: A Guide to Children's Books for Ages 1 to 8, by Edythe M. McGovern & Helen D. Muller. Prometheus Books, 1994. In this practical guide to the selection and use of books with young children, you will find annotated book lists by subject matter, including many titles that relate to competence and self-esteem.

The Magic of Encouragement: Nurturing Your Child's Self-Esteem, by Stephanie Marston. Pocket Books, 1992. (Not in print — please check with your librarian.) A lively, readable, practical book on topics parents care about such as: self-esteem, feelings, and discipline. It is a valuable resource for parents of children from preschoolers through teens.

The Divorced Parent: Success Strategies for Raising Happy Children After Separation, by Stephanie Marston. Pocket Books, 1995. The author has spent the last 12 years as a successful family therapist dealing with all the complicated parenting issues divorce raises. She brings to the topic her empathy, common sense, and years of case histories, in this important book.

Resources for Early Childhood: A Handbook, by Hannah Nuba et al. Garland Publishing, 1994. An invaluable reference tool, this handbook "is designed to meet the informational needs of all concerned with the well-being of young children."

Your Child's Emotional Health, by The Philadelphia Child Guidance Center with Jack Maguire. Macmillan, 1995. A comprehensive family reference to a child's emotional well-being written for parents with children of any age. In easy-to-understand language it guides parents through every stage of development, and uses timelines to let them know what to expect at each particular stage. "The Early Years" section provides advice for parents of children under the age of six. It covers problems such as tantrums, separation anxiety, nightmares and fears.

Me, Myself and I: How Children Build Their Sense of Self, by Kyle D. Pruett, M.D. Goddard Parenting Guides, 1999. In this accessible and beautifully written volume, the author's focus is on the child from 18 to 36 months, "one of the most engaging and vibrant periods in your child's life." He offers parents practical information about current child development research, understanding differences in temperament, and the importance of the interaction of nature and nurture.

Helping Young Children Flourish, by Althea J. Solter, Ph.D. Shining Star Press, 1989. (P.O. Box 206-85, Goleta, CA 93116.) This useful book includes a chapter on "Playing and Pretending" that discusses the question: *How can I be a helpful participant in my child's play?*

The Self-Confident Child, by Jean Yoder, M.D., with William Proctor. Avon Books, 1990. This pediatrician/mother advises parents about the steps they can take to build a child's self-confidence so that outward abilities and achievements will naturally follow. The authors provide real-life case studies as illustrations.

FOR CHILDREN

Sara's City, by Sue Alexander. Clarion, 1995. The story is told from the point of view of a little girl living in Chicago in the 1940s. We hear about Sara's school, her trip to the department store with Mama, the games she plays with her friends, and how Daddy listens to the radio with her before bedtime.

Bub or The Very Best Thing, by Natalie Babbitt. Michael di Capua, 1994. "One day in the castle the King and the Queen had an argument." They quarreled about this question: what is the very best thing for the Prince? Is it toys? Is it lessons? The King looks in his books for the answer. The Queen talks to everyone she meets in the castle. But every book says something else, and each person has a different answer. Finally, they ask the cook's daughter, who asks the young Prince. He answers, "Bub." The cook's daughter is clever enough to understand. The King and Queen might even figure it out some day too!

Benjamin's 365 Birthdays, 2nd ed. by Judith Barrett. Aladdin, 1992. Benjamin has so much fun at his birthday party, especially unwrapping his presents, that he figures out how he can make the fun last 365 days a year!

American Too, by Elisa Bartone. Lothrop, Lee & Shepard, 1996. When Rosina, an Italian immigrant, is laughed at by some neighborhood girls, she asks her father, "Why do we always have to do *Italian* things? This is America not Italy!" In a moving ending to the story, Rosina is the queen at the feast of San Gennaro. She is dressed as the American symbol that she treasures most, and is glad to have two countries as part of her heritage.

Mad About Madeline, by Ludwig Bemelmans. Viking, 1993. Collected in this one volume, including Bemelmans' childlike illustrations, are all the classic tales about brave, self-confident, adventurous Madeline. As Anna Quindlen states in her introduction, "...it would not be stretching it too far to say that, for little girls especially, Madeline is a kind of role model."

Paddington Bear Board Book and Rattle, by Michael Bond. HarperFestival, 1999. Packaged in a cardboard "suitcase" like the one in the classic story, this appealing book and stuffed bear rattle would make a lovely gift for toddlers.

The Important Book, by Margaret Wise Brown. HarperTrophy , 1990. Each page tells, in rhythmic prose, the most important facts about one particular thing. And the book ends with, "The important thing about you is that you are you."

The Secret Birthday Message, by Eric Carle. HarperFestival, 1998. Think of the excitement of finding a secret message under your pillow on the night before your birthday. The reader accompanies the boy on the treasure hunt through the cutout shapes of this board book, until the treasure is found — a surprise birthday present.

Sleepytime Rhyme, by Remy Charlip. Greenwillow, 1999. This book is a love song from a mother to her baby. It tells how she loves every part of her baby: "I love your hands, your teeth, your nose, your ankles, feet, and all ten toes." There are whimsical illustrations by the author/illustrator.

Mama, Coming and Going, by Judith Caseley. Greenwillow, 1994. After Jenna's baby brother was born, life got so busy that Mama forgot to do some things like defrost the chicken for dinner. Absentminded Mama also left the water running in the bath, locked the car with the keys and the baby inside, and went to a birthday party on the wrong day. But Jenna is always there to help, and with the use of problem solving and lots of love, they work it all out very well.

This Mess, by Pam Conrad, Hyperion, 1997. Dad tells the children to clean up the mess in the living room. They do it, with imagination and originality, even throwing a rainbow across the ceiling.

So Much, by Trish Cooke. Candlewick, 1994. The doorbell rings and one by one the relatives come to visit. And they all want to hug and kiss and squeeze the baby because everybody loves the baby so much! The author is a Caribbean native and the illustrations reflect the cuddling that her own baby receives from her family. The pictures, by master illustrator Helen Oxenbury, are brimming with love.

Tell Me Again About the Night I Was Born, by Jamie Lee Curtis. Joanna Cotler Books, 1996. A little girl, who knows the story of her birth and adoption by heart, wants to hear it again, with all the loving details.

The Most Beautiful Kid in the World, by Jennifer A. Ericsson. Tambourine, 1996. Grandma is coming for dinner, and Annie wants to look beautiful. She tries on all different clothes until she thinks she looks perfect. Although Mama may not completely approve of the outfit Annie chooses, Grandma thinks she's the most beautiful kid in the world.

I'll See You When the Moon Is Full, by Susi Gregg Fowler. Greenwillow, 1994. Abe's Daddy is going on a trip and Abe will miss him. But Daddy promises that he will be back when the moon is full. Although some nights the moon will be hidden, it will always be back. "You can always count on the moon, and you can always count on me," Daddy says.

Adoption is for Always, by Linda W. Girard. Albert Whitman & Co., 1986. Cecilia's parents had always told her that she was adopted, but she paid little attention. However, when Cecila realizes that she had another mommy and daddy, she is afraid that her birthparents didn't keep her because she was bad or ugly. With love and understanding her adoptive parents help her learn that there was nothing wrong with her and that they will be her mommy and daddy for always.

Chatting, by Shirley Hughes. Candlewick, 1996. The little girl in this story loves to chat. She chats with the cat, with friends in the park, and on the telephone with Grandma and Grandpa. The author/illustrator is well known for her *Alfie* books, and her pictures are filled with affection and understanding of family life.

My Bike, by Donna Jakob. Hyperion, 1994. The exhilaration of mastering a new skill is expressed by a boy who has just learned to ride his bike. "Yesterday I fell a lot in a tangled heap. Today I ride with the wind in my face."

My Happy Birthday Book, by Lisa Jahn-Clough. Houghton Mifflin, 1996. A little girl is overjoyed that today is her birthday. She describes how she will enjoy the day with cake, presents, and a parade. An exuberant little book that celebrates the joy of having a special day of one's own.

What Will Mommy Do When I'm at School? by Dolores Johnson. Simon & Schuster, 1998. No more cooking muffins together; no more singing songs together. This little girl is off to school tomorrow and is really worried about how her mother will get along without her. When they talk it over, the girl finds out that her mother will begin a new job tomorrow, so they'll both have adventures with lots to tell each other when they get home.

Mama, Do You Love Me? by Barbara M. Joosse. Chronicle, 1998. A loving dialog between an Inuit mother and child, this book has become a favorite. *Mama, Do You Love Me?* Video, based on the book. Sony Wonder video. 30 minutes. (Book also available in Spanish, entitled, *¿Me quieres, mamá?,* Chronicle, 1998.)

Horace, by Holly Keller. Mulberry Books, 1994. At bedtime, Horace's mother (a tiger with stripes) always tells him the same story, "We chose you when you were a tiny baby because you had lost your first family and needed a new one." Horace doesn't look like his parents: he has spots and his parents have stripes. He runs away and finds children who look just like him to play with. But Horace misses his own family and returns to them at night, providing his own ending to the story of how he was chosen.

The Day We Met You, by Phoebe Koehler. Simon & Schuster, 1997. A mother and father remember with joy the day they met their adopted baby. They tell their child all the details about their preparations, the formula, the teddy bear, and the cradle, and how they hung wind chimes in the window and filled the room with flowers.

The Carrot Seed, by Ruth Krauss. HarperFestival, 1993. This classic tale of a child's faith in his ability to grow a carrot from a carrot seed has been reissued with cardboard pages for the youngest preschoolers to enjoy. As in the original, this new version uses the appealing illustrations by Crockett Johnson.

You're Just What I Need, by Ruth Krauss. HarperCollins, 1998. A question and answer game between a mother and her little boy begins as mother sees a bundle under the covers of her bed. Could it be a bundle of laundry? A bundle of carrots?

My Wicked Stepmother, by Norman Leach. Macmillan, 1993. Tom and his dad were happy together. But now he has a wicked stepmother, and nothing she does will make Tom like her. Then Tom learns that even a wicked stepmother can cry when he says mean things to her. So Tom gives her a kiss. Then and there Tom decides that he must be a wizard, because guess what happened when he kissed her!

When Frank Was Four, by Alison Lester. Houghton Mifflin, 1996. The reader learns about seven boys and girls and their accomplishments and adventures as they grow from age one to seven. A creative format in which children will recognize some real experiences and enjoy some humorous ones.

My Monster Mama Loves Me So, by Laura Leuck. Lothrop, 1999. This monster child knows his mama loves him. In this humorous tale in verse, the child tells all of the reasons. She "combs the cobwebs from my bangs and makes sure that I brush my fangs." Truly a loving mother.

In The Beginning, by Miriam Ramsfelder Levin. Kar-Ben Copies, 1996. With words that parallel the story of creation, a little boy named Adam wakes up, makes some order out of his room, waters his plants, feeds his fish, and finds that all is good. He says good morning to his parents, declares that everything is perfect, and, nestling between them, Adam rests.

I Love You As Much..., by Laura Krauss Melmed. Lothrop, Lee & Shepard, 1993. Animal mothers tell their babies how much they love them in this story in rhyme, ending with a human mother telling her baby, "I love you as much as a mother can love."

Little Bear, by Else Holmelund Minarik. An I Can Read Book®. HarperTrophy, 1978. There are four stories about Little Bear in this book, with pictures by Maurice Sendak. Whether he is deciding what to wear out in the snow, or cooking birthday soup, or flying to the moon, or telling his mother his wishes, Little Bear seems childlike and engaging.

Cinder-Elly, by Frances Minters. Viking, 1994. An updated Cinderella story with a lively rhythm featuring a heroine who is capable and lovable.

A Big Day for Little Jack, by Inga Moore. Candlewick, 1997. Little Jack Rabbit gets an invitation to a party. But he's never been to a party before, and he's afraid to go alone. So he asks each member of the family to go with him. Grandpa suggests that he take his toy bunny instead, with happy results. A gentle story about a youngster facing new experiences.

The Adventures of Isabel, by Ogden Nash. Joy Street, Little, Brown, 1994. The poet, known for his humorous verse, tells the story of Isabel in rollicking rhyme. No matter what she encounters, Isabel is undaunted and handles each situation with confidence.

Waiting for Noah, by Shulamith Levey Oppenheim. HarperCollins, 1990. Noah loves to hear his loving Nana tell him time and time again about the day of his birth — how Nana waited to hear from his Daddy that he was born, and of all the dreams she had of the things she and Noah would do together.

Coat of Many Colors, by Dolly Parton. HarperTrophy, 1996. Based upon a song written by the country music star, this story tells of a poor little girl who proudly wears her coat of many colors. It was made by her mother and though it was put together from rags, she sewed every stitch with love.

The Chalk Doll, by Charlotte Pomerantz. HarperTrophy, 1993. Rose's mommy tells her daughter stories about her girlhood in Jamaica. She tells about the time she had three pennies to spend, about the pink taffeta dress her mother sewed for her, and about the rag doll she had. Then mommy and Rose make a rag doll together.

Princess, by Susan L. Roth. Hyperion, 1993. Although the little girl in the story hears her mother say, "Wake up, Princess!" every morning, she knows she's not a princess. If she were a princess, she'd sleep 'til 10, eat chocolates for breakfast, and wear diamond-studded shoes. Children will love the imaginative and colorful cut-paper collage illustrations in this book.

Trade-in Mother, by Marisabina Russo. Greenwillow, 1993. Nothing is going right for Max. His mother is saying no to everything he wants. He tells her she is the worst mother in the whole world and he wishes he could trade her in for a different mother. His mother says, "I would never trade you in." And the day ends with a good-night kiss.

Why Do You Love Me? by Dr. Laura Schlessinger and Martha Lambert. Cliff Street Books, 1999. A little boy asks his mother why she loves him. Her reassuring answer is that it's not because of the things he can do, but just because he's the one and only Sammy, and her son. She lets him know that she will always love him, no matter what.

Brave as a Mountain Lion, by Ann Herbert Scott. Clarion, 1996. A contemporary Shoshone boy, Spider, is afraid because has to get up on a stage in front of an audience to participate in a spelling bee. He asks his father, brother and grandmother what to do to feel brave, and they give him wise advice.

Someday Rider, by Ann Herbert Scott. Clarion, 1991. Kenny is impatient to learn to ride a horse as his father and the other cowboys do. But his mother tells him he is not ready yet. He tries riding a goose, a sheep and a calf, but it just doesn't work! His mother watches and decides that it is time to teach him to ride. And when his father needs some more hands for the roundup, both Kenny and his mother can join the group.

I Am Really A Princess, by Carol Diggory Shields. Puffin Unicorn, 1996. The heroine of this book lives every child's fantasy — that she is above the ordinary and should not be made to do the workaday chores required of regular children. Great fun!

Busy! Busy! Busy! by Jonathan Shipton. Delacorte Press, 1991. A little boy's mother is in a such a bad mood, she says she is too busy to play with him or read him a story or anything. So he plays by himself for a while. Then he creeps downstairs and sees his Mom at the kitchen sink with two big tears rolling down her cheeks. So he wipes her tears, gives her a kiss, and takes her outside to share a wonderful moment in the sunshine.

Baby Dance, by Ann Taylor. HarperFestival, 1999. This board book for the youngest preschoolers pictures the joy of a father and his little girl dancing happily together.

You are My Perfect Baby, by Joyce Carol Thomas. HarperFestival, 1999. This board book for the newest arrivals is a celebration of the wonder of a baby, perfect in every way.

Galimoto, by Karen Lynn Williams. Lothrop, Lee, & Shepard, 1990. Kondi is a seven-year-old boy who lives in a village in Malawi, in Africa. He is determined to make a galimoto of his own. This is a push-toy fashioned from bamboo, corn, wire, and other found materials, and is much prized by the children of Malawi. After many adventures as he goes about the village looking for materials, this ingenious, self-reliant little boy succeeds in making a wonderful galimoto.

Section Two

Being
an
Individual

Section Two
Being
an
Individual

Introduction

Parents know that each child is different right from the start. Research has shown that all of us have our own particular inborn personality traits. These differences in personality are referred to as temperament. The author of chapter 8 outlines the nine attributes of temperament, as researched by Stella Chess and Alexander Thomas, and helps the reader to see that these attributes are neither "good" nor "bad" ; there are advantages and disadvantages to each.

In Chapter 9, parents, teachers, and caregivers are urged to observe their youngsters in detail. To observe is much more than to look. It is to watch, listen, and think about what is happening.

By observing children, parents and teachers can note their health and development. They can see how problems may be solved, and how to plan for future events. Observation is a way to know your child even better than you do now.

SECTION TWO
BEING AN INDIVIDUAL

Chapter 8
Understanding
Differences
in Temperament

Elizabeth Kuhlman

*Every parent who has
more than one child
recognizes that each has
a very different personality
from birth.*

Your Child's Temperament
Every parent who has more than one child recognizes that each has a very different personality right from birth. Parents whose first baby slept through the night during the first three months of life and cried only when hungry are not prepared for a second child who sleeps irregularly and bellows out every need.

One child may enter nursery school eagerly with never a backward look, yet her brother may need mom or dad around for the first few days while he gets used to the new environment. Such differences in personality are referred to by psychologists as temperament.

Temperament means those qualities possessed by each of us which were present when we were born and which remain relatively unchanged throughout life.

Nine characteristics make up temperament
They are: regularity, intensity, distractibility, persistence, activity level, adaptability, approach/withdrawal, mood, and sensory threshold. Developmental psychologists see these as inborn personality traits — qualities that are relatively unchanging throughout life.

Examples of Differences in Temperament
The following are examples of differences in temperament which are representative of those commonly observed.

Two eight-month-old twin babies are playing on the floor. Willie crawls over to an electrical outlet (which is covered with child-proof caps) and begins to explore it with his hands. His twin sister Clara follows him. Their mother leaves the clothes she is folding and calls them. She rattles a milk container full of clothes pins and pours them out onto the floor. Both babies leave the outlet for the clothes pins. After a minute, while Clara is still totally absorbed with the clothes pins, Willie heads back for the outlet.

At age 2 1/2, Willie and Clara go on a car trip with the rest of their family. Clara settles into her car seat and is content to ride for hours. However, Willie fights against being restrained after only about an hour of driving. His parents discover that if they stop at a rest area and let him run for five minutes, he is willing to go back into the car seat without complaint. When visiting, Willie enjoys meeting new relatives and has no trouble going to sleep in strange beds. Clara, on the other hand, becomes grouchy after one day of so many changes. Her parents get worn out with her refusal to eat in restaurants and her resistance to sleep. When introduced to adoring aunts and uncles for the first time, she hides behind her mother and clings to her leg.

<u>In nursery school, at age four,</u> Willie and Clara's teachers say that both children have adjusted well to their classrooms, although they note that while Willie is loud and exuberant, with intense mood changes, Clara is more quiet, self-contained and even-tempered. The teachers are concerned, however, that Willie is having difficulty in the gym. Every day he runs around wildly, bumping into other children and literally bouncing off the walls. The teachers have discovered that he calms down quickly when they take him out of the noisy gym into a quiet environment. *Willie and Clara are twins* — two babies born within minutes of each other, raised in the same family, but very different in their responses to life.

While both babies are easily <u>distracted</u> from the electrical outlet, Willie's interest <u>persists</u> and he returns. <u>Active</u> Willie cannot tolerate the car seat and needs frequent opportunities to run off his energy; he <u>adapts</u> easily to all the changes he experiences during the family trip. Clara, however, is thrown by change and <u>withdraws</u> from new situations and people.

At school, Willie's <u>intensity</u> shows up in his exuberance and in the strength of his <u>moods</u>. Clara's moods are less changeable. Finally, the teachers discover that Willie's difficulties in the gym are the result of his inability to deal with the noise level created by the excited voices of twenty children echoing throughout the gym's cavernous space; this is because he has <u>low sensory</u> <u>threshold</u>.

Descriptions of the Nine
Attributes of Temperament

Researchers Stella Chess, M.D., and Alexander Thomas, M.D., describe the nine attributes of temperament in their book: *Know Your Child: An Authoritative Guide for Today's Parents.* (See Resources, page 70).

Activity Level
Some children are full of energy and always on the go. They require lots of exercise. Others are content with relatively little activity.

Intensity
Some children are loud and exuberant while others express themselves in a more quiet, self-contained way.

Distractibility
Some children have a hard time concentrating. Others can be easily distracted from an activity they are involved in. Still others continue their chosen activity despite distractions.

Persistence
Some children will leave what they are doing easily when a new activity is offered. Others stick to what they have chosen "through thick and thin."

Adaptability
Some children adapt readily to changes while others are "thrown off" by them.

Approach/Withdrawal
Some children are enthusiastic about new people and new experiences while others prefer to watch for a while and "warm up."

Sensory Threshold
Some children are acutely sensitive to light, sound, texture, temperature, while others are not bothered by a barrage of sensory stimuli.

Mood
Some children have predominantly positive reactions to what is happening while others have predominantly negative reactions.

Regularity
Some children have very regular sleeping, eating, and digestive rhythms, while others are not hungry or sleepy on a predictable schedule.

Each Attribute Has Advantages and Disadvantages
It is important to understand that all the variations of each quality have their advantages and disadvantages in later life. The very active three year old may wear out his teachers and parents, but his energy level will enable great accomplishments as he matures. The quiet child may get into less trouble, but also runs the risk of being overlooked.

Distractibility can be a stumbling block in learning, but it is an asset in being able to "switch gears" easily and quickly. The person who is active and distractible, yet persistent, can learn to give himself frequent activity breaks which will allow him to return to a task refreshed and see it through to completion.

An important part of growing up is learning to understand and accept one's own temperament, to make best use of temperamental strengths, and to accommodate temperamental difficulties. That is why it is important for parents to understand their preschooler's individual temperament.

Responding to Your Child's Temperament

The possibilities for differences in temperament between children, even in the same family, are vast when one considers the number of different qualities involved in temperament and the possible levels for any child within each quality. Understanding, accepting, and appreciating your child's individual temperamental qualities can make life easier and more pleasant for both of you.

Suppose your preschool child enjoys new situations, adapts easily to change, has regular eating and sleeping habits, is moderately active and moderate in the intensity of his moods. It would probably have been easy to get him onto a regular schedule when he was a baby, easy to toilet train him, and he probably will have made a happy adjustment to preschool. As he progresses through school, however, you may need to help him learn to stand up for his rights, rather than adapting readily to any situation which presents itself.

On the other hand, if your preschool child is very active and distractible, intense in mood, and irregular in body functions, you've probably had your hands full since he was born. It helps to let such a child know, both in words and by adjusting your expectations of him, that you understand his temperament. This does not mean that you tolerate unacceptable behavior (no matter how active he is, he may not run across the street; no matter how intense his anger with a younger sibling, he may not hit or kick). Acceptance of such a child means making sure there is enough physical activity in a day; periods of relative quiet should be followed by time at the park or playground; car trips can be broken up by stops to run around a rest area.

It is helpful to separate the issue of nutritional intake from mealtime, and the issue of adequate sleep from bedtime. You may require that your child "attend" mealtimes with the rest of the family, but allow her not to eat much if she is not hungry. Nutritional "snacks" can be available in the refrigerator for her to help herself at times when she is hungry. Similarly, you may require that she be in bed at a reasonable hour, that she stay there, and that she be quiet. But if she cannot go to sleep, she may be allowed a quiet activity such as listening to a favorite tape with ear phones.

The basically quiet child presents another "cluster" of temperamental qualities. If your child is not very active, has mild moods, is slow to warm up to new situations, and not very adaptable to change — she may need considerable support from you in preschool so that she doesn't get "lost in the shuffle." It is important not to label such a child as "shy," but to allow her to take her time in adapting. It will also help to arrange for time for getting used to new situations. For example, when choosing a preschool, make sure the staff plans for a gradual adjustment period when your child enters. Plan to be able to stay with her for several days. She may need to go for shorter periods at first. She must be allowed to stand and watch until she is ready to move into group activities on her own.

As your child matures, successful integration of temperament with life experiences depends on the match between your expectations and her temperament. Sometimes parents expect conformity to a lifestyle or "schedule" of achievements which are ill-suited to a child's temperament. A classic example would be the expectation by a parent that an irregular child be toilet trained by age two. Such a "mismatch" of expectation and temperament results in a "no win" struggle between parent and child which can ultimately result in emotional and behavioral problems.

A good match between parent and child involves mutual respect. When a parent understands and manages temperamental issues with sensitivity and respect, the child learns to accept and appreciate herself. She also learns to make whatever adjustments are necessary to accommodate her temperamental peculiarities. Such self-awareness is the foundation of maturity.

We are indebted to Dr. Stella Chess for reviewing this work by Elizabeth Kuhlman and offering comments and suggestions.

Chapter 9
Observing: A Major Way
of Knowing Your Child

Harriet Heath

*Observing
is often
the first step
in solving
a problem.*

"You should have seen Katie at the park today," Maggie was reciting to her husband her experience with their eighteen-month-old daughter. "She headed straight for the jungle gym. I felt it was too high. It was higher than I am (Maggie was five feet ten inches tall). And the bars were too far apart. She could barely reach the next one.

"First, I picked her up and headed toward the swings, telling her I'd swing her. She just squirmed and kept saying, 'Me climb. Me climb.'

"I tried her on the little merry-go-round and the sand box with no success. She just kept heading off for the jungle gym.

"So finally I let her try. I stood right behind her ready to catch her if she fell. But she didn't. It was amazing. She seemed to know just how to do it. First, with both hands she got a solid grip on the bar just over her head. Then she moved her feet to the lowest bar, one foot at a time, the instep of each foot resting on the rung. Then she grabbed the next bar up with her right hand. She could barely reach it but she grabbed it tightly. When that hand had a firm grip the left hand went up. Then one foot and then the other. Her eyes were fixed on the bar above her. She did not look around or smile. She went up that tall jungle gym like an experienced pro. I didn't need to worry.

"The funny thing is that the books on development talk about kids climbing at this age. I just didn't believe they could!"

Maggie had given her husband a detailed observation.

Observing is noting what is going on. It entails watching closely and listening carefully. Observing is the parents' basic way of gathering information about their children: How does she act when she really wants to do something? How does he explore a new object? How competent is he?

Observing strengthens our parenting.
By closely observing her daughter, Maggie was able to tell whether or not her child was safe and could manage this adventure of climbing the jungle gym. Observing was a means for Maggie to know what her child could do and how she did it.

By observing and checking with a resource about development, Maggie could confirm that her child's pattern of growth was comparable with that of other children's.

By observing Maggie was able to share the event. She described to her husband, Ted, each of her maneuvers to divert Katie's attention from the jungle gym and exactly how Katie had climbed it. Giving Ted these details helped keep him in touch with his daughter and the kind of person she is. Observing provided Maggie a means of sharing with Ted her experience with Katie.

Teachers and child care providers observing the children in their care are in an excellent position to keep parents in touch with their children in the same way Maggie kept Ted in touch.

By observing, parents determine the health of their children.
Johnny's parents noticed that on some days their three-year-old would respond quickly when they called — but on other days he wouldn't move. Observing him closely they realized that on those days when he ignored them, he would also turn his music and the TV on louder.

A trip to the doctor on a day when Johnny wasn't as responsive revealed he had liquid behind the ear drum which was interfering with his hearing.

Careful observing of how Johnny was responding to sound in different situations gave his parents information that something might be wrong and that Johnny wasn't just being rebellious.

Observing is often the first step in solving a problem.
Regardless of the time of day, Bill and Mary's children seldom were able to play happily together. Five-year-old Tim was forever hitting four-year-old Gail. After ten minutes of playing in the same room Gail would be in tears and accusing Tim of hitting her. All kinds of punishments did not seem to teach Tim not to hit. His explanation, "She's always bothering me," did not seem to his parents to justify his actions.

The parents were at a loss over what to do about the problem. "We just don't have enough information," they concluded.

At the next opportunity they planned that one of them would try to follow the interaction between the two children. One rainy afternoon when the children settled in their play area with paper and crayons, Mary took the laundry to be folded and worked in an adjoining room. That evening she reported to her husband what she had observed.

"As they were getting settled, Tim announced, 'I'm going to draw a space ship.'

"Immediately Gail commented, 'You can't make one that looks real,' or something like that.

"Tim snapped back 'I can so.'

"Then there was a short quiet. I peeked in and they were both sitting on the floor busy coloring. Tim was sitting strangely, though. He had himself sort of curled around his drawing with his back towards Gail, as if he were protecting it.

"While I was still watching, Gail scooted over, around Tim, looked at his drawing and laughed. 'I told you that you couldn't draw a spaceship. It needs a captain's deck. Here, I'll show you.' And she actually raised her hand with a crayon as if she were to start to draw. Tim's hand came up, fist clenched, and I moved in," finished Mary.

By observing, Mary and Bill could better understand both Tim's and Gail's role in their conflict and, consequently, how better to deal with it.

Observing is usually the first step in planning for an upcoming event.
As she started to prepare supper, June watched her four-year-old son, Sam, coloring on the floor next to her. He had been working on this type of picture for over a week now, drawing one after another after another. First he would draw curving lines that intersected and twisted back on themselves, covering the whole 18"x12" size paper. Using a variety of colors he carefully planned what colors to put next to each other. Then he would meticulously color in each open space. June was continually amazed at the differences in his pictures though he always started with large sweeping lines that twisted and curved around the page.

"This is so typical of Sam," she thought. "He takes an idea and reworks it again and again." He had done the same when drawing figures. He'd drawn hundreds, it seemed, before moving into these abstract designs. She thought of her plan to return to work. "I'll want to find a preschool program that will provide him the freedom to experiment with coloring and with art materials," she thought. "I would not want to jeopardize his creativity." June's observations were guiding her planning.

The ability to observe is an important skill for parents and caregivers to have. Through their observations they come to know the children in their care, keep in touch with their development, better deal with problems that evolve and plan more adequately for them.

The Ingredients
of a
Useful
Observation

For an observation to be useful it must be objective and include detail.
So often parents are told their child has been so good. If parents stop to
think about this observation, they quickly realize they know nothing about
their child's life while they were absent. Had their child been involved
with other children, or had she sat passively without participating? Had
he slept all afternoon, sat in front of a TV, had a walk, a story, a snack, or
any combination thereof? Interpretations, judgments, and even summaries
of events are quick and easy but they provide little specific information
about what has happened. They provide little knowledge on which to build
an understanding of the child.

Observations to be useful need to include detailed information about three components of an event:

• One is the *setting* of the event. This description should include details about the time and the objects and equipment in the setting. Maggie's description of the jungle gym is a good example. Her details about its height and the distance between the bars is important if the listener is to grasp the feat eighteen-month-old Katie accomplished in climbing it. Johnny's parents related his lack of response to them to the loudness of the TV and music. Mary and Bill noted that their children seemed to fight at any time of the day not just when they were tired or hungry, a time many children are more apt to fight.

• The second component of an observation is a *description of the people involved* with details as to each person's expression and body language, and how they moved. The description of how Katie climbed the jungle gym, how Johnny responded to his parents, or how Tim protected his drawing from his sister's view — all added to the understanding of these events.

• The last component is recording *the sequence of events.* Mary could not understand Gail's role in the conflict between the siblings, if she had not noted the sequence of events leading up to the eruption.

A useful observation freezes what has occurred. It captures the essence of the event. The observation may be kept in memory, written and/or described verbally. Written ones, of course, are most permanent. But the important point to remember is that useful observations need to record all information because one never knows which piece will be important. Observations give us the information on which we, as parents or teachers, can base the guidance and planning needed to help our children.

Write an observation of your child or children when they are occupied. As you read back through, can you see the event? Read it to your parenting partner. Can your partner see the event? What additional information does she/he wish you had given her/him?

Observing is not easy. It takes practice to develop the skill. But it is a skill that parents constantly rely on. Being able to make detailed, objective observations will facilitate any parent's nurturing efforts.

Resources for Section Two: Being an Individual

FOR ADULTS

Know Your Child: An Authoritative Guide for Today's Parents, by Stella Chess and Alexander Thomas. Aronson, 1996. This is an comprehensive overview of various theories of child development, with an emphasis on the authors' research into children's temperament. It explains the nine categories of temperament and discusses the importance of coming to terms with the child's basic temperament.

Observing & Recording the Behavior of Young Children, by Dorothy Cohen & Virginia Stern. 4th ed. Teachers College Press, 1996. An invaluable resource that describes methods of observing young children in different settings.

The Kindergarten Teacher's Very Own Student Observation & Assessment Guide, by Judy Keshner. Modern Learning Press, 1996. Developed by an educator and author, this paperback provides a wealth of information for teachers about observing and assessing young children's activities.

Me, Myself and I: How Children Build Their Sense of Self, by Kyle D. Pruett, M.D. Goddard Parenting Guides, 1999. In this accessible and beautifully written volume, the author's focus is on the child from 18 to 36 months, "one of the most engaging and vibrant periods in your child's life." He offers parents practical information about current child development research, differences in temperament, and the importance of the interaction of nature and nurture.

The Difficult Child, by Stanley Turecki and Leslie Tonner. Bantam Books, 1989. Using a step-by-step approach to difficulties in temperament, the authors focus on helping children whose behavior is difficult to manage.

FOR CHILDREN

Annabel, by Janice Boland. Dial Books for Young Readers, 1993. Annabel is a little pig who wants to be important and do something wonderful. She asks other animals what makes each one so special. She soon discovers that everyone is unique — including herself!

Michael, by Tony Bradman. Andersen, UK, 1998. Michael is different. He doesn't do what he's told and his teachers say he will come to no good. But like many other unique personalities, Michael suddenly blossoms and astonishes them all.

Blue-Ribbon Henry, by Mary Calhoun. Morrow, 1999. Henry the cat is entered in a pet show at the county fair. He may not be as big or as beautiful as the cat in the next cage, but he has exciting adventures at the fair, and becomes a hero with a blue ribbon of his own.

The Mixed-Up Chameleon, by Eric Carle. HarperFestival, 1998. The chameleon has the ability to change into the color of its background. But when it tries to change its shape too, becoming like each of the animals in the zoo, things get all mixed up. Being yourself is best. Children will love this colorful story, in its first board book edition.

All About All Of You, by Sue Clarke. Hyperion, 1994. A set of 4 boxed books entitled, *Bodies, Clothes, Faces,* and *Feelings,* telling how children are alike and different. Everyone has feelings, faces and bodies, but each child sees a different face in the mirror. The message comes through that every person is special.

How I Was Adopted: Samantha's Story, by Joanna Cole. Morrow, 1995. A cheerful and loving story told by a little girl about her adoption. The author has written "A Note to Families" at the start of the book. In it, she explains that "...this is not a "problem" book. Instead, it tells the youngest children what adoption is and how it happens..."

Dottie, by Peta Coplans. Houghton Mifflin, 1994. Dottie is a dog who loves gardening. Never mind that dogs don't usually grow things. Dottie is unique. And eventually even her parents learn to appreciate her individuality.

The Other Emily, by Gibbs Davis. Houghton Mifflin, 1990. Emily loves her name. On her first day of school, she wears a T-shirt with the words: *The 1 & only EMILY.* But that very first day, she finds out that there is another Emily in her class — and she thought she was the only Emily in the world. She doesn't feel special anymore. But soon she finds that sharing a name can lead to sharing other fun things together.

You're My Nikki, by Phyllis Rose Eisenberg. Puffin, 1995. Nikki is afraid her Mama will forget all about her when she starts her new job. But while Mama may be tired and busy when she gets home, she can offer love and reassurance that she will never forget her Nikki.

The Chick and the Duckling, by Mirra Ginsburg. Aladdin, 1988. In this simple tale translated from the Russian, a chick and a duckling find many ways in which they are alike but they learn that there are differences when they both try to go for a swim .

All the Colors of the Earth, by Sheila Hamanaka. Mulberry, 1999. With lyrical language and glorious colors, this book celebrates our love for children's beauty and diversity.

Chrysanthemum, by Kevin Henkes. Greenwillow, 1991. Chrysanthemum was a perfect little mouse, with a perfect name. When she started school, though, the other children teased her about her name: imagine — she was named after a *flower!* Chrysanthemum didn't think her name was perfect any longer; she felt terrible. And then the music teacher, Mrs. Delphinium Twinkle, arrived, and everything magically changed for Chrysanthemum.

Harry and Tuck, by Holly Keller. Greenwillow, 1993. Harrison and Tucker were twins. They did everything together. They liked it that way. Then they started kindergarten, and were placed in different rooms with different teachers. They missed each other, but they each found things to do. Some things they did were the same; some were different. They liked it that way!

Leo the Late Bloomer, by Robert Kraus. HarperTrophy, 1971. Leo the little lion can't do anything right: he can't read; he can't write; he can't draw. His father is worried but his mother says Leo is just a late bloomer. Father waits and waits. "Then one day, in his own good time, Leo bloomed!" *Also available in HarperChildren's Audio (Share a Story™ My First Book and Tape).* Young listeners will want to hear this gentle story again and again, about a little tiger who develops in his own good time.

Little Louie the Baby Bloomer, by Robert Kraus. HarperCollins, 1998. Fans of Leo the Late Bloomer, will want to read about Leo's little brother Louie, who couldn't do anything right. Leo tries to teach him to throw a ball, to pull a wagon, and to do other important things, and finally, in his own good way, Louie learns.

Story of Ferdinand, by Munro Leaf. Viking, 1985. This is the classic story of Ferdinand the bull, an individualist, who does not want to fight as the other bulls do, but prefers to smell the flowers.

Speak Up, Blanche! by Emily Arnold McCully. HarperCollins, 1991. Blanche loves the theater, but she is too shy to say her lines loudly enough, or even to sell tickets. They are ready to send her home. But Blanche does finally speak up for herself, in a strong voice, to tell the actors that she has a talent. She can design and paint their stage sets. She is an artist.

Amanda's Perfect Hair, by Linda Milstein. Tambourine, 1993. Everyone thinks Amanda's thick, curly, blonde hair is magnificent. But Amanda is worried that her hair is the only thing people ever notice about her, and that they miss seeing the special person she really is. So Amanda takes matters into her own hands...

Regina's Big Mistake, by Marissa Moss. Sandpiper, 1995. Regina and all the other children in class are supposed to draw a jungle or a rain forest on the big blank piece of paper in front of each of them. The others don't seem to have any trouble drawing trees, and lions, and birds, but when Regina begins, she is afraid she has made a mistake, and she crumples up her paper. She tries again and finally creates a beautiful picture that is all her own.

The Ugly Duckling, adapted and illustrated by Jerry Pinkney. Morrow, 1999. In this lovely adaptation of the Hans Christian Anderson tale, the ugly little duckling must overcome many obstacles until he finally grows into a beautiful swan.

Why Does That Man Have Such a Big Nose? by Mary Beth Quinsey. Parenting Press, 1986. Twelve physical and ethnic differences are pictured and explained in a respectful way that emphasizes each person's uniqueness and value.

Ruby the Copycat, by Peggy Rathmann. Scholastic, 1997. Ruby copies everything that her classmate Angela wears, says, or does, until Miss Hart, their teacher, helps Ruby to discover something unique that she can do herself.

Oscar's Spots, by Janet Robertson. Troll, 1996. The leopard in this story is named Oscar. He is so bored with his spots, he tries a magician's potion that goes much too far. When the magician finally straightens it all out, Oscar realizes, "It's lovely to be myself again."

Supergrandpa, by David M. Schwartz. Mulberry, 1998. This is a true story about Gustaf, an elderly man with a white beard who rides his bicycle everywhere. When he reads about a bicycle race called the Tour of Sweden, he decides to enter. Although the judges will not permit him to join the race, he rides anyway. Gustaf becomes a celebrity as all of Sweden learns about this Supergrandpa who wouldn't let anyone tell him to "Go home to your rocking chair."

Why Am I Different? by Norma Simon. Whitman, 1993. This book identifies various ways in which children see themselves as different. Through these differences, they can see that our world is made more colorful and interesting than if everyone were the same.

Which One Is Whitney? by James Stevenson. Greenwillow, 1990. This is a story about a family of dugongs (aquatic mammals). Of the five children, Warren's the cheerful one; Winnie's the polite one; Wally's the friendly one; Wendy's the funny one; and Whitney is none of the above. Or is he all of the above? Another humorous tale by the inimitable author/illustrator.

Cherish Me, by Joyce Carol Thomas. HarperFestival, 1998. With a text that is a lovely poem, and joyful pictures of an African-American girl, this board book celebrates the uniqueness and importance of every child.

But Names Will Never Hurt Me, by Bernard Waber. Sandpiper, 1994. Children will sympathize as they read this funny, touching story of how Alison Wonderland got her name and how she learned to live with it.

Yoko, by Rosemary Wells. Hyperion, 1998. Yoko goes to school and greets all her friends. When it's time for lunch, the children bring out their peanut butter sandwiches and their egg salad on pumpernickel. Yoko opens her lunch box. Inside is her favorite sushi. The other children laugh at Yoko's lunch. So the teacher decides to have an international food day, where everybody needs to try everything.

Section Three

Ways of
Encouraging
Children
as
They Grow

Section Three
Ways of Encouraging Children as They Grow

Introduction

I met my neighbor's little grandson today, for the first time. His grandmother brought him to our home while delivering an invitation to a party. He talked to me about the previous night's thunderstorm, and the picture on the party invitation. Later, at the corner luncheonette while having lunch with his grandmother, he waved to us in a sociable way. Although he had just met us, he was open and friendly. As one author points out in this section, self-confident children interact with other people with the expectation that they will be well received.

In innocence, a child may make his parents uncomfortable by asking, "Why does that [pregnant] lady have such a big tummy?" Chapter 12 offers appropriate responses to this question and others, and explains how answering children's questions is an ongoing process.

If your toddler doesn't talk very much, chapter 10 explains that the normal range for expressive language is huge — from six months to almost two years. "All children...have their own unique rate and pattern of development during the early years," states the author, who offers a common sense approach to developmental guidelines.

A common sense approach is also important when you consider that boys and girls behave differently. Are they born that way — or are they taught to be different? Chapter 14 offers parents and teachers important insights into the research about gender.

WAYS OF ENCOURAGING YOUNG CHILDREN AS THEY GROW

Chapter 10
Making Sense
of
Developmental Milestones

Michael K. Meyerhoff

Like snowflakes, sunsets,
and other miracles of nature,
no two children are exactly alike.

"Why isn't David talking yet? He's 18 months old. His brother Danny was saying 'Mama' and 'Dada' by nine months."

"Your Jennifer isn't walking yet? My Sharon was born two weeks before her, and she's been walking for a month!"

"Do you mean to tell me my grandson still isn't toilet trained? He's almost three years old! I had you and your sister trained before you were two."

"I don't care if they aren't teaching reading in Emily's kindergarten class. Her cousin Laura was reading by the age of five, so she should be able to handle it too."

The first words...the first steps...toilet training...reading readiness. For most parents, the "as expected" appearance of major developmental milestones is a source of relief, happiness, and pride. Unfortunately, for some mothers and fathers, the "off-schedule" emergence of these achievements produces considerable anxiety, alarm, and confusion. However, while a child "missing the mark" may, indeed, be cause for genuine concern on occasion — *in many cases the real problem is simply a basic misunderstanding of what developmental milestones are all about.*

The Myth of the "Normal" Child

All children — even genetically identical twins — have their own unique rate and pattern of development during the early years. Like snowflakes, sunsets, and other miracles of nature, no two children are exactly alike. Of course, when psychologists and educators study young children as a group, various norms may be established. The standards resulting from such studies are merely statistical concepts. They do not represent a distinct and precise timetable, and they are not intended to describe something that routinely occurs in the real world. In fact, if researchers come up with a "typical" rate and pattern of progress based upon a study of 100 children, it is highly unlikely that the development of any one of those children will match every detail of the collective description.

For that reason, psychologists and educators usually do not like to pinpoint the expected appearance of new abilities, preferring instead to offer reasonable "ranges." For example, the average age at which a child can sit up by herself may be calculated as 5 1/2 months, but the deviations from this date may be so wide and numerous that anything between 4 1/2 and 6 1/2 months must still be regarded as perfectly acceptable. Parents often receive the wrong impression that the designations of what is "normal" are far more rigid than they actually are.

The plague of inappropriate comparisons

While parents appreciate the notion of normal ranges on an intellectual level, a lot of parents can't help feeling that something is wrong if their child's development is slower than the children of friends or relatives.

Comments like "Your Andrew still can't button his own coat? My Adam is two months younger and he can dress himself completely!" while insensitive and inappropriate, are hard to ignore.

Development is not a race but a process

The problem seems to lie in our inevitable tendency to view all comparisons in a competitive light. We seem to have trouble acknowledging that "differently" does not automatically mean "better" or "worse" and that "equal" does not necessarily mean "identical." It is therefore important for mothers and fathers to keep in mind that development is not a race, it is a process. *In the long run, most children end up in pretty much the same place at roughly the same time, even though they may take separate routes and proceed at varying paces along the way.* So it usually is meaningless to refer to a child's progress at any point as "advanced" or "slow" just because she reached one or another milestone earlier or later than a neighbor, cousin, sister, or brother.

The emergence of speech is perhaps the best example of this. No one knows what prompts a child to begin speaking, and no one knows how to accelerate the acquisition of this skill. Yet one couple will boast that their Camille said her first words at seven or eight months, while another couple will lament that their Tina has yet to say anything at 17 or 18 months. The fact of the matter is that despite the apparently large discrepancy, neither Camille nor Tina has demonstrated anything unusual; and it is still a safe bet that both children will be using complex phrases and complete sentences shortly after the second birthday — and there even is a reasonable chance that Tina will start doing so before Camille.

Undue pressure can retard development

Perhaps the most distressing examples of inappropriate comparisons concern the completion of toilet training and the onset of reading readiness. Clearly, these are important milestones in the overall span of development. However, the precise point at which they emerge during the early years really is of relatively little significance. Unfortunately, many parents believe that anything past the average age reflects a lack of intelligence or poor quality parenting. Consequently, they put strong and improper pressure on their children to take on tasks for which they are not ready, and this results in failure, frustration, and the pursuit of counterproductive practices that actually delay the natural course of development.

Labeling can be harmful

Parents also should beware of the common inclination to make inappropriate judgments based on comparisons between different aspects of their own child's development. For instance, if a child is "early" with the first smiles and "late" with the first steps, some mothers and fathers may unconsciously and unfairly start thinking of her as very "social" but not very "physical." Remember, the rate and pattern of individual development are both rather irregular, so this is not likely to be accurate as a lasting characterization. And to the extent that it shapes parent/child interactions and parental expectations, it can lead to potentially detrimental practices and disappointment.

When to be concerned

The primary purpose for mapping out developmental milestones is to help parents determine when their child needs professional help. While they should be concerned when their child gets to the upper end of an age range, or approaches the upper ends of all age ranges, they should not panic. Instead of looking just at the age ranges, mothers and fathers should learn more about the underlying developmental processes involved in a particular milestone.

This point can be illustrated by using language development as an example. As noted earlier, the normal range for the emergence of **expressive language** (when children say the first words) is huge — from six months to almost two years. On the other hand, the normal range for the emergence of **receptive language** (when they understand the first words) is rather narrow — from six months to eight months at most. Therefore, if their child is approaching her first birthday and hasn't yet started speaking, there probably is no reason for parents to get upset or fear that she is in imminent danger of developing serious problems. But if she is not responding properly to her name or simple instructions (such as "wave bye-bye" or "give me a kiss"), then it is possible that she is suffering from a mild to moderate hearing loss, and she should be checked out by a pediatrician soon so that an undetected congenital dysfunction or persistent ear infection won't cause further delays.

Some children skip milestones

Many parents, upon further independent investigation, may be surprised to discover that various "intermediary" milestones may be missed entirely without any damage ensuing whatsoever. For instance, a small number of children skip crawling and go right to walking; some children go directly from one-word utterances to complete sentences without passing through a stage of using two- and three-word phrases; and a few children never exhibit "parallel play" (playing alongside other children without actually interacting) before engaging in true peer play activities. There is absolutely no solid evidence to support the idea that these lapses are disadvantageous (or advantageous) in any way.

The Need to Anticipate

In addition to their usefulness in alerting parents and professionals to potential problems, developmental milestones are very helpful to mothers and fathers in planning appropriate childrearing strategies. It is wise not only to note each achievement as it passes by, but to pay attention to what might be coming along in the months ahead as well.

For safety: Perhaps the best examples of this point concern the need to anticipate the emergence of new physical abilities in order to ensure that proper safety precautions are put into place. Although the majority of children do not start crawling and climbing until they are well into the second half of the first year, it is a good idea to remove or replace anything in the house that could be harmful to a child (or that she could harm) long before that in case she decides to pull off an early surprise. And while most children do not become capable of throwing a ball or swinging a bat with any real power until sometime around the third birthday, it would be wise to institute some relevant rules and set aside some appropriate areas well in advance instead of waiting for an accident to occur.

For intellectual development: Although the majority of children do not show signs of reading readiness until five or six years of age, they do enjoy and profit from pointing-and-naming games with picture books starting at around two years of age, page-turning exercises starting at around one year of age, and being read to at almost any age.

The need to show appreciation
Another thing to keep in mind is that some milestones in one area of development may be key players in promoting optimal progress in another area as well. For example, with regard to the emergence of new physical abilities, anticipating and safety-proofing accordingly is only half the game. In order for a child to develop healthy self-esteem and pride in achievement, it is necessary for her first successful episodes of walking, climbing, throwing a ball, pedaling tricycle, etc. to be accompanied by reactions of excitement and enthusiasm from her mother and father.

Preparing for behavioral milestones
Anticipating the appearance of behavioral milestones may help mothers and fathers maintain their own mental health. Knowing that virtually every child enters a period of "negativism" (constantly pushing limits, refusing requests, and testing wills) during the latter part of the second year prevents parents from taking it personally when their sweet, innocent infant turns into an occasionally nasty toddler. Knowing that almost all three-year-olds develop an intense interest in imitating adult activities and "acting grown up''' helps parents to be patient about the initiation of toilet training. And knowing that most four-year-olds go through a phase of asking "Why?" incessantly enables parents to avoid becoming overly annoyed when subjected to a seemingly endless round of questioning.

Final Comments

While all children have their own unique rate and pattern of development, some groups go through the milestones in a fashion distinctly different from depicted "norms." For example, children born prematurely routinely tend to achieve early physical abilities according to a schedule that is more appropriately standardized from their original due date rather than their actual birth date. And first-borns routinely tend to be "early" while later-borns routinely tend to be "late" with regard to initial achievements in language development. Nevertheless, there are always exceptions, and everyone and everything tends to even out as the months go by.

The important thing to remember is that established milestones can provide a general picture of "typical" development during the early years, *but they cannot provide a precise blueprint for the progress of any particular child.* Although books, articles, and charts often may describe it in a concise and organized manner, the fact of the matter is that early development is never a neat and orderly affair. And while parents may want to compare their child's progress to that of other children and standard norms from time to time, they should never forget to appreciate and enjoy the special individuality demonstrated by their own child.

Chapter 11
Helping Young Children Achieve a Sense of Competence

Neala S. Schwartzberg

*Autonomy begins
with the development
of a sense of basic trust:
a baby's belief that she can rely
on her caregivers.*

Mikey is crying in his crib. He has just awakened from his nap and he's ready to leave the confines of his bed. As Mikey's father comes into the room Mikey grins broadly and reaches out his little arms. "Me out," he calls. His father grins back, "Hi little guy, had enough nap time?" He picks Mikey up, "Come on then, let's roll."

We often think that a toddler exhibits autonomy when he is determined to walk across the floor by himself, or when the preschooler rejects adult help to make the letter *B*. But autonomy is something which begins in infancy from the experiences caregivers provide from the earliest moments of a baby's life. And it is shown in small ways: a mother sensing that her baby doesn't want to play peek-a-boo right now; a baby toddling across the floor secure in the knowledge that his mother standing near will be there if he needs her; little Mikey calling out, knowing someone will "rescue" him from his crib.

Basic trust

Autonomy begins with the development of a sense of basic trust: a baby's belief that she can rely on her caregivers. We create a sense of trust when we provide sensitive care of our baby's needs, when our baby knows that we will be there. With this certain knowledge that if they need help, help will be there, toddlers begin to reach out and explore.

We foster autonomy and competence when we encourage children to take on and succeed in new skills. These capabilities grow when children realize they can communicate their needs to us, and we will listen. We foster autonomy by being a resource for children, helping them to discover the solutions to their problems calmly and gently without overwhelming them with *our* solutions.

Developing a sense of initiative

Children develop a sense of initiative by exploring and manipulating objects. When they are little it may be seen in activities as simple as piling up blocks, placing stickers on a page, or writing a story in scribbles. As they get older they will start to develop little projects on their own: making a birthday card, setting up a party for their dolls, pretending to dress up as adults and go to the store, making incredible machines. This kind of play helps them develop a sense of autonomy and competence — *an "I can do it" attitude.* If you listen you can hear them actually put this into words — "Look at the machine I made!" "Don't you think my birthday card is nice?" They'll do this with physical activity also. "Look at me swing, I can swing so high!" "I can run so fast, faster than you." You should validate and encourage their independence and achievements. "That's a great machine. Look how well you put the parts together." "What a lovely card. Aunt Jean will love it." "You sure are a fast runner!"

Sometimes this exploration and experimentation doesn't match what adults would like to see happen. Many a baby has exasperated his parents by tossing food over the side of the high chair and watching with delight as it splatters on the floor. Other babies watch food squish through their fingers. Troublesome children? No — children learning about gravity, about cause and effect, about the way things operate, and their ability to cause things to happen.

The importance of communication
Communication is a big part of autonomy and competence. Help children express their ideas and listen to them when they do. The ability to communicate helps children affect the world around them. It doesn't have to be only verbal communication. Some children are very late talkers and use mime to help convey their meaning. Babies express their thoughts and feelings through their body language. When baby is tired of playing peek-a-boo, she will turn her head away to signal that she's had enough, at least for now.

It's also important to encourage children's explorations and celebrate their successes. When children and adults believe their own efforts are responsible for their successes, they see a direct relationship between effort and achievement. Children know that if they want something they can work to achieve it. Psychologists call this an *"internal locus of control."* Children and adults who feel they are buffeted by chance and the actions of others have an *"external locus of control."* Examples of this are: a child can't cut out a paper doll because the scissors are *stupid,* or the dough won't roll because the rolling pin is *broken.*

How adults can help
A sensitive adult encourages a child to see situations he can control and help him control them. Let's see how this would work. Four-year-old Timmy's shout of frustration brings his father to the kitchen table. Timmy has been trying and failing to cut out a picture from a magazine. "These scissors are stupid," he complains. His father says, "Well, maybe, but I've never seen a pair of stupid scissors. Why don't you cut out another picture and let me see what's going on?" As his father watches he sees Timmy wildly chopping with the scissors. "Whoa!" says his dad. "Why don't you cut really slowly and follow the outlines. If you have trouble seeing the outlines, I'll make them darker for you." Timmy follows his father's suggestions and successfully cuts out a picture.

Angela is trying to put on her shoes by herself. No matter how hard she tries she just can't seem to get her foot into the shoe. She carries the shoe to her mother. "This is broken," she announces as she drops the shoe on the floor. Her mother looks carefully at the shoe. "Do you think the opening is too small for your foot?" "Yes!" agrees Angela. "Do you think there is some way for us to make that opening larger?" asks her mother, "Maybe something to do with opening up these laces? Do you want to try that?" Angela nods as she tugs at the laces. "Now it's bigger," says Angela as she puts on the shoe.

What are the characteristics of autonomous and competent children? They approach tasks with the expectation that they will be successful, and interact with people with the expectation that they will be well received. They have confidence in themselves and their ability to achieve. They trust themselves to be able to handle situations and activities. They believe that they will be successful because they are competent and because they know how to work hard and solve problems which confront them.

Dos and Don'ts

• Don't leave babies (less than 12 months of age) to "cry it out" as a regular policy. They can come to decide that the world is not a caring or responsive place. Babies can't be "spoiled" in the sense that they come to demand extraordinary amounts of attention. They cry and fuss because they are unhappy and upset. Yes, it is true that some babies need more attention than others. But they aren't being unreasonable from their point of view. They don't want to be alone or be in that crib. Babies should be treated as the center of the universe.

• Toddlers are ready to confront the world. Make their environment interesting and stimulating. They want to walk, investigate, explore. If they want to take everything out of drawers within their reach, why not set aside one or two baby drawers, full of interesting and safe objects for them to play with. But also remember that safety comes first.

• Toddlers are also ready to begin to solve challenges. Provide them with shape sorters, blocks, etc. But it isn't easy for them. Do make sure they have age-appropriate materials. Tiny blocks and shape sorters with intricate forms which are too similar to each other will frustrate these young preschoolers. Help them learn the shapes and share in their joy when one of those shapes is finally pushed through the opening.

• At each stage of development, let them proceed on their own until they reach their limits. Then step in and offer gentle suggestions: "Let's count the corners," "Are all the sides the same length? Let's measure." Make sure puzzle pieces are large and easy to use. And work with the youngster helping her to see where the piece goes. But if she wants to put a piece where it obviously won't fit, let her. The purpose is to learn and she can learn from mistakes too. Remember that the idea is to build a sense of competence and autonomy. If she is not allowed to make her own decisions, she may get the puzzle perfect, but she won't have done it herself.

• Don't take over projects — resist the temptation. You know you've taken over if you find yourself saying "Here, let me do that," or "That will never work." Then it's time to sit back and remember that the child is doing the playing and the learning. There is usually a thin line between providing the support to be successful and doing the puzzle for the youngster. Walk it carefully and with awareness.

• Do give them choices rather than open-ended options. Don't ask "Do you want to drink your milk?" it is too easy for youngsters to say, '"No!" It's one of their favorite words anyway. Give them a choice of drinking cups, or whether to drink milk or juice. If you say, "We're going out now; get something to wear," you could end up with a child holding a bathing suit insisting that it is appropriate clothing for February. Instead, say, "Pick one of your jackets to wear outside." It is better to create a situation in which all the decisions are choices you can be satisfied with.

Chapter 12
Answering Preschoolers' Questions About Pregnancy, Birth, and How Their Bodies Work

Neala S. Schwartzberg

Don't feel that
you have to push
your child beyond
what he wants to know.

When your preschooler asks, "How was I born?" your first thought might be, "Isn't this too soon?" But it really isn't. Like children at any age, preschoolers are curious about the world around them. Their questions about the human body — its parts and functions — is just another example of their constant curiosity. Answering, "Where did I come from?" is not much different from answering, "Why is the sky blue?" or even, "How does that big tree grow from that little seed?" Be open and natural. How much information is enough? Provide as much information as you feel is appropriate to the situation and your child's developmental level. But, don't underestimate his ability to understand information which is presented simply and clearly.

Some children have more curiosity than others. Don't feel that you have to push your child beyond what he wants to know. As long as he knows that you will be there to answer his questions, he will come to you whenever something puzzles him. Try to be aware of, and sensitive to, the situations in which questions are likely to arise. Open the topic naturally using something going on in your child's life, a pregnancy in the family (including pets), or a trip to the zoo. Reading books with your youngster is another good way to bring forth your child's questions.

Although you may feel uncomfortable, and wonder if "professionals" could do a better job — *you*, as the parent, are the best teacher. No professional could be as sensitive and aware as you are of the needs of your individual child. The most important qualification is not an academic degree, it is the willingness to talk honestly and openly. Resist the temptation to avoid answering the topic with non-information or misinformation.

Teaching your youngster about reproduction is only part of the educational process. Your preschooler also wants to know about her body, how it works, and how it changes as she grows. While she is too young to understand the mechanics of sexual behavior, she's not too young to understand the emotional caring that makes a man and woman love each other, and the child they produce.

Dealing with inappropriate behavior
Sometimes a preschooler will engage in an activity which upsets parents and other primary caregivers. They worry about children examining themselves and the bodies of their friends, preferring to be nude at inappropriate times, and using sexual language in their play. According to Jennifer Birckmayer, of the Department of Human Development and Family Studies at Cornell University and author of the monograph, "Beyond the Birds and Bees," unless these behaviors are extreme, occupying most of a child's waking hours, these activities should not be regarded as problems.

Children (as well as adults) like to do things which give them pleasure. Children will touch their genitals because it feels good. Your child will not harm himself or herself, from this kind of touching. But acceptance of this behavior doesn't mean they can do it in the living room or the playroom. Gently remind your child that there are things we do in private and this is one of them.

When an adult discovers children "playing doctor" she may be unsure of how to react. If you feel uncomfortable with the game, react honestly by saying, "I'd rather you kept your clothes on when you play together," or "People's bodies are private. Let's find some books so that we can see how people are made by looking at the pictures."

What is the parents' role?
Be an information resource so your child can come to you anytime she has a question or doesn't understand something. Children need to feel comfortable asking about words they hear and don't understand, things other kids have said that sound wrong, even an idea which has just popped into their heads.

It is also helpful to *learn what your child already knows or believes.* According to Anne Bernstein, Ph.D., author of *The Flight Of The Stork,* (See Resources, page 106) the adult who asks "What do you think?" when asked a question, learns what the child knows or thinks he knows. The adult can now correct misinformation or reassure the youngster about troubling fantasies. Once you find out the kind of information your child knows, you can gear your explanation to his level of understanding. But Dr. Bernstein cautions never to make children feel silly or foolish about their ideas. Use them as a starting point, correct misinformation (gently), and provide additional information.

Answering your preschooler's questions is an ongoing process. It is not a one-time, "sit down and let's discuss the birds and bees" topic. They cannot absorb everything at once. As their ability to think and ponder grows they will want to come back and clarify the points which puzzle them.

The article on the next page gives suggestions as to how to answer your preschooler's questions.

Responding to Children's Questions and Behavior

There is no one "right" way to answer a child's questions, or handle a behavior. It depends on the youngster's age, circumstances, and prior knowledge. The following are suggestions which parents may find helpful. But the most important thing is to be sensitive to your youngster, open, and available for discussion.

What do you say —
When your daughter asks, "Can I marry Daddy when I grow up?"
It is very common for a little girl to want to marry her father and a little boy to want to marry his mother. They've watched mommy and daddy enjoy one another's company, and they want to have that kind of relationship. Their solution, to marry mommy or daddy makes sense from their perspective. Respect these feelings but tell them that it is not possible for children to marry their parents. They will find someone when they are older to love and marry.

When your preschooler asks,
"Why do boys and girls go to the bathroom differently?"
Although this is a fairly simple question, it often leads to more complicated ones. The basic explanation is that boys have a penis so they can stand up and urinate. Girls do not have a penis so they need to sit down. Ending the explanation there may leave a little girl feeling short-changed so a parent might want to add a bit more about the differences in male and female anatomy. Girls have a uterus or womb where babies grow and a vagina which is the opening babies use when being born. Don't be too surprised if this leads to further discussion about babies, or about which gender is better designed.

When your child sees an infant nursing
at her mother's breast and asks you about it.
After a woman has a baby her breasts start producing a special form of milk for the baby to drink. It contains all the protein and vitamins babies need to grow. When a baby nurses at her mother's breast she is drinking this special milk. Not all babies are nursed by their mother. Some mothers feed their infants a specially prepared drink, infant formula, which also contains all the protein and vitamins a baby needs.

When your child wants to walk around
without clothes when you're having company.
It is common for a young child to prefer to be undressed, but it can become a problem when company is expected. Parents can bring up the idea that there are some parts of the body which are private and which we don't show everybody. There are also some things we can do when we are alone which we can not do when other people are present. In this culture we wear clothes when people come over to the house.

When your preschooler wants to be with you when you are using the toilet.
Parents often use the toilet in the presence of their very young children. A parent may feel it is safer to know the whereabouts of their inquisitive youngsters rather than discovering them creeping into mischief. Babies may cry at being separated from a parent. But at some point a parent is going to decide they want use the toilet without company. When this happens it is time to have a discussion about privacy. If the youngster already has the concept then just add bathroom time to the list of "private" times. Otherwise a parent has to explain that there are some things people do alone, without others being there, and using the toilet is one of those activities. Your child may return with the idea that HE doesn't need privacy when he uses the toilet. The implication is clear that if HE doesn't need privacy, neither do you. But a parent who is made uncomfortable by the presence of a onlooker is entitled to have that privacy. Tell him you'll be out very soon. If your child seems to be afraid that you will disappear, talk to him through the door and let him know that you are still there.

Basic Information
Appropriate to All
Preschoolers

How their bodies work, and the correct names for their parts.
Some adults do feel reluctant to use the correct name for the parts of the body, but such false modesty has no place in teaching youngsters. Every child needs to know his or her body and understand how it works. Teaching children the right names for the parts of their body is just as easy as using babyish substitutes.

A feeling of respect for their bodies.
Children who grow up feeling they are worthwhile human beings are less likely to do things harmful to their bodies or allow others to do so. A preschooler can be taught that he "owns his own body" with the right to refuse physical advances of any kind.

How the bodies of the other gender differs.
Once a child understands and respects her own body she is ready to understand that a boy's body is different (and vice versa). Not better or worse, but different. Parents can use books, pictures, or models to educate their youngsters about the internal and the external differences between males and females.

How the sperm and the ovum meet.
Not all preschoolers are ready for this topic. Once they feel comfortable with the notion of sperm and ovum and where the baby develops, they will have more questions and want to know exactly how this happens.

How a child develops inside the mother.
You can also use the resources listed on pages 106-113, many of which have photos or drawings to explain how the fetus develops.

Respect for new life (and a sense of wonder).
The creation of new life is wonderful. To grow a baby, to watch a puppy being born, to see kittens nurse is to watch nature at it's finest. It is a manifestation of the continuity of life.

Chapter 13
Helping Youngsters
Reach Their Potential

Michael K. Meyerhoff

*...paying too much attention
to specific skills
often means ignoring —
or at least interfering with —
what is really essential.*

> *Education is the kindling of a flame, not the filling of a vessel."*
>
> Socrates

The "Superbaby Syndrome"

One-year-old Rebecca lives with her affluent, college-educated parents in a large, neatly-kept house in the suburbs. Her nursery is stocked with all the latest educational toys, and she spends much of her time in a well-equipped playpen that is placed in front of the television so she can be exposed to "Sesame Street." Her parents each set aside 45 minutes a day for "learning sessions," during which they teach Rebecca to recognize numbers, letters, and objects in pictures. They have her enrolled in a professionally-run playgroup three mornings a week; and in a few months, they will send her to a high-tech academy where she will receive extensive instruction in reading, writing, math, science, music, and art.

At first glance, it might appear that Rebecca is getting all the advantages, and that her parents are helping her to achieve the best possible start in life. However, my 20 years of research on early learning have convinced me that while Rebecca's mother and father are well-motivated, they have been badly misguided, and they actually are preventing their daughter from developing into a bright, well-adjusted, competent preschool child.

What is early education all about?

Like most mothers and fathers, Rebecca's parents want their child to be happy and to make the most of her potential. Unfortunately, by being too structured, trying too hard, and focusing too closely on the contents of her achievements, they are misconstruing or obscuring what early education is all about. Whether it is basic capacities such as reciting the alphabet, counting to one hundred, and categorizing shapes and colors — or amazing talents such as playing the piano, producing poetry, or operating a personal computer, *paying too much attention to specific skills* often means ignoring — or at least interfering with — what is really essential.

Young children are learning how to learn.

During the first years of life, children are learning all the time, and they are learning to do a lot of different things which may or may not include any or all of the activities mentioned above. But above all else, *they are learning how to learn* — and much of that they are doing on their own.

As they indulge their innate inclinations to explore, investigate, and experiment, they are developing general skills that will enable them to absorb from, and adapt to, the ever-changing environment around them for the rest of their lives.

Infants and toddlers who have been encouraged to develop these fundamental abilities fully and freely will be far better off than those whose initial educational experiences have been directed into relatively restricted channels — no matter how well-intentioned their instructors, and no matter how impressive their early academic or artistic accomplishments.

There is overwhelming evidence to suggest that if you use a variety of elaborate and expensive procedures, and if you expend enough time and energy, you can teach an infant or toddler to do just about anything. I've seen graduates of intensive intelligence institutes who could recite Shakespeare and reconstruct sophisticated mathematical models well before their third birthdays, and I've seen graduates of special music schools who could play Vivaldi pieces quite proficiently on tiny violins while still in diapers.

However, there is no evidence to suggest that programs designed to produce such early talents provide any lasting educational advantages. Furthermore, while serious, systematic, scientific instruction of this sort may produce immediately impressive results, it can be quite counter-productive in the long run. *Young children cannot be rushed into comprehending things before they are ready.*

What makes for an accomplished preschool student?
The finest preschool students — those with whom teachers can work most efficiently and who continue to perform superbly and show constant improvement with each passing year — are characterized not by their accomplishments of the past, but rather *by how prepared they are to cope with whatever is in store for them in the future.* Moreover, they also possess interpersonal skills which enhance and balance their intellectual abilities, thereby preventing them from becoming "lonely geniuses" — social cripples with high test scores and few friends. And finally, it is clear that the learning process is self-sustained for such children. They regard educational endeavors not as dreadful chores to be completed solely in order to obtain adult approval, but as exciting and enjoyable challenges.

Suggested Strategies for Parents

To help make the most of your child's potential, consider some of the more productive and less stressful strategies outlined in this section:

Allow your child to develop a true understanding of basic concepts instead of training him to perform a meaningless repertoire of tricks.

Impressive performances do not necessarily reflect equally impressive brainpower — Roy Rogers taught his horse, Trigger, to count, but I wouldn't let that horse balance my checkbook. With extraordinary techniques, you can teach your baby to do almost anything, but he is not yet mentally capable of comprehending and appreciating the processes involved.

For example, if you painstakingly teach your toddler to operate a personal computer, he may acquire the rigid set of skills required to use an IBM PC; and it may appear that this gives him an advantage over his agemates. But considering the rate at which technology advances, those skills soon may be as obsolete as knowing how to use a slide rule is today; and it is likely he will be stymied by the new technology. Meanwhile, another child who may have learned a lot less about computers, but who had more opportunities to absorb information from many different items and adapt her emerging skills to a variety of situations, will easily and eagerly deal with whatever technology she is confronted with any time.

Therefore, it is a good idea to avoid over-controlling your child's environment and feeding him pre-formulated solutions to selected questions. Once he is able to get around on his own, simply make as much of your home safe for and accessible to him as possible, then let him loose to satisfy his natural curiosity about everything. By exploring under the bed, investigating the properties of things in the kitchen drawers, and experimenting with the bathtub faucets among an infinite number of other apparently "non-educational" activities, he will be able to collect unlimited stores of knowledge and gradually construct universal rules for coping with a multitude of problems and projects.

Concentrate on enhancing your child's horizontal development and let his vertical development advance by itself.

Developmental progress can be viewed as a series of successively higher stages with each one serving as a base of support for the next. If your child is prodded to move on to a higher stage too soon, he may exhibit seemingly appropriate behavior for a while, but he will be standing on shaky ground and probably will fall back before long.

For example, during the early years, children learn to categorize objects according to similarities and differences — shapes and colors being two initial schemes. Once your child displays this basic capacity, it is possible —- using flashcards and other devices — to get him to distinguish a Renoir painting from a Matisse, or a symphony from a sonata. However, this takes a lot of his mental energy — and leaves him with very little fundamental categorizing ability at all. Conversely, another child who was permitted to just exercise her simple sorting skills over and over again (sorting various buttons, blocks, seashells, etc.) will be far more confident and competent in expanding this aspect of development as time goes by.

Therefore, when your child displays the lower levels of any ability, don't take it as a sign to push him quickly past them. Instead, simply provide him with ample opportunities to practice his rudimentary skills and wait for him to move ahead at his own pace. By filling in around him as he develops *(horizontal development)* rather than forcing him upward *(vertical development),* you will be helping him to build wide and firm foundations so he can maintain a solid hold on the more complex capacities that come later.

Be available to encourage your child, but don't dominate his decisions.

Obviously, the parents of outstanding preschool students are not idle bystanders in the early learning process; but it is clear that they act as consultants rather than instructors most of the time. Instead of super-imposing their own schedules and lesson plans on their children's activities, they simply set up open environments, let their children make their own choices and set their own agendas, then stand by to provide assistance, expansion, and enthusiasm as indicated. While they observe their children carefully, they make sure to use their children's interests, abilities, and requirements of the moment to guide their input.

For instance, one-year-olds often exhibit a strong inclination to browse through books. Over-anxious parents may misread their infant's signals and obtrusively rush out to buy a series of books with long stories, so they can start reading sessions. But at this point, the baby probably does not have the attention span to sit still for stories, much less the memory capacity to follow plots, so the result will be a discouraged student and frustrated teachers. On the other hand, more relaxed and laid back parents may realize that this first fascination with books is based on their infant's fondness for operating simple mechanisms, with the hinge action of the book binding being irresistible. Hence, they will just let her turn the pages back and forth, and perhaps introduce her to a couple of related items such as a cabinet door and the lid of a lunch box. The result will be an educational experience that is as enjoyable as it is enriching for everyone involved.

Remember that your child is a person, not a project,
and that there is more to life than academic excellence.

Two qualities often associated with young children who have been pushed too far too soon are *low self-esteem* and *poor social skills*. If you value your child according to his intrinsic characteristics rather than his accomplishments; if you take the time to simply enjoy him rather than only seek to educate him; and if you give him the opportunity to share, cooperate, and just play with other people rather than restrict his experiences to the intensive study of subjects, you may or may not end up with a precocious preschooler — but you'll be much more likely to produce a child who will have healthy interpersonal relationships, and who will have no difficulty truly loving anyone, including himself.

Chapter 14
Gender Considerations in Early Childhood: How Parents' Expectations Influence Their Sons and Daughters

Warren Speilberg

...parents continue to treat
boys and girls
in vastly different ways.

David's mother is talking to his teacher: "David and Emily are so different. He's always moving, always active, always knocking things over. He's aggressive too. Not like Emily. She's a pleasure: loving, quiet and able to sit still. She also talks to me more. I always understand what she is feeling and needing, unlike David. Sometimes I get so exasperated with him. Frankly I just don't understand how he got to be that way."

Parents and teachers often echo these sentiments. Research shows that in general boys are more active, more violent and less communicative than their female counterparts. In contrast girls are usually quieter, less active, more interested in relationships and generally more loving. Of course there are differences in individuals — gentle and communicative boys as well as aggressive and adventurous girls. In general, however, the differences in behavior between boys and girls are so striking that most parents and professionals believe gender differences are due to biology — *boys and girls are just "born different."*

While boys and girls do behave differently, it isn't clear <u>what</u> is responsible for these differences. Are boys and girls born that way — or are they taught to be different? Research has helped to demonstrate that biology has only a partial impact on male and female behavior. In order to fill their expected roles in society, boys are taught to be more aggressive, more active, and to take more dangerous risks than girls. Girls, on the other hand, are discouraged from such behaviors and are socialized into their particular gender role. This role advocates that girls should be seen as being attractive, non-aggressive, nurturing, and able to receive nurturing from others.

Parents and Traditional Roles
Despite enormous changes in our society where the traditional roles of men and women are no longer as well defined, parents continue to treat boys and girls in vastly different ways. They treat boys in a harsher and less supportive way than is the case with girls. Study after study indicates that young boys are held less, communicated with less, and given less help for both major and minor illnesses and mishaps than is the case with their female counterparts. Boys are still taught that they should strive for independence, be tough, competitive and aggressive — and never ask for help. Boys as young as four years old are capable of telling interviewers what it is to be a "real man." One four year old boy recently said to me that a man "don't cry and act like a baby."

Girls — on the other hand — are given more help in both academic and nonacademic tasks, and are encouraged to be less independent and exploratory than is the case with boys. When it comes to enforcing rules, parents punish boys more harshly for both minor and major infractions than is the case with girls. Boys tend to be subject to physical punishment, while girls are subject to milder forms of punishment. In addition boys are punished more harshly for deviating from their expected behavior (for example, when they cry or whine) than when girls deviate from their expected behavior (for example, when they get their clothes dirty or punch another child).

Negative aspects of traditional roles

Boys are taught to suppress their feelings and emotional needs. They are encouraged constantly to strive for achievement and to fight at the slightest provocation. These kinds of messages leave boys and later, men, more lonely, frustrated, anxious and tense than they need to be. Because of this early learning, boys are conditioned to fear and avoid intimacy which easily might lead to dependency. Also because boys and later, men, are taught to be contemptuous of their own needs for support and help, *they are less likely to seek help for both their emotional and physical problems.* This is largely responsible for the often quoted seven year difference in longevity between men and women. Because boys are taught that men must risk their lives to earn their manhood, males suffer from much higher rates of violent death than is the case with females. In addition, since boys and men are taught to be tough and to ignore their physical problems, they become much sicker than they should.

Finally, because of the traditional male role model and parent expectations for their sons, boys tend to cut off those qualities of character which represent their most human and unique aspects. In this connection, by the time a boy is about five years old he has learned that compassion, sensitivity and tenderness are qualities that are more appropriately female. This also applies to those skill areas which are considered to be less masculine: music, the arts and an interest in relationships between people.

For girls the tragedies of their traditional role playing are somewhat different. Because girls are taught to be non-aggressive and non-assertive they are more prone to depression and bouts of sadness than is the case with boys. Since girls are often encouraged to be inexpressive and "good" they tend to hold their angry and anxious feelings inside. This difficulty with the expression of anger can often make girls and later, women, more susceptible to turning their feelings against themselves. Both depression and inhibition can result from such a condition. Girls are often discouraged from fully developing and using the array of their competencies and skills. Parents, it appears, discourage girls from emotional and physical separation, from risk taking and from a full exploration of their environment. Therefore, girls fail to develop a greater sense of confidence about their abilities and their capacity to try new things successfully. This accounts, in part, for women's greater conflicts with being both successful and competitive in their future academic and career life.

How to Be a Gender-sensitive Parent

• *Be aware of your own gender attitudes.* Many of us have grown up with our own set of prejudices about appropriate activities and qualities for both boys and girls. Many of these attitudes, which were taught to us, are antiquated and no longer functional. While most of us applaud changes in our views of both men and women ("Isn't it wonderful to have a woman astronaut!") ("Isn't he doing a great job raising two young children!") many of us are usually unaware of our own inherent gender prejudices. Recently, a client of mine became extremely angry at his four-year-old son who began to weep after being hit in the head with a ball. When he examined his feelings more closely, he began to realize that his negative attitudes about his son's crying were more related to his own ties to the traditional male role model than to any failing of his young son. As a result of this self inspection he has become more able to provide the nurturing and closeness his son needed from him.

Many parents are confused by their child's interest in opposite-sex role play. For example: a boy playing with dolls, a girl climbing trees. A child's occasional interest in such activities should be tolerated and accepted.

• *Encourage boys to seek affection and support.* Although boys are often more interested in activity than in relationships, they still require a great deal of support and nurturing, more than has been allowed them under traditional notions of male rearing. Boys should be encouraged to be both independent and to seek support and comfort when they require it. Boys must be taught that they should not fear or be ashamed of their needs for emotional connection and support.

• *Encourage girls to be more independent and competent.* Although girls are apt to be more interested in playing with others, it is important that they also be encouraged to become competent in other skill areas that interest them. It is vital that girls be taught that they can be successful at whatever activity they choose. In addition it is important that girls not be overprotected, that they be allowed to explore their environment freely and engage in physical play as well. The overprotection of children by fearful parents often leaves children feeling frustrated, resentful and ultimately frightened about the world they will eventually need to inhabit.

• *Encourage both boys and girls to learn effective means for asserting themselves.* For boys, learning how to get what they want often entails more exposure to verbal strategies designed to help them to achieve their goals — for example, asking for what they want and expressing their feelings. ("Give me back my toy because I want to play with it now.") These kinds of strategies can help boys to learn to become less aggressive and violent in the world. For girls encouraging them to stand up for themselves, even at the cost of temporarily losing affection can go a long way towards helping them to become more effective in the world.

• *Get Dad involved.* For boys, a male role model who can be both tender and strong can help them to accept both their assertive and affectionate sides. Research suggests that boys who have a positive relationship with their fathers are able to make better adjustment to both the academic and social world. Girls who have a healthy relationship with an encouraging father figure have been shown to be more successful in their academic and career endeavors.

This is not to minimize the importance of Mom as a role model. Because mothers and teachers spend so much time with children, they too must be sure to spread the right messages about the promises and opportunities of being either a boy or a girl.

Resources for Section Three: Ways of Encouraging Children as They Grow

FOR ADULTS

Your One-Year-Old; Your Two-Year-Old; Your Three-Year-Old; Your Four-Year-Old; Your Five-Year-Old; Your Six-Year-Old; Your Seven-Year-Old (series), by Louise Bates Ames & Frances Ilg. Delacorte Press, 1976-1985. Each book in this series is a practical guide that parents can use as a child development resource during the early years.

The Flight of the Stork: What Children Think (and When) About Sex & Family Building, rev. ed. by Anne C. Bernstein, Ph.D. Perspect Indiana 1994. Part research and part advice, this book combines Dr. Bernstein's investigation into the way children think about human reproduction at different ages with practical suggestions about what children need to know and how parents can provide that knowledge.

The Hurried Child: Growing Up Too Fast Too Soon, 2nd ed. by David Elkind. Addison Wesley, 1988. A solid survey of what happens when kids are pushed too far too soon.

The Magic Years, by Selma Fraiberg. Simon & Schuster, 1996. A perennial favorite that explores the non-academic aspects of the early years.

The Preschool Years: Family Strategies That Work — from Experts and Parents, by Ellen Galinsky and Judy David. Ballantine, 1991. This comprehensive book covers a wide range of topics relating to preschoolers, including information about children's interest in sex differences and reproduction.

In a Different Voice: Psychological Theory & Woman's Development, by Carol Gilligan. Harvard University Press, 1993. This book discusses the psychological differences between boys and girls and men and women.

"I Think I Can, I Know I Can!" Using Self-Talk to Help Raise Confident, Secure Kids, by Susan Isaacs and Wendy Ritchey, Ph.D. St. Martin's Press, 1991. The authors explain to parents how their children can change inner negative voices into positive ones.

Boys Will Be Boys, by Miriam Miedzian. Anchor Books, 1992. In examining boys and violence, this book covers the psychological development of boys, the effect of television and toys on boys, and violence and fathering.

A Child Is Born: The Completely New Edition, by Lennart Nilsson. Dell, 1986. Following a chronological, week-by-week format throughout the nine months of pregnancy, this book features astonishing photographs, in brilliant color, of the journey from fertilization to birth.

Finding Our Fathers: How a Man's Life is Shaped by His Relationship with His Father, by Samuel D. Osherson. Fawcett Books, 1987. This work is about the importance of fathering.

The First Five Years, by Virginia E. Pomeranz. St. Martin's Press, 1987. The author of this book takes a relaxed approach to child rearing.

A Toddler's Life: Becoming a Person, by Marilyn Shatz. Oxford University Press, 1995. A scholarly, interesting study, through the story of one little boy's passage through the toddler years.

The First Three Years of Life, (revised edition), by Burton L. White. Prentice-Hall, 1985. An excellent guide to child development between birth and three years of age.

The Too Precious Child, by L.H. Williams, H.S. Berman, and L. Rose. Warner Books, 1989. This book tries to help parents let go of the super-parent syndrome, and to understand why children should not be pushed more and more to achieve faster and faster.

FOR CHILDREN

My Feet; My Hands (Let's-Read-and-Find-Out Science Book® series) by Aliki. HarperCollins, 1992. In these two books, the author/illustrator explains in clear and simple terms the many different ways our feet and hands are important to us.

How Babies are Made, by Andrew C. Andry and Steven Schepp. Little, Brown, 1984. Colorful paper cutout illustrations convey basic information about reproduction and birth in humans, plants, dogs, and other animal species.

Paddington's Things I Do, by Michael Bond. HarperFestival, 1994. The beloved Paddington Bear is seen in daily activities that will be familiar to young children. Each colorful page illustrates another activity, with only a few words as text. For example: I wake up, I exercise, I get dressed, I eat, and on through the day.

Big Sarah's Little Boots, by Paulette Bourgeois. Scholastic, 1992. Sarah loves her yellow rubber boots, but one day they don't fit anymore. She gets new boots, and her younger brother wears her old ones, so they can splash in the puddles together.

Hey, Little Baby! by Nola Buck. HarperFestival, 1999. Not only can big sister brush her teeth, dress herself, and stir up a batch of cookies, she can tell her baby brother about those and all the other accomplishments she has mastered. And she'll teach them all to him, when he gets older. A lively and humorous book, brimming with self-confidence.

How a Baby Grows, by Nola Buck. HarperFestival, 1998. In this charming board book with appealing pictures by Pamela Paparone, the first page begins, "These are the things that babies do: Cry, wet, sleep, coo." It looks at people and things in a baby's world, and describes them in gentle rhymes. This book should delight babies from newborn through toddlerhood.

The Growing-Up Feet, by Beverly Cleary. Morrow, 1987. The four-year-old twins are growing and Mother takes them to buy new shoes. But their feet haven't grown enough to get the next size, and the twins are disappointed. So instead they each get a pair of bright red boots that will stretch and grow as their feet grow. At home, Daddy helps the twins find a reason to use the new boots, even though it isn't raining.

Janet's Thingamajigs, by Beverly Cleary. Mulberry, 1997. Janet collects little treasures like a paper clip, a wheel, and a shiny bead, and calls them "my thingamajigs." She won't let her twin brother play with them, and keeps them safe from him in paper bags in her crib, which makes him want to play with them all the more. Mother is at her wit's end until she plans a surprise for the twins: real beds to replace their cribs — and they are delighted to realize that they are growing up.

How You Were Born, rev. ed. by Joanna Cole. Mulberry, 1994. With black and white photographs and drawings, the author describes pregnancy and birth in a simple, matter-of-fact tone. The book begins with an informative section called, *A Note to Parents,* in which the author offers suggestions about discussing the story of birth with children.

My Puppy Is Born, by Joanna Cole. *Revised and Expanded Edition.* Morrow, 1991. The story is told from the point-of-view of a little girl who will get to keep one of the neighbor's puppies. The color photographs show the birth of the puppies and follow the progress of the little girl's puppy for eight weeks, when she is ready to leave her mother and go home with her new owner.

When I Grow Bigger, by Trish Cooke. Candlewick Press, 1994. Preschoolers Sam, Leanne, and Natalie are boasting about the things they will do when they're bigger. But Thomas is a little baby and he can't even talk about growing bigger. Then Dad places the baby high on his shoulders so that Thomas is bigger than anybody.

When I Was Little: *A Four-Year-Old's Memoir of Her Youth,* by Jamie Lee Curtis. HarperFestival,1999. In this charming book with whimsical pictures by Laura Cornell, a little girl tells about all she has learned since she was just a little baby.

Before You Were Born, by Jennifer Davis. Workman, 1997. A lively story in rhyme in which a mother tells what went on month-by-month as she was pregnant with her child. As you find out what is happening to Mom on the outside, there are flaps to lift that show what is happening with the baby inside her belly.

The Egg, by Pascale de Bourgoing. *A First Discovery Book.* Scholastic Cartwheel Books, 1992. Looking at this book with vivid, glossy illustrations and unique transparent pages, preschoolers can learn how an egg develops inside the mother hen, and find out about other animals that hatch from eggs.

I Eat Dinner, by Margery Facklam. Boyds Mill Press, 1992. A child compares the way he eats with a variety of animals' eating habits. An inviting book with simple text and cheerful illustrations.

On My Own, by Miela Ford. Greenwillow, 1999. A polar bear cub can do many things on his own: he can wiggle; he can stretch; he can roll. Some toddlers would love to do the same, after seeing the photographs and hearing the text of this playful board book.

Just My Size, by May Garelick. HarperCollins, 1990. In a story about growth and a treasured article of clothing, a girl remembers a beautiful blue coat that had been given to her when she was little. She loved the coat, so as she outgrew it, it was cut down to a jacket, then to a vest, then to a knapsack and finally to a doll's coat, a replica of the coat she wore many years before.

Good Morning Chick, by Mirra Ginsburg. Mulberry, 1999. A little chick is hatched from its egg and explores his world and the creatures in it. When his adventures do not go very well, his mother warms and coddles him.

Aaron's Shirt, by Deborah Gould. Bradbury Press, 1989. Aaron has a red and white shirt that he can't bear to part with, even when he outgrows it. But he won't give it away, and instead finds just the right wearer, who will never outgrow it—his teddy bear!

I Look like a Girl, by Sheila Hamanaka. Morrow, 1999. With buoyant, poetic words and exuberant illustrations, this book has as its heroine a young girl who imagines she is a tiger, a dolphin, a condor. You believe, as you read, that nothing can keep this child from being just what she wants to be.

The Biggest Boy, by Kevin Henkes. Greenwillow, 1995. Billy can eat with a fork. He can get dressed all alone. His mother and father tell him he is growing bigger and bigger. That starts Billy and his parents imagining how it would be to be the biggest boy in the world, where he would wear the roof as a hat, and could move the clouds by blowing on them. But right now, his parents agree, "You are just the right size for a big boy your age."

Bernard On His Own, by Syd Hoff. Houghton Mifflin, 1996. Bernard is a little bear who is trying to find independence. He attempts to stand on his hind legs and growl, climb tall trees, and explore caves, but each effort is unsuccessful. His parents reassure him, and promise to help him learn to growl and stand on his hind legs tomorrow.

Amazing Grace, by Mary Hoffman. Dial, 1991. Grace loves stories and wants to act out the most exciting parts herself. When Grace's class acts out *Peter Pan,* Grace wants to play the part of Peter. One classmate says, "You can't be Peter—that's a boy's name." Another says, "You can't be Peter Pan. He isn't black." Grace's family tells her that she can be anything she wants, if she puts her mind to it. A wonderful story, beautifully illustrated, about a very real little girl.

Pots and Pans, by Patricia Hubbell. HarperFestival, 1998. Baby's in the kitchen with the pots and pans. Boom! Bang! Clash and clang! Sure is fun.

New Shoes for Silvia, by Johanna Hurwitz. Mulberry, 1999. In a package from Tía Rosita in America, Silvia gets a pair of bright red shoes. She loves them but they are too large for her. As the weeks pass, Silvia uses her shoes in creative ways: first for her dolls to sleep in, next to hold shells and pebbles, until she has grown enough to wear them happily on her feet.

When You Were a Baby, by Ann Jonas. Greenwillow, 1991. This board book will remind toddlers of the things they couldn't do when they were babies, and make them feel good that they can do those things now.

Jacob's Tree, by Holly Keller. Greenwillow, 1999. Jacob is smaller than all the members of his family. He is too small to get a cookie from the cookie jar, or to see himself in the mirror over the bathroom sink. His Mama tells him, "You'll be bigger soon." And his Papa makes a mark on a tree to see how much Jacob grows. But Jacob hates to wait. What happens at the end of the winter and the end of the book will be satisfying to all young children who are waiting to grow bigger.

Look, I'm Growing Up, by Marilyn Knoepfel and Betty Farber. Standard Publishing, 1995. A variety of children tell how much they have learned to do since babyhood, such as: dress themselves, snap their fingers, sing a song, and so much more! Includes an "I Am Growing" song.

The Growing Story, by R. Kraus. HarperCollins, 1947. An endearing story about a little boy's discovery that he is growing.

Where Do Little Girls Grow? by Milly Jane Limmer. Albert Whitman & Co., 1993. A little girl asks her mother, "Where did I come from?" And the two of them laughingly concoct fantasies about her arriving in a balloon from the sky, a shelf in a grocery store, or a nest in a tree. Until the mother tells her daughter the true answer: "I carried you within myself, safe and warm, secretly. / I felt you grow close to my heart, curled up inside of me."

Jess Was the Brave One, by Jean Little. Puffin, 1995. Of the two sisters, Jess is the brave one, when they go to the doctor for shots, or climb trees, or watch a scary movie. Claire, on the other hand, has an overactive imagination. But one day, Claire's imagination saves the day, and she finds that she can be brave too.

Duck, by David Lloyd. Lippincott, 1988. A little boy is learning about words. At first he calls all animals "duck," and all vehicles "truck," but with Granny's help, he starts to figure out the differences.

I Want To Be, by Thylias Moss. Dial, 1993. The author, a prize-winning poet, opens up the reader's imagination with beautiful, exciting images, as she tells how a young African-American girl answers the question, "What do you want to be?"

How Was I Born? by Lennart Nilsson & Lena K. Swanberg. Dell, 1996. A Photographic Story of reproduction and birth for children put together by the same group that did *A Child is Born.* (See Adult Resources, page 107.)

Maybe My Baby, by Irene O'Book. HarperFestival, 1998. With color photos by Paula Hible, the youngest toddlers will love this board book in which diverse babies are dressed in different hats, while the parent wonders what the baby will become. Will the child grow up to be an astronaut, police officer, actor, or something else? All the while, the parent affirms that, "I'll love you whoever, however you are."

I Can, by Helen Oxenbury. Candlewick Press, 1995. A Baby Beginner Board Book that tells, with one word on each page, many things that a baby can do, like: sit, crawl, jump, and wave. A book for the youngest toddlers to enjoy.

It's Fun To Be One; It's Great To Be Two, by Fiona Pragoff. Aladdin Books, 1994. These two books will appeal to the youngest preschoolers. And their parents will like the fact that the thick pages cannot be torn easily. The glossy color photographs are of real babies and toddlers performing familiar activities. The text tells the toddler about all the things he or she can do.

Bathtime; Playtime (Look At Me Books series), photographs by Stephen Shott. Dutton, 1991. In these two board books, there are a variety of babies and toddlers engaged in their favorite activities. Young children will enjoy pointing at familiar items in the color photographs, such as socks, soap, and shampoo in the first book, and blocks, train, and wagon in the second.

Rolling Rose, by James Stevenson. Greenwillow, 1992. Baby Rose rolls everywhere in her rolling walker. And, in this funny, fantastic tale, when the family isn't paying attention, she rolls right out the door and down the road, with 85 other babies joining her parade.

The Smallest Stegosaurus, by Lynn Sweat and Louis Phillips. Puffin, 1995. His mother and father are nearly twenty feet long, but the baby stegosaurus is much smaller. He has not yet grown armor, and feels quite helpless. His parents bring him into the safety of their large nest and teach him to guard the egg that will hatch soon. The small stegosaurus finds he can help his family by warning them that another dinosaur, the ornitholestes, is coming to steal the egg. An endearing story about a capable little dinosaur.

The Brass Ring, by Nancy Tafuri. Greenwillow, 1996. The author/artist uses bright, bold colors, and clear and simple language to tell about a little girl who is growing bigger. Once she was little, and didn't know about the fun of a vacation, the pleasure of taking a swim, or the excitement of riding the carousel and catching the brass ring. Now that she is "big" she can do all these wonderful things.

Show Me! by Tom Tracy. HarperFestival, 1999. As they go through the day's activities, a mother playfully names her baby's body parts, such as nose, chin, knees, and toes, Cardboard pages make this a perfect book for babies and toddlers.

Gina, by Bernard Waber. Houghton Mifflin, 1997. In this lively tale in verse, a little girl, Gina, moves to a new apartment building, where there are only boys to play with — not a girl in sight. But the boys won't play with Gina, until she shows them how well she does with a baseball and bat. Then they find that she's good at lots of things. An appealing story about a fun-loving heroine.

Once There Were Giants, by Martin Waddell. Candlewick Press, 1995. In a wonderful book about growing older and bigger, a little girl describes the days when there were giants in her house, when she was a baby and everyone around her was huge. The illustrations show her as she grows until she is the giant in her house, and there is a new baby, her own daughter!

The Baby's Word Book, by Sam Williams. Greenwillow, 1999. Babies love to point and name objects. This book gives them the opportunity to see a variety of little children with the clothes they wear, their body parts, the toys they play with, and other things in their world.

Step by Step, by Diane Wolkstein. Morrow, 1994. A little ant travels to visit a friend, making its way step by step, with a feeling of accomplishment at journey's end.

I Like to Be Little, by Charlotte Zolotow. HarperTrophy, 1990. When a mother asks her little girl the question, "What do you want to be when you grow up?" the girl helps her mother understand how she is happy doing the things that children enjoy — watching a raindrop roll down the window, sitting under the dining room table, or just doing nothing.

William's Doll, by Charlotte Zolotow. HarperCollins, 1985. William is good at sports and playing with electric trains, but he'd like to have a doll, too. Everybody in the family is astonished, except his sensible, understanding Grandma.

Section Four

Balancing Activities and Relaxation

Section Four
Balancing Activities
and
Relaxation

Introduction

An important book called, *The Hurried Child: Growing Up Too Fast Too Soon,* appears in the resource list in this section. Young children are often pushed to achieve skills that previously were expected only of older children. Carrying the scenario to fantastic lengths, one author in this section comes up with a plan for a three-year-old's schedule that (thank heavens!) can still be called outrageous.

Adults, too, often overprogram themselves. Ask most people how their lives are, and they answer, "I'm so busy, I hardly ever have a chance to relax."

But it doesn't have to be that way. Another contributor discusses the benefits of relaxation and offers suggestions about ways to relax using games, music, and imagery. Read the chapter, take a deep breath and ....

SECTION FOUR
BALANCING ACTIVITIES AND RELAXATION

Chapter

Chapter 15
Should You Enroll Your Preschooler in "Extracurricular" Activities?

Michael K. Meyerhoff

*...for most preschool children,
no one has demonstrated any method
which has proven to be effective
in bringing them up to the "genius" level...*

An outlandish scenario:
5:00 A.M. — Three-year-old Elizabeth is driven to the local ice rink for her figure skating lessons.
7:30 A.M. — Elizabeth is picked up at the ice rink and taken to her prestigious preschool which features rigorous classes in reading, writing, science, and math.
3:00 P.M. — Elizabeth is picked up from preschool and taken to her music teacher for her piano lessons.
4:30 P.M. — Elizabeth's parents sit with her at the family's personal computer and follow a special manual that will teach her how to run a variety of software systems.

❈ ❈ ❈

During the preschool years, most parents want their children to become well-balanced, capable, caring people who are comfortable with themselves and others. By "capable" these parents simply mean "making the most of whatever potential they were born with."

Parents also want to expose their children to experiences in physical activities, the arts, and intellectual pursuits. This ordinarily does not include pre-professional skills in tennis and piano playing, genius capacities in reading and mathematics, or the acquisition of highly impressive vocabularies and overwhelming amounts of factual material. Although these kinds of accomplishments would be appreciated, parents usually do not set such lofty goals and have the strong desire to follow through.

However, some mothers and fathers do, indeed, desire extraordinarily high levels of achievement for their children as quickly as possible. Today, there are numerous programs for preschoolers that promise to produce impressively talented behavior in one or all aspects of development.

❈ ❈ ❈

6:30 P.M. — Elizabeth and her parents sit down to dinner. They all are too exhausted to talk.
8:00 P.M. — Elizabeth is in bed, tossing and turning. Her parents are sitting at the kitchen table, looking at their checkbook balance and wondering where all the money has gone. They fall asleep before they can figure it out.

Questions for parents to consider
Do the people operating such programs really know dramatically better ways to deal with preschoolers, or are they merely exploiting the exaggerated hopes of anxious mothers and fathers? Will learning special skills at an unusually early age guarantee a child a lasting advantage over

his peers, or will everyone else catch up soon enough? Should parents be supplying their little ones with extra stimulation right from the start, or will any benefits gained by such practices be outweighed by unhealthy side effects? (See Risks on page 121.)

Opinions of psychologists and educators

Answers to these questions vary from one type of program to another, and even among individual programs of the same type. However, most psychologists and educators who have spent many years studying the development of young children do share the following opinions when it comes to "extracurricular" activities for preschoolers:

• There are, undeniably, some truly "gifted" children around. But no one is quite sure how they got to be that way. However, for most preschool children, *no one has demonstrated any method which has proven to be effective in bringing them up to the "genius" level — intellectually, physically, or artistically.* Researchers have been able to put together a fairly clear picture of how the mind grows during the preschool years, but they have not been able to determine how that growth can be significantly accelerated.

• Psychologists and educators are virtually unanimous in recommending that parents be very cautious and skeptical with regard to "intelligence institutes" that proudly proclaim they can take anyone's child and turn him into a little genius. Few of these institutes have permitted independent groups to observe and evaluate their procedures in order to verify the results being claimed.

• While there are several respectable programs which do have solid records of success in teaching preschoolers *specific* skills (such as reading and writing) a few years before they typically would learn them, *there is no such course of study which has proven to have lasting advantages for preschoolers without educational handicaps.* In other words, children who are developing well in general and did not participate in these special programs will be performing on a par with those who did participate by the time everybody enters the second or third grade.

• Most believe that *if benefits are achieved through procedures which involve intensive drills for long periods, the children's spontaneous interest and pleasure in learning are likely to be jeopardized.* During the preschool years, children learn to relate to other people, to use their bodies, and to employ their mental functions in a variety of ways — and that learning takes time. Preschoolers spend a large portion of their day just observing and exploring the world around them in a relaxed and unhurried fashion.

• Most children do not benefit in the long run from special programs. However, children with early educational handicaps which prevented them from learning certain fundamental skills may, indeed, be better off if they attend a high-quality compensatory program. Eliminating disadvantages during the preschool years does seem to produce enduring results.

Before Enrolling Your Child...

If parent and child have certain passions, an extracurricular activity of some sort may be pleasurable and productive. However, if it is decided to involve a preschooler in a special early learning program, it is wise to make sure that the following factors have been considered carefully.

1) <u>Goals</u>. Will the child be learning something that is really valuable? Learning to swim, to play the violin, or any number of other activities can provide him with skills he may enjoy and value for the rest of his life. On the other hand, there are skills which may appear to be significant at first glance but may, in fact, turn out to be useless or superfluous as time goes by.

For example, there are several popular programs that teach three and four-year-olds how to use a personal computer. Given our high-tech society, this may seem like a good idea. However, with the rapid technological advances that are being made is it wise to devote a good portion of his day to mastering a machine which could be totally obsolete by the time he enters kindergarten? Might it not be far better for a preschooler to simply indulge his natural curiosity and develop his general learning skills?

2) <u>Effectiveness</u>. Can the program actually do what it says it can do? Just because the goals are admirable does not mean they are attainable. As indicated earlier, there are several programs with reliable records of success in teaching very young children a variety of skills. On the other hand, there are many more with miserable past performance charts. Consequently, it would be wise to ask any ambitious and/or expensive program for a list of parents whose children have previously participated and check those references thoroughly.

3) <u>Risks</u>. Is there anything about the procedures that might cause serious harm? It already has been mentioned that high-pressure, time-consuming, academically-oriented activities may be severely detrimental to a preschooler's well-balanced development. It also should be noted that some activities may be potentially hazardous from a medical standpoint. Therefore, it is a good idea to solicit input from a pediatrician before enrolling a preschooler in any program that may subject his body to unusual physical conditions.

For example, preschoolers can reap enormous benefits from many activities that promote physical fitness, from figure skating and dance to swimming and gymnastics. But it is important to keep in mind that their bones and joints are not nearly as strong as they will be in later years. Consequently, health professionals favor simple exercises with a strict concentration on recreation. They warn against programs that involve serious competition and aspirations toward high levels of proficiency as they may push young children to perform difficult jumps and twists that can produce inappropriate stress on still-tender body parts.

4) <u>Atmosphere</u>. Will the child truly like the program? The most successful offerings of this sort usually revolve around activities that capitalize upon the basic interests and abilities the preschoolers bring with them. Moreover, since Mom and Dad are the most important people in their lives, any activities which allow the children to share their excitement and achievements with their parents will have a greater likelihood of producing both enrichment and enjoyment.

For example, a sophisticated science program in which the instructor requires active and alert preschoolers to sit still for a prolonged slide show on the solar system defies the fact that children in this age range do not have long attention spans. They are constantly curious about everything, and they would much prefer to be doing something with their mothers and fathers. On the other hand, a parental participation program featuring a nature walk and a variety of "hands-on" experiments designed to feed into the children's strong desire to practice and perfect their emerging mental and motor skills probably will produce a lot more fulfillment and fun.

Most parents recognize that the preschool years constitute a critical period for learning. However, too many fail to realize just how rich, exciting, challenging, and "educational" the whole world is when it is being observed, explored, and interacted with for the very first time. And they often overlook the value of the many lessons that preschoolers learn through the thousands of ordinary experiences which constitute their day-to-day lives.

It is not surprising that Pablo Picasso, Maya Angelou, Albert Einstein, and Chris Evert, along with most other superachievers, did not begin to exhibit their particular talents until well after the preschool years. Instead of being urged to emulate the specific accomplishments of such notables right from the start, a child's preschool years probably will be a lot more productive and pleasurable if his parents simply encourage and help him to build a wide and firm foundation for whatever may come along in the future.

Chapter 16
Making Relaxation
Part of Children's Lives

Rae Pica

*More than ever,
children need to know
how to relax.*

• *Weekday mornings, Jennifer awakens, gets washed and dressed, eats breakfast, and brushes her teeth in the 45 minutes before her mother drives her to preschool. There she spends mornings and afternoons participating in the business of playing, learning, and socializing.*
• *Late on Tuesday and Thursday afternoons, Jennifer's father picks her up and takes her to gymnastics.*
• *On Fridays, Jennifer has violin lessons.*
• *Every evening after dinner, which is often rushed and seldom enjoyed by all family members due to hectic schedules, Jennifer watches a little TV, takes a bath, and goes to bed early in preparation for another busy day.*

Such is the life of many preschoolers. Gone are the carefree days of leisurely play, of unscheduled hours that could be filled with alternating rhythms of physical activity and such leisurely pursuits as lying in the grass, imagining creatures in the clouds.

Not only are today's young children maintaining busier, adult-like schedules, but they are also confronted with stresses and anxieties that their predecessors could never have imagined. If they aren't facing family crises or problems of poverty in their own lives, they have friends who are. Or they're bombarded by the media with images and examples of society's many ills.

Learning to relax
More than ever, children need to know how to relax. They must be able to find a quiet place inside themselves that allows them to cope — in order to maintain control of their bodies and feelings. Just "resting" is generally not enough; children must be capable of immersing themselves in total relaxation. Clare Cherry, author of *Think of Something Quiet* (see Resources, page 128), tells us children are entitled to experience serenity. She writes: "If children never learn how to turn inward they may be affected adversely by unrelieved stress."

Though most would agree relaxation is beneficial, many people are unaware relaxation is a learned skill; it must be encouraged and practiced. Moreover, relaxation must be valued by the important adults in children's lives. If it is, children are more likely to take some quiet time during the course of each busy day to "turn everything off."

Benefits of relaxation
More and more, researchers are discovering the correlation between stress and physical and mental illnesses. This means the child who does learn to relax will have the ability to manage stress and, therefore, live a healthier (not to mention more tranquil) life. Knowing when and how to relax also ensures a more energetic life, as stress is most certainly an energy robber. Relaxation techniques, however, help "recharge the batteries."

On a more basic level, experience with relaxation helps children gain greater motor control. Children who can voluntarily relax will have more control over their bodies in general. This means they will be able to start and stop their movements with ease and to execute slow and sustained, as well as fast, movements. A child who takes the time to relax will have the chance to experience motionlessness, giving more meaning, in contrast, to the body's movement. Whether or not the child chooses to participate in sports, dance, or other organized physical activities, such coordination leads to greater poise and self-control and an overall feeling of comfort with one's own body.

If imagery is used to encourage relaxation, the child's ability to imagine is enhanced. With so many ready-made images available to children in today's world (with television, computers, videos, and the like), the ability to imagine is becoming less and less necessary. How frightening to envision a world in which people are incapable of seeing beyond what already exists, of imagining the solutions to problems and challenges, or putting themselves in the place of others (i.e. feeling empathy).

Similarly, if music is used to encourage relaxation, the child is exposed to the world of quiet, peaceful music (in contrast to what is commonly heard on radio or television). This can result in a greater appreciation for aesthetics — heightening the child's awareness of, and sensitivity to, beauty.

Finally, the research of Dr. Edmund Jacobsen, a leading authority on the subject of relaxation, demonstrates tension control helps children learn better. In all probability, tension control helps anyone, of any age, do *anything* better!

Suggestions for Parents

Any number of physical signs can warn you that your preschooler is feeling stressed. These include excessive or rapid talking, muscular tenseness, a belligerent attitude, unusual listlessness or hyperactivity and unprovoked tears. Taking the time to relax should be a routine part of every day — for children and adults alike. But relaxation techniques will be especially needed if your child shows any of these symptoms of stress.

Setting the stage
Whether it's a daily routine or required because of a stressful situation, you can set the stage for relaxation by darkening the room, speaking slowly and softly, and moving gently. If you decide to use music to promote

tranquillity, choose pieces you're already familiar with — that you've found to be peaceful and soothing. Most often, that means instrumental selections, although a number of children's recordings now available for relaxation include lyrics intended to soothe.

With or without lyrics, the songs should be arranged simply, with few changes in rhythm or tempo. If the music is only intended to set the stage while your child performs relaxation exercises (see below), keep the volume much lower than if the music itself were the focus of the activity. (Too much external stimulation will defeat the cause.) If the music *is* the focus, you can sometimes encourage your child to lie quietly with eyes closed. Other times you might suggest that your preschooler listen for something specific, like a certain sound or instrument.

Using imagery
If you choose to use imagery to promote relaxation, be sure it's imagery your young children can relate to. Show them a rag doll or a wet dish rag, or talk to them about the difference between uncooked and cooked spaghetti. Then ask them to pretend to be one of these objects.

You can also paint a picture in their minds. Ask them to lie on the floor and imagine, for example, they're at the beach. Talk to them (softly) about the warmth of the sun, the cool breeze, and the gentle sounds of the waves and the gulls circling overhead.

Breath control
Breath control plays an important role in relaxation. When we inhale slowly and then exhale twice as slowly, we decrease the supply of oxygen and increase the amount of carbon dioxide in the blood, thus slowing down the activity of the nerves and brain. To promote deep breathing, you can ask the children to expand (by inhaling) and contract (by exhaling) just like a balloon, alternately (and slowly) inflating and deflating. Initially demonstrating with an actual balloon can help make this image more vivid.

Controlling muscular tension
The ability voluntarily to control muscular tension is also critical to relaxation. Because preschoolers won't understand the terms *contract* and *release*, you can play a game based on the words *calm* and *nervous*. Explain that calm is a very relaxed feeling — like that experienced just before falling asleep at night. Other times that children might have experienced a feeling of calm include: sitting by a lake, observing a bird soar through the sky, or watching the sun set. At such times, muscles feel loose and "liquid." Nervous, on the other hand, is something like a combination of scared and worried. Preschoolers may have worried it might rain on the day of a big outing, or they may have lost sight of parents in a big store and felt nervous until spotting them again. How did their muscles and bodies feel at those times? Were they loose or tight? Ask them to demonstrate.

Once your children have the idea, explain that when you say the word *calm*, they should make their bodies as relaxed as possible. When you *say nervous,* they tighten up. (Vary the time between verbal cues, and use the quality of your voice to invoke the proper response.) Do this first with the children standing. Then repeat the process with the children kneeling, sitting, and, finally, lying down.

"Melting" is also a wonderful — and fun — relaxation activity. Talk about the melting of ice cream cones, snow sculptures, and ice cubes. Then ask your preschooler to pretend to be one of these things and to show you just how slowly he or she can melt.

And don't forget — relaxation is important for adults, too. Don't just encourage your children to relax; whenever possible, do it with them!

Resources for Section Four: Balancing Activities and Relaxation

FOR ADULTS

Think of Something Quiet, by Clare Cherry. Fearon, 1981. Although this book is subtitled "A Guide for Achieving Serenity in Early Childhood Classrooms," this fine publication is for any adults who want to help their children find serenity. It's filled with techniques for responding to the tension and stress children experience, and activities for helping children learn how to reduce their own tension and experience relaxation.

Drama & Music: Creative Activities for Young Children, by Janet Rubin and Margaret Merrion. Humanics Learning, 1995. A sourcebook of ideas and activities for nurturing and expanding children's creative potential. It includes more than 100 games, stories and rhymes, plus activities with rhythm instruments, creative movement and drama.

Quiet Times, by Louise Binder Scott. T.S. Denison, 1986. This resource deals with the problems of tension, restlessness and inattentiveness due to overstimulation and feelings of insecurity in young children. It features 11 child-oriented stories for relaxation, 35 helpful devices to induce relaxation, 23 action rhymes for relaxation, and 16 child-centered poems for quiet feelings.

FOR CHILDREN

The Sleeping Porch, by Karen Ackerman. Morrow, 1995. Jonathan and his family are thrilled to move to a big house from their small apartment. But one hot summer night, there is a terrible storm and the roof starts to leak. Where can they sleep? The whole family troops onto the sleeping porch, where the stars twinkle, the breeze softly blows, and everybody watches the fireflies until they fall asleep.

Taxi, Taxi, by Cari Best. Orchard Books, 1997. There are Spanish phrases sprinkled throughout this upbeat story, in which Tina spends every Sunday with her papi, who comes to pick her up in his taxi. This Sunday, they drive into the country to have lunch by a pond, and papi buys Tina a special present. Winner of the Ezra Jack Keats award.

Rabbit's Good News, by Ruth Lercher Bornstein. Clarion Books, 1995. A little rabbit peeks out of her warm burrow to discover the soft green sound of spring.

D.W. Flips! by Marc Brown. Little, Brown, 1987. D.W. can't even do a forward roll in gymnastics class. But with persistence and much practice, she finally learns to do flips!

A Child's Good night Book, by Margaret Wise Brown. HarperCollins, New Edition, 1992. A classic bedtime book that was first published in 1943, the soothingly repetitious words tell how each little animal, and finally, the children, all go to sleep.

Goodnight Moon, (Board Book, Comb & Brush Set), by Margaret Wise Brown. HarperFestival, 1997. In a package with this longtime favorite story, there's a comb and a brush and a sleepy little bunny. This charming set will add to the goodnight fun.

Good Morning, Pond, by Alyssa Satin Capucilli. Hyperion Books, 1994. As the pond comes to life with frogs, ducks, dragonflies, and other creatures, three little children come to peek quietly and to look up at the soft white clouds.

From Head to Toe, by Eric Carle. HarperFestival, 1999. With an "I can do it!" attitude, children imitate animals' movements, in a book that could inspire youngsters to hours of movement activities!

Just Another Ordinary Day, by Rod Clement. HarperTrophy, 1995. Amanda gets dressed for school, plays with her friends, and cuddles with her cat. While the text tells of an ordinary day, the pictures depict Amanda riding to school with a dinosaur, playing with an alien, and cuddling with a lion. Just an ordinary day with an author/illustrator who has an extraordinary imagination.

If Once You Have Slept on an Island, by Rachel Field. Mulberry, 1995. The poetry of Rachel Field and the enchanting watercolors of Iris Van Rynbach combine in a tribute to the peace and joys of island life.

In the Woods: Who's Been Here? by Lindsay Barrett George. Greenwillow, 1995. As we follow two children along a woodland trail, we learn what bird or animal had been there before and left its trace behind. A beautifully illustrated journey of discovery.

Catch the Wind! All About Kites, by Gail Gibbons. Little, Brown, 1995. In this informative book, Katie and Sam go to Ike's Kite Shop and learn about the history of kites, how they are made, and how to fly them. They each buy a kite to fly in the kite festival. Includes instructions on how make your own kite.

I Pretend, by Heidi Goennel. Tambourine, 1995. Throughout her every-day activities, such as playing in the sand, mixing paint, or playing with her cat, a little girl pretends all sorts of wonderful things. (The daily activities are pictured with black and white line drawings, while the products of her imagination are in vivid colors.)

Sleep, Baby, Sleep: Lullabies and Night Poems, selected and illustrated by Michael Hague. Morrow, 1994. A collection of nighttime poems written by such poets as William Blake, Robert Louis Stevenson, and Nikki Giovanni, as well as traditional folk lullabies. Also included are several musical arrangements. The illustrations depict children of many different cultures.

Rosie's Ballet Slippers, by Susan Hampshire. HarperTrophy, 1996. Rosie's mother buys her pink ballet slippers, so that she can learn to dance. The colorful pictures by Maria Teresa Meloni capture the expressions of joy and concentration on the faces of the children at the ballet lesson as they learn how to plié, sauté, and just have fun.

Sleep Tight, by B.G. Hennessy. Puffin, 1995. In the bedtime ritual in this family it is "Night time/Quiet time/Read our favorite book time." Everything and everybody everywhere is asleep, and soon the children are sleeping too.

What Can You Do in the Rain? What Can You Do in the Snow? What Can You Do in the Sun? What Can You Do in the Wind? by Anna Grossnickle Hines. Greenwillow, 1999. The author of many, many appealing books for toddlers adds four more to her impressive list. These board books help children celebrate the changing seasons, enjoying activities in every kind of weather.

Sewing by Hand, by Christine Hoffman. HarperCollins, 1994. Older preschoolers, working closely with an adult, might enjoy sewing a circle pillow, a beanbag cat, or a flower girl doll as described in this introduction to sewing.

Sidewalk Trip, by Patricia Hubbell. HarperFestival, 1999. A little girl takes a joyful jaunt with her mother through her neighborhood, with a delicious treat at the end.

The Sweet and Sour Animal Book, by Langston Hughes. Oxford University Press, 1994. This unique book includes 27 never-before-published poems about animals by Langston Hughes. The poems are perfect for young children, and the colorful, creative illustrations were made with paints and clay by students at the Harlem School of the Arts.

The Big Alfie Out of Doors Storybook, by Shirley Hughes. Lothrop, Lee & Shepard, 1992. In this new collection of stories and poems about Alfie, we see how Mom and Grandma buy pretend groceries from a shop that Alfie sets up in the backyard; we go on a trip with the family to the seashore where Alfie (almost) loses his favorite stone; and we learn how Alfie and his Dad spend the night outdoors in a tent, until their sleep is interrupted by a curious pig.

The Quiet Evening, by Thacher Hurd. Greenwillow, 1999. It is evening and everyone is thinking quiet thoughts. The family is settling down for the night, and far away every aspect of life seems to be serene: people in boats, the fish in the ocean, even the earth itself. A perfect book to evoke tranquil feelings.

Wilson's World, by Edith Thacher Hurd & Clement Hurd. HarperTrophy, 1971. "Wilson liked to paint pictures, and sometimes he wrote stories to go with them." Wilson paints the world, the sea, and the sky. Soon little green things begin to pop up everywhere: trees, grass, and flowers. Animals appear and people too. But when his world becomes full of pollution, Wilson paints another picture of the world he really wants.

Bouncing on the Bed, by Jackie French Koller. Orchard Books, 1999. This book with bouncy text tells about a lively little boy, who goes bouncing, wiggling, and singing through his day's activities. It is winningly illustrated by Anna Grossnickle Hines.

What Is the Sun? by Reeve Lindbergh. Candlewick Press, 1996. In a bedtime dialog between a boy and his grandmother, she answers his questions about the sun, moon, wind, and rain with love and understanding.

All the Places to Love, by Patricia MacLachlan. HarperCollins, 1994. With words of love and remembrance, a little boy tells about the beauty of the land where he grew up: "The valley, The river falling down over rocks, The hilltop where the blueberries grew." (The author of this poetic story won the 1986 Newbery Medal for *Sarah, Plain and Tall.*)

The Greatest Gymnast of All, by Stuart J. Murphy. HarperTrophy, 1998. Confident Zoe dazzles us with her gymnastics while she demonstrates opposites, such as: UP and DOWN, ON and OFF, and FORWARD and BACKWARD.

Good Night! by Claire Masurel. Chronicle, 1995. In a little girl's nighttime ritual, she fluffs up the pillows and brushes her teeth. She gathers all of her bedtime friends: bear, rabbit, clown and all, and scolds them gently for wanting to stay up longer. Then at last everyone is tucked in and ready to sleep.

Fireflies for Nathan, by Shulamith Levey Oppenheim. Puffin, 1996. Nathan visits his grandparents, and spends a magical evening catching fireflies just as his daddy did when he was a boy.

Long Ago Yesterday, by Anne Rockwell. Greenwillow, 1999. Ten little stories are included in this book by artist/author Rockwell. The themes vary: playing in the snow, a trip to a lake, a new tricycle, a little boy's original lullaby. They come straight out of young children's experiences, and should be favorites with toddlers and preschoolers.

The Goodbye Walk, by Joanne Ryder. Lodestar, 1993. A girl says goodbye to the special places she loved as her summer vacation ends.

Bijou, Bonbon & Beau: The Kittens Who Danced for Degas, by Joan Sweeney. Chronicle, 1998. Did it really happen? A mama cat delivers her kittens back-stage in a ballet theater in Paris. As they grow, they get into trouble, but everyone loves them — even the artist who sketches the dancers. On opening night, the little kittens run on stage, pouncing on the dancers' ankles. The manager is furious, but the kittens are the talk of Paris. The story could be true. Do you see the tiny paw prints in Degas' painting?

The Big Big Sea, by Martin Waddell. Candlewick Press, 1994. A little girl and her mother take a nighttime walk to the sea. They are all alone on a moonlit beach as they splash in the water, and then walk on the sand. It's an experience to treasure always.

Me Too! Me Too! by Harriet Ziefert. Harper & Row, 1988. In a story of family fun, Molly and her little sister play dressup indoors and then splash in the rain outdoors where Mommy joins them, marching with their umbrellas.

Section Five

Understanding Feelings

Section Five
Understanding Feelings

Introduction

Have you taught your child the names of the colors and shapes? They need to learn the vocabulary for *feelings* too! Knowing words for basic feelings like *mad, sad, frustrated,* and *happy* help youngsters to manage their feelings more readily.

Adults need to explain that feelings are different from behavior. It's okay to express in words whatever emotions you have inside. It's not permitted to act on those feelings to hurt others.

Taking a "life-affirming and self-affirming" approach, some authors of this section explore the feelings of joy and hope. And one contributor shares a recipe that won't be found in *The Joy of Cooking*. "A Recipe for Growing Happy Children," however, is about the joy of parenting.

SECTION FIVE
UNDERSTANDING FEELINGS

Chapter 17
Understanding Feelings

Elizabeth Crary

Children need to know
that feelings change.

Mad is not bad. Mad is a feeling. People often think love is good and anger is bad. However, love and anger are both feelings and neither is good or bad. Feelings can be expressed in both constructive and destructive ways. For example, when you express love by being overprotective and refusing to let your child experience the consequences of his decision, that love is not healthy. When you use anger to open communication and confront injustice, that anger is healthy.

Children need to understand feelings. There are three things children need to know:
• First, they need a feeling vocabulary.
• Second, they need to understand the nature of feelings.
• Third, they need to understand how to use those feelings constructively.

Feeling vocabulary.
Children need to learn *feeling words.* They need a feeling vocabulary as much as they need to learn their colors and letters. When you give your child words to explain his or her feelings, the feelings become more manageable.

Start with basic feelings like *mad, sad, happy,* and *frustrated.* Then add more types of feelings *(proud, lonely, scared)* and various intensities *(contented, cheerful, pleased, excited).* It is easier for children to notice they are getting mad when they understand feelings like *concerned, annoyed,* and *upset.*

Nature of feelings.
Children need to know that feelings change. And different people feel differently about the same things. They need to know that there is a difference between *feelings* and *actions.*

Young children and many school-age children live in the "now" zone. If they are happy, they believe they will always be happy. If they are mad, they believe they will always be mad. For most children the worst threat they can give someone is, "I won't invite you to my birthday party." The birthday can be nine months away yet the threat is as powerful as if it were the next week. When we can help children realize that feelings change, they can begin to use the feelings effectively.

Interestingly enough, many parents also act as though feelings last forever. They are uncomfortable with their child's anger because they are afraid that it will last forever, and they don't know how to "fix it." However, if parents try to make or keep their children happy, they deny the children the chance to learn the skills to be happy themselves.

Children need to know that people feel differently about the same things. One child may prefer strawberry ice cream, another vanilla. One child may prefer the dump truck and another the fire engine. *When children know people feel differently, that knowledge opens the door to discussion and negotiation.*

Feelings are different from behavior. Feelings are on the inside, behavior is on the outside. When children have names for their feelings they can think about them. They can separate the angry feeling on the inside from the action on the outside. Some actions are hurtful, like hitting; some actions are helpful like taking three deep breaths. You can help children separate feelings and actions when you establish clear limits. For example, "It's okay to be mad. And I will not let you hurt your brother. You need to find another way to let him know him you are mad."

Dealing with feelings.
When someone is upset, there are two parts to the problem — the *feelings* and the *situation.* Children need tools to deal with both.

Feelings give information and energy. The information tells you something is happening. The energy gives you the strength to deal with the situation. Sometimes the energy is so strong that it gets in the way of thinking about the problem. As a parent, or a teacher, you can teach children ways to use the energy constructively.

Ways to use energy constructively. Give your children physical, verbal and imaginative ways to use their energy. Kids can stomp their feet, take deep breaths, imagine the anger draining out, or ask for help. They can listen to music, count to ten, or do a "Mad Dance." Long, smooth motions are better for releasing energy than short, chopping motions. Help your children practice using calming tools <u>before</u> they need to use them "for real."

Ways to deal with the situation. We tell kids to use their words, but that fails many times. They need more ideas. For example, if your child wants the toy another child is using, she can ask for it. Or trade. Or wait. Or make a deal. You can teach these tools by demonstrating them for your children. "Here is a toy. See if Mary will trade with you." You can also teach by modeling. "I'm frustrated because I don't like to stand on a long line at the supermarket. But I will wait my turn."

When you acknowledge your children's feelings you help them understand themselves. When you offer them tools to deal with feelings and situations, you help them act effectively and feel good about themselves.

Feeling Activities

You can help your children understand feelings and deal with them effectively by modeling and by introducing feeling discussions into your daily activities.

• **Talk about feelings.** Use a variety of feeling words. Make a list of feeling words and try to introduce two or three each day in your conversations. Use both comfortable feelings (like *happy* and *proud*) and uncomfortable feelings (like *angry* and *scared*).

Share how your feelings change and what you do about the feelings. For example, if someone cuts you off while you are driving, you could say, "Boy, I feel angry when someone cuts me off. I feel like cutting <u>him</u> off, but I am going to take three deep breaths instead. One. Two. Three. That's better, but I think I need to do it again."

• **Read feeling books.**
Use books like *I Feel: A Picture Book of Emotions* (George Ancona, Dutton, 1977) and *Feelings Inside You & Outloud Too* (Barbara Kay Polland, Celestial Arts, 1984) to introduce new words. Books (see Resources, page 157) like *What Is a Feeling; All My Feelings at Home: Ellie's Day;* and *All My Feelings at Preschool: Nathan's Day* illustrate what feelings are and how they change. *I'm Mad; I'm Frustrated, and I'm Proud* offer children ways to deal with their feelings. *I Want It; I Can't Wait; I Want to Play;* and *My Name is Not Dummy* teach children negotiation skills.

Use the books as a springboard for discussing feelings and options. Help your child realize that there are many right ways to deal with feelings. You can ask your child, "When have you felt like that little boy in the book? What did you do when you felt that way? What else could he have done?" Once you get used to discussing feelings you can introduce them while reading any book to your child.

• **Do art and craft activities.** You can use playdough, paper plates, and pictures of feelings to introduce feeling discussions.

Make playdough faces.
Label the feeling *(happy, sad)*. Ask your child, "What does your playdough face feel? When have *you* felt that way?" Squish the playdough up and make a new feeling face and discuss it. Observe that feelings can change like the playdough faces.

Make a feeling wheel.
 Take a paper plate and divide it into six segments. Draw or paste a face (cut from a magazine) in each segment. You might have *mad, scared, proud, happy, sad,* and *contented.*
1)　Talk with your child about when you, the parent, felt these different feelings.
2)　Put a paper clip on the segment that describes how you feel now.
3)　As your feelings change, move the clip.
4)　Ask your child to follow steps 1,2 & 3 with his or her own feelings using a different kind of paper clip.
This shows how feelings change.

Introduce feelings while you exercise.
You can take turns "Walking mad" or scared, or proud. You can get a broom and take turns "Sweeping scared," or silly, or happy. You can also explain how running or dancing uses up extra feeling energy. Have your children pretend they are angry and suggest they walk until they feel better. Practice will make it easier for kids to use the techniques when they are really angry.

Sing songs and play music.
An easy place to begin is with a children's song like "If you're happy and you know it ..." or "I'm so mad I could scream ..." (Miss Jackie). You can sing the traditional songs first. Then make up your own verses.

People often have emotional responses to music. Play some music and talk about how you feel listening to it. Marching band music evokes *happy, proud* feelings. Flute or violin music often evokes a *sad* or *lonely* feeling. Some children will sit and listen to the music, others will need to move to the music.

Make up games to illustrate feeling ideas.
For example, *Inside Outside.* Explain that feelings are on the inside and behavior is on the outside. Give a situation: "You meet a lion walking down the street." Have your child get into a large box or an area marked off with blocks or string, and say "On the inside I feel ...*(scared)*." Then, climb out and say "On the outside I ...*(run away)*." Encourage children to offer different feelings and behaviors for the same situation. Use the same game with different situations.

Imagine a calm place. Your child needs a calm place in his mind to go to when things get rough. The calm place can be a rocking chair with a blanket, or under a tree in the park or looking out at a lake, for example. When you are physically in a calm place, talk about how it feels. Then later in a different place, recall the feeling. When kids can recall the feeling elsewhere you can tell them when they are *mad, scared,* or *lonely,* they can go to the calm place in their mind. Eventually they will be able to go there by themselves when they are upset.

Practice with puppets. You can make it easier for your child to learn new things by using puppets. Set up a situation with the puppets and ask the child what the puppet could do to resolve a conflict.

For example, if you had two puppets playing with blocks, one could knock down the other's tower. You could ask your child what the other puppet might do. Guide her through the thought process without judgment.

For example, if she says, "Hit him," you could say, "Yes the puppet could hit the other puppet. What might happen next?" thereby helping your child realize there are consequences to the decision. Your goal is to teach your child the *process* of dealing with the feelings, not to memorize a set of rules.

Chapter 18
A Recipe for
Growing Happy Children

Katrina Katsarelis

The positive approach takes practice.

There's an old 1940s song with a terrific message for growing happy children — "You've got to accentuate the positive, eliminate the negative...." This simple philosophy can sometimes be difficult to carry out when the normal frustrations and time constraints of raising children come into play. But, parents who make the effort to retain a positive focus by providing a warm and nurturing environment are more likely to have their children blossom into happy, well-adjusted persons.

Start with realistic expectations.
Every family has certain limits, but it's important to keep your expectations appropriate to the child's age and ability. Diane, a mother of a 3-year-old daughter and 2-year-old son wastes a lot of time and energy trying to keep her young children "in line." Because of past encounters with what she refers to as "spoiled children," Diane is determined to raise well-behaved children.   A few of Diane's expectations are:
• Children must remain at the dinner table throughout the entire meal.
• Children must answer all instructions with "Yes, mommy."
• Children must not climb all over Diane when she gets home from work.

Any variation from these rules results in the children being reprimanded, given a time-out or a spanking, depending on Diane's mood and the severity of the offense. When the children conform to her "rules" they are seldom praised or rewarded. As a result, Diane has set up a negative parenting style which has placed her family in a frustrating cycle of punishment. Diane, often feeling out of control, can't understand why her 3-year-old daughter is acting out with excessive tantrums. Unfortunately, her children get so little attention by pleasing her that they've learned to how to command attention by misbehaving. Diane feels like an inadequate parent when in fact her expectations far exceed the developmental abilities of her young children.

Resolve issues through communication first.
Even young children comprehend a great deal more than many adults give them credit for. A lot can be accomplished by simply conveying realistic expectations to a child before problems arise. Janine, the mother of a five year old was constantly at odds with her son Conrad over one issue. Conrad's only job each morning was to make his bed, but for some reason, despite his numerous attempts the bed was always in disarray.   At wits end, Janine finally sat down with her son and together they discussed the issue. Conrad admitted to his mom that he didn't know how to make the bed. Once she patiently showed him what to do, the problem was solved.

Use positive approaches when discipline is necessary.
Discipline is a misunderstood concept. The term discipline is derived from the word *disciple* which means, "one who receives instruction from another;

a pupil." In these formative years, parents have the ultimate responsibility of teaching children what is acceptable behavior and what is not. There are four basic steps to disciplining a child while maintaining a positive focus.

1. *Choose your battles wisely.* Once you've established which issues are important to you, inform your child why these boundaries are needed as they come up. If, for example, it's important to you that your child not jump on the furniture, use specific reminders and offer alternatives. As your child begins to climb on the sofa, walk up to him (as opposed to yelling from across the room) and get down on his eye-level. "Furniture is not for jumping on. If you feel like jumping, you can go outside and jump off the back step."

2. *Give a warning.* It's appropriate to give a preschool-aged child one clear warning on a minor transgression. "Remember, I told you furniture is not for jumping? If you jump on the sofa again, I'll need you to go to sit on the stairs for 3 minutes." Inform the child exactly what will happen if he disobeys again.

3. *Follow through.* If and when a child deliberately crosses the line, act swiftly and initiate the consequence. Remind the child that each time he jumps on the sofa, he'll need to go to back on the stairs. Then interest him in an acceptable activity. After the issue is over avoid dwelling on it; move on.

4. *Use praise as a reward.* When you see your child make a conscious decision to follow a rule you've set forth, delight him with a hug and a big dose of positive reinforcement, "You remembered to pick up your toys — I knew you could do it!" This response will get you the results you want more quickly than scolding, punishing, or reprimanding.

Following this type of format consistently will teach the child that your rules need to be followed. The child also learns that gratifying attention is received when he follows the rules and that, by itself, is a terrific incentive.

The positive approach takes practice.
Accentuating the positive is more a *way of life* than a parenting technique. It involves taking the time to recognize and acknowledge the ordinary *and* extraordinary things children do everyday. It takes a bit of our time and attention to "catch them being good" but with practice it gets much easier. By accentuating the positive, children begin to feel cherished simply because of who they are, not what they do. If a seed is planted into the ground and given no nourishment it cannot bloom. On the other hand, take a child, drench with love, shower with attention and sprinkle with regular doses of positive messages. You'll be helping your child grow into a confident, warm-hearted, unique person.

Growing Happy Children: 20 Things You Can Do Today!

1. Greet your child with a hug and a kiss each time you come home.

2. Notice at least three small things each day that your child does RIGHT. Tell the child about it.

3. Start a journal about your child. Write down memorable events or comical sayings in your child's life as they happen. Continue writing in it monthly until your child is an adult. Give it to your child for a graduation or wedding gift.

4. Read to your child. Start early with durable cardboard baby books and read as much as the child's attention level will allow. Visit the public library often. Most libraries encourage young readers with specially-designated children's areas and story hours.

5. Frame and display a piece of your child's artwork. Pick out a special drawing and put it in a picture frame. Hang it proudly in an obvious place and see how long it takes your child to notice. Let your child know how good it makes you feel when you look at that drawing.

6. Be honest. Answer questions honestly and appropriately for the child's age level. Also, if you make a promise, keep it. Children need the security of knowing their parents will always be truthful with them.

7. Appreciate nature. Point out the beauty in a rainbow, the wonderful smell of mountain air or the happy sounds of chirping birds. Soon your child will be pointing these things out to you.

8. Allow occasional messes. Some of the best learning experiences come in the form of a mess. Puddle stomping, fingerpainting, rolling in a pile of leaves or making shave cream sculptures create some of the sweetest childhood memories ever.

9. Give your child a little power. Offer choices and let your child make some small decisions. Forcing a child to do everything your way may some-day backfire in a big way. Retain limits but be flexible on unimportant issues. Making little decisions today will help prepare your child to make serious decisions in the future.

10. Establish a Family Night. Set aside one day a week for creating closeness through outings together. Go to a movie, ice-skating or just stay home and play games. Let children help think of ideas for family night. This is a tradition children will remember for years to come.

11. Touch your child. Hold hands, stroke your child's hair, hug and kiss at will. Nothing expresses love more than a warm comfortable bear hug from mommy or daddy. Sadly, many adults can't remember ever being hugged or kissed as children. Don't let your child be one of them.

12. Minimize good and bad labels. Being told, "You're bad" repeatedly can damage a child's self-esteem. Instead, point out the actual *behavior* that bothers you. Conversely, instead of saying, "good boy / good girl" when your child does something right, try praising in specific ways, "I like the way you put your toys away."

13. Get along well with your spouse. Go on dates, communicate, resolve conflicts and be affectionate toward one other. One of the best gifts a parent can give is to be a positive role model for your child's future relationships.

14. Be an example yourself. If you curse and swear, expect that your child will too. From the time they are infants, children learn almost everything from mimicry. Unfortunately, children can't disregard your negative traits and adopt only your positive ones.

15. Ask questions. What's your favorite color? What do you want to be when you grow up? What did you dream about last night? Let children know their thoughts and opinions are valued.

16. Play. Play. Play. Children learn a great deal through play. Get down on the floor and build blocks, play dress-up, make up silly stories or play board games. Let yourself go sometimes and just have fun together.

17. Have regular sit-down dinners. Studies show that families who eat a daily meal together form a better connection by keeping the lines of communication open. Keep mealtimes relaxed and encourage conversation by asking an open-ended question such as, "What was your favorite part of the day?"

18. Sing with your child. Whether or not you were blessed with the gift of song, a singing parent is a happy parent. Play, "Name that Tune" by taking turns humming a song until someone guesses correctly. Music *brings* together the family who *sings* together.

19. Say "I love you.." Your child may not really know it unless you say those three little words.

20. Respect your child. Show your child the same courtesy and respect you would a treasured friend. You can enforce limits without yelling, name-calling, or shaming. The respect demonstrated for your child <u>now</u> will be reflected in the way he treats others <u>later</u>.

Chapter 19
The Joy in
Your Preschooler's Life

Fredric C. Hartman

*Joy will come to your preschooler
from many different sources,
many activities.*

In *Freedom and Destiny,* ROLLO MAY *says that joy is an overflowing of inner energies leading to awe and wonderment. It is a release, an opening up; it is what comes when one is able genuinely to "let go." Joy points toward the future; it is both the thrill of new continents to explore and the discovery of new continents emerging within oneself...it is an unfolding of life.*

Joy will come to your preschooler
from many different sources, many activities.
Imagine you are inside your child's mind as she is sitting on the seat of her two-wheeler bicycle getting ready to start riding by herself as you are walking alongside her holding her seat getting ready to let her go. Imagine that moment inside of you and her when you let her go and she pedals and pedals down the sidewalk wobbling, trying so hard to do it — you're worrying and rooting for her so much — and then suddenly that magical moment occurs and you know she has found her balance and pedals away and she says, "Daddy, look at me, I can ride, I can ride, look at me!" This bursting of joy in a child can bring the happiest tears to a parent's eyes.

The feeling of joy is our most life-affirming and self-affirming feeling. When it is a physical activity that brings joy, such as the joy of being able to ride a bike, it affirms the pleasure your child's body can give her. When it is the joy that occurs when your preschooler is able to appreciate nature, such as a snowfall, it affirms his sense of the wonder of the world. As he is enraptured with the snow falling, his feeling of joy is telling him that the world can give him gifts like this and let him feel good in such quiet mysterious ways. It will tell him there is an endless supply of natural joys.

Mental joys affirm your preschooler's sense in her ability to think, reason, and solve problems. When she builds a house out of blocks that her stuffed animal or dolls can live in comfortably and happily, and it gives her joy, she is feeling that there is enough material in the world for her and that she can use her own mind to make a happy home within it. Her joy will be letting her know that problems <u>can</u> be solved and that <u>she</u> can solve them.

Social joys will affirm your child's faith and trust in others. When your son makes his first friend and feels joy in anticipating playing with him — his joy will be telling him that people who are not from the same family can enjoy being together — and feel a special affection for each other.

Emotional joys affirm your preschooler's ability to experience and express her feelings. When you praise her or give her a hug, she will enjoy these moments because she will feel that she is lovable and that other people can be loving. Also she will learn that it is good for this to be expressed freely. Her joy will be telling her that there are treasures like this to be found in her emotional life and that they are worth searching for.

Infants can experience joy in the most unexpected ways. I'll never forget one afternoon when I was 8 years old, my brother was sitting in his highchair and suddenly burst out giggling as the tennis ball on the table rolled off and bounced on the floor. At first, I thought he was laughing at something else. I rolled it off again and he burst out laughing again. He was giggling so hard and for so long that I began laughing myself. I kept rolling the ball off the table and we laughed so much together that day. Such a simple act can create so much joy. It doesn't take expensive toys, and you don't have to travel far. Joy can be hidden in the most unexpected places.

Children are born with an enormous potential for feeling joy. How much this potential is realized and the way joy is ultimately experienced and expressed can be shaped to a large extent by the love, sensitivity, and communication that exists in the most intimate and important relationships the child has at home. Along with their potential for joy, children have a wonderful ability to model whatever it is they experience around them.

One of the most important things parents can do for their children is to help them experience joys whenever possible. And the joy you can build into your preschooler's life will become the joy she derives later in her life from her career, her own family, or from simply looking at the night sky or a flower. And she, in turn, will be able to give this joy to her own preschooler.

Ways to Help Young Children Experience the Feeling of Joy

As parents, think about how much and what kinds of joy you're finding in your lives, in your work, in your relationships, and in your children. It is so important to keep in mind that the joy a child sees demonstrated by adults is the joy that will be deeply instilled in him or her.

• *Encourage your child to engage in creative activity.* Play music to dance to, give him crayons to draw with, tell him stories, and sing songs with him. When your child attempts new things (whether he succeeds or fails) praise him liberally for his efforts. Your child will absorb the encouragement and praise you give and will reexperience it as a flash of joy when he attempts a new task.

• *Get excited with your child.* Become silly with her. If she wants to pretend to be the mommy and have you be the baby, let her pretend to feed you and tuck you in bed. Try to experience as she does the excitement of the moment as she runs to catch snowflakes on the tip of her tongue. Let her spontaneity excite yours and let go with her.

• *Look through family photographs.* Reminisce with your child. Let him become immersed in recalling past experiences of joy, sadness, or danger. Remembering joyful times will enhance the present. Reminiscing about the sad or dangerous times can help him feel stronger and more self-confident, especially knowing that life is good and secure now, and that he is loved and enjoyed.

• *Start a family journal* in which each member of the family records things that have happened which have brought joy to him or her. Read the entries to your child and talk about them with her. This helps children learn how people can differ in what brings them joy.

• *Still another way to instill the value of joy in preschoolers is to build traditions in their lives* that enable them to experience various joys on a regular basis as a part of family life. For example, you can decorate a shoe box on which you write the words, "Treasure Chest." In it would be placed a gift of some kind that you would give to your child each week. The gift could be an inexpensive thing like a crayon, a book, or a rubber ball. The gift-giving wouldn't necessarily have to be tied to any behavior on your child's part but would be given to convey the idea that he or she is special and special things should come their way. Each week your child would look forward to receiving some interesting surprise. The pleasure would be akin to that special pleasure a child feels when looking forward to the coming of the tooth fairy or Christmas or Hanukkah and anticipating receiving a gift for simply being who they are.

Chapter 20
Encouraging Hope
in Young Children

Amy Houts

*Having a hopeful attitude
is closely related
to being optimistic,
having high self-esteem,
and having firm beliefs.*

Remember the story of *The Little Engine That Could?* The little blue engine puffed, "I think I can, I think I can..." when trying to pull toys and food to boys and girls over the mountain. The little train was willing to take on this task and achieved his goal because he had hope. He puffed steadily down the mountain: "I thought I could; I thought I could."

Dr. Charles R. Snyder, a psychologist at the University of Kansas who studies hope, defines hope as more than the simple notion that everything will turn out all right. "Having hope means believing you have both the will and the way to accomplish your goals, whatever they may be."

Should We Teach Hope?
In the world we live in today, with crime, violence, and war, you may wonder if it is healthy to teach children to hope. You might reason it is better to be realistic and teach preschoolers that ours is a cold, cruel world without hope. If you teach children to hope, is it just setting them up for disappointment when they grow to adulthood? What is the right answer?

Research shows that when persons, young or old, are hopeful — they are healthier, happier, and have better relationships with family, friends, and their community. Children have more chance to be successful in school. Grownups have more chance for better paying jobs and rewarding careers. If you teach your preschoolers to hope, they might not have better circumstances than another child, but they will be able to thrive with whatever challenges they face.

Attributes of Hopeful People
Dr. Snyder's research included discovering what attributes hopeful people have, so we can learn how to be more like them. Hopeful people:

   * turn to friends to help achieve their goals
   * tell themselves they can achieve their goals
   * tell themselves things get better with time
   * are flexible in finding ways to achieve a goal and take small steps to get there
   * aim for another, possibly similar goal, if they find they cannot achieve a desired goal.

Grownups, as well as preschoolers, set goals for themselves that have many similarities. Both children and adults hope for friendship with a peer, either a preschool classmate or co-worker. Both children and adults hope for a loving companion: a teddy bear or a spouse. Both hope to master a sport: learning to jump rope, or learning to ski. Goals and hopes of any age need to taken seriously.

As a parent, you are the one who is most capable of helping your preschooler acquire the attributes of hopeful people listed above:

* You can be the friend to help her with a goal.
* You can tell her, "You can do it!"
* You can remind her she is growing and when she is a little older she will be able to reach her goal, for example, of jumping rope.
* By taking small steps you can help her learn. Maybe you'll point out she could jump over the rope, if you lay it flat on the ground. And take the next step of swinging it gently back and forth, low to the ground, while she jumps.
* If it's not the right time to achieve this goal, you could help with another, similar goal: hopping on one foot, walking backwards, skipping.... Whatever the goal, you can help your preschooler by actively using the attributes of hopeful people.

One important point to remember is: a hopeful attitude is not a sit-back-and-wait attitude. Hope stimulates motivation. When your child says, "I hope I get a sled for my birthday," he has already begun the process of hope. He is going to find a way to accomplish this goal. There are several different approaches he can take: telling you is one, because you are the number one person who gets him a present. He could continue to finalize his goal by pointing out his favorite sled in the store, the one with the blue stripe, or he could dictate a letter to Grandma about how much he wants this gift. He might not request any other toy for his birthday. If you, his parents, believe this would be a good gift for him, and can afford it, then his hope will be realized.

Optimism, Self-Esteem, and Firm Beliefs
Having a hopeful attitude is closely related to being optimistic, having high self-esteem, and having firm beliefs.

Optimism is "an inclination to anticipate the best possible outcome." Martin E.P. Seligman, Ph.D., points to parents as models for optimism. He has been researching optimists and pessimists for over 25 years and is the author of *Learned Optimism* (Pocketbooks, 1998.). He states that his research indicates that children are likely to acquire views similar to those of their parents, and that the key to optimism is changing the destructive things that you say to yourself.

There are many opportunities for changing from the use of destructive language to teaching positive language to preschoolers. We can make choices in how we can explain events to our children. Dr. Seligman says children listen intently to the explanation of *why* something happened.

For example, my preschooler was watching me when I dropped a heavy bag of groceries which contained a jar of barbecue sauce. The jar broke. I could have explained this misfortune with a negative statement about myself such as, "I'm so clumsy: I never do anything right," or I could have used Dr. Seligman's four step process. One, state a fact, "The bag was heavy." Two, consider the alternative, "I'll baste the chicken with orange marmalade instead of barbecue sauce." Three, consider the consequences, "The barbecue sauce cost a dollar," and four, transform the event into a learning experience, "Next time I won't carry such a heavy bag."

He emphasizes this four step process of stating a fact, considering an alternative, considering the consequences and transforming the event, as a way to teach children and parents to use positive language and promote optimism. You will have to use simple language when using this approach with your preschoolers. Start out with, "What happened?" Then, "What else could we do?" "What didn't you like about this?" Finish by asking, "How could we make this have a happy ending?" Visualizing and hoping for a happy ending is the first step toward one.

Self-esteem, the second link to hope, has three parts. In order to feel self-esteem, to feel good about oneself, a young child needs to have a sense of worth, a sense of competence, and a sense of belonging. You are the mirror of your child's self-esteem. You can help your preschoolers' self-esteem by believing and showing them you feel good about them and helping them to feel good about themselves. Helping them to learn the tasks they are ready to learn at each age level, such as buttoning their coat, encourages self-esteem. If a child feels that she is loved, capable, and that she belongs to her family and community, she has a better chance to accomplish her goals, and to hope for her dreams to come true.

Hope is intangible. We cannot touch it. Hope is a desire based on human beings' most intimate needs — the hope for love, for health, for happiness.

Hope is based on *firm beliefs*. When you believe you can do something, you can see yourself doing it, just as the little engine believed that he could get over the mountain. His attitude made his goal possible. With hope you can believe not only in yourself and your family, but in a "greater good."

Ways to
Encourage Hope

Through language

Use of positive language is one of the most prevalent ways you can encourage hope because you can use positive language every day. Listen to yourself and how you relate to your preschooler. Do you encourage or discourage?

One example of how to encourage hope by using language involves children's desires to imagine what they will do when they grow up. A preschooler might say, "I want to be an astronaut." It is important to emphasize the feeling, "How exciting, to zoom into outer space!" rather than take away her hope because of far-into-the-future adult concerns.

Dr. Seligman cautions against parents using the words "always," "never," and "so." Examples: "You *always* do it wrong." "You *never* do it right." "You are *so* lazy." Instead of saying, "You will never be able to jump rope" (even if that's the way you feel after trying for an hour) encourage the hope of accomplishing this goal in the future by saying, "You tried hard; let's work on it more tomorrow."

Through Action

Listen to your young child's hopes. If he says, "I hope Grandma sends me a letter," you can help realize that hope by taking steps to make it into a reality. Sit down with your preschooler and let him dictate a letter to Grandma. Tell her to write back soon. Include a picture he drew. By taking action, hope becomes reality.

Dramatic Play

Dramatic play encourages problem solving and achievement of goals in a safe environment. The goal here could include defeating the bad guys or being a lovely princess. Whatever it is, your preschooler can use his or her imagination to achieve their goals. And it's safe, because in the security of your room you are in control of the bad guys. And when you tire of being a princess, you can be a normal preschooler who spills milk on her jeans.

Traditions

During the holiday season, children have so many hopes! The one they verbalize is usually for a specific toy. But one of the things children really want is to be a part of family traditions. Hope is connected to anticipation and expectation. Children look forward to events that happen year after year — ones they can look forward to and feel secure with. When you carry out family traditions, you reinforce the hopeful attitude that events looked forward to will indeed take place.

Stories

When we read a book or see a show where evil is defeated and good reigns, we reinforce the hope for a better world, a truth that good is stronger than evil, and that there are courageous people who will protect us. We might even imagine we are that valiant person.

Or we might see a story of a person who overcomes a difficult situation, so we can have hope for our own situation. Adults and children need these role models — people who don't give up.

In the book, *The Carrot Seed,* a little boy plants a carrot seed. His mother says, "I'm afraid it won't come up." His father says, "I'm afraid it won't come up." His brother says, "It won't come up." But the boy has hope. His goal is to grow a carrot seed. He still waters it and pulls up the weeds every day. He firmly believes in his abilities, and he is rewarded on the last page of the book with a wheelbarrow-sized carrot .

We need to read stories about people who used the attributes of hope. See what they accomplished. If they can, then surely we can, too.

Resources for Section Five:
Understanding Feelings

FOR ADULTS

Pick Up Your Socks... and other skills growing children need! by Elizabeth Crary. Parenting Press, 1990. Parent educator and author, Elizabeth Crary offers tools and insights to help parents teach their children responsibility.

Without Spanking or Spoiling, A Practical Approach to Toddler & Preschool Guidance, 2nd edition, by Elizabeth Crary. Parenting Press, 1993. "No one child guidance method works with every child all of the time," says the author, "so what parents need are lots and lots of ideas." This helpful book draws information from four major parenting approaches and invites parents to choose a guidance method that fits best with their child's temperament and their family values.

The Mother's Almanac, by Marguerite Kelly and Elia Parsons. Doubleday, 1975. A feast of joyful activities for mothers and small children. (See *The Father's Almanac,* below.)

Love and Anger: the Parental Dilemma, by Nancy Samalin. Viking, 1992. The Director of the Parents Guidance Workshops in New York City, Samalin offers valuable suggestions about how parents can direct their anger into constructive expression, which results in growth for everyone.

The Father's Almanac, by S. Adams Sullivan. Doubleday, 1992. Another feast of joyful activities for fathers and small children. (See *The Mother's Almanac,* above.)

FOR CHILDREN

The Candlewick Book of Bedtime Stories, Candlewick Press, 1995. Many favorite authors and illustrators contributed to this appealing collection of stories. You will find *Good Night, Lily,* by Martha Alexander, *Tom and Pippo's Day,* by Helen Oxenbury, and Martin Waddell's *Can't You Sleep, Little Bear?* among the 17 stories that will delight youngsters at bedtime.

Charlie Anderson, by B. Abercrombie. Aladdin, 1995. This book tells about the joy of having two loving families.

What Makes Me Happy? by Catherine and Laurence Anholt. Candlewick Press, 1995. Different children ask, "What makes me laugh?" "What makes me cry?" "What makes me scared?" And then they answer these questions with rollicking rhyme and whimsical pictures.

Grandfather and I; Grandmother and I, by Helen E. Buckley. Lothrop, Lee & Shepard 1994. These classic stories, published originally in 1959, have been newly illustrated by Jan Ormerod. They tell of the special relationship between a grandparent and a young child, encouraging a sense of worth and a feeling of belonging.

Cannonball Simp, by John Burningham. Candlewick Press, 1994. Simp is a sad, hungry, homeless dog. In her wanderings, she evades the dangers of the streets and the dog pound, until she at last finds hope and a home, when she saves the day for the circus clown.

Life Is Fun! by Nancy Carlson. Puffin Books, 1996. With a positive outlook on life, a cheerful youngster gives the reader simple instructions on how to be happy on earth in this funny and upbeat book.

What If It Never Stops Raining? by Nancy Carlson. Puffin, 1994. Tim worries about everything, but somehow things usually have a way of working themselves out in a positive way.

Why Did It Happen? Helping Children Cope in a Violent World, by Janice Cohn, D.S.W. Morrow, 1994. A little boy, Daniel, has a friend named Mr. James, the owner of a neighborhood grocery store. When the store is robbed and Mr. James is hurt, Daniel is frightened and angry. His parents help him to talk about his feelings. Mr. James takes a hopeful point of view, saying that many people were helpful and caring when he was injured by the robbers, and adding, "We can appreciate the good things that happen — like picnicking in the park, and going sledding in the snow, and just being together with our family and friends who love us..." The book includes a *Note to Parents* with suggestions for helping to counteract the influence of violence on children and helping children to cope with their feelings.

All My Feelings at Home: Ellie's Day, by Susan Conlin & Susan Levine Friedman, *Let's Talk About Feelings Series,* Parenting Press, 1989. This helpful story follows a young child through the ups and downs of feelings in a single day.

All My Feelings at PreSchool: Nathan's Day, by Susan Conlin & Susan Levine Friedman, *Let's Talk About Feelings Series,* Parenting Press, 1991. The authors explore a range of feelings from confident to rejected, happy to mixed-up.

Dealing with Feelings Series, by Elizabeth Crary. Parenting Press, (1992-1994). These books explore common feelings everyone experiences. They provide an interactive format that allows the reader to make decisions for the character in the story:

I'm Excited. Annie and Jesse are very excited because it's their birthday; young children will love helping them find a way to release their high energy.

I'm Frustrated. Alex wants to be able to roller-skate perfectly the first time he tries, but gets very frustrated when he falls down.

I'm Furious. Matt is furious when his little brother ruins his best baseball card. Readers help Matt choose a better way to handle his anger.

I'm Mad. Katie is angry that rain has cancelled a picnic with her dad. What can she do?

I'm Proud. Mandy rushes to tell her family she's learned to tie her shoes, only to find that everyone is too busy to notice.

I'm Scared. Tracy is terrified of the new neighbor's big dog, and needs help deciding what to do about her feelings.

Children's Problem Solving Series, by Elizabeth Crary. Parenting Press, 1996. These interactive picture books focus on different issues, offer several alternatives and illustrate the possible consequences for several different responses. The following books in the series help teach children negotiation skills: *I Want It; I Want to Play; and My Name Is Not Dummy.*

Today I Feel Silly & Other Moods That Make My Day, by Jamie Lee Curtis. Joanna Cotler Books, 1998. Humorous rhymes and illustrations help to describe the many moods children have: silly, cranky, lonely, or joyful, among others. There's even a picture at the end of a young girl's face, with a wheel to turn, changing the expression on the face so that the reader can express her own mood.

Annie Flies the Birthday Bike, by Crescent Dragonwagon. Macmillan, 1993. Annie gets the bicycle she wanted for her birthday, but never realized how difficult it would be to learn to ride. The book is a touching chronicle of her trials and successes as she slowly masters the skill that is so important to her.

Go Away, Big Green Monster! by Ed Emberley. Little, Brown, 1993. Little by little, as you turn the cutout pages, the features of a monster's face are revealed: eyes, nose, hair, etc. But when you continue to the end, you can also make the monster go away, little by little. An ingenious book — giving children a feeling of control over what they fear.

A Rainbow of My Own, by D. Freeman. Puffin, 1978. This book tells about the joys of using your imagination.

How Are You Peeling? Foods With Moods, written and illustrated by Saxton Freeman & Joost Elffers. Arthur A. Levine/Scholastic, 1999. Pears, peppers, tomatoes, and strawberries are among the expressive fruits and vegetables that illustrate this whimsical book. The words in rhyme help youngsters to recognize and accept their feelings. Both parents and children will enjoy the charming illustrations.

Look! Snow! by Kathryn O. Galbraith. McElderry Books, 1992. In this almost-wordless book, children, adults, and animals in the town share in the excitement and joy of the first snowfall.

Honey, I Love, by Eloise Greenfield. HarperFestival, 1994. A little African-American girl tells about all the things she loves — like her cousin from the South and the way he talks, the cool stream of water from a hose on a hot day, and her mama's soft, warm arm. And she ends with the thought that she loves herself too, in this appealing story in rhyme.

Peas, by Nicholas Heller. Greenwillow, 1993. When Lewis says "Yuck!" and refuses to eat his peas, his mother tells him he will hurt the peas' feelings. "Peas don't have feelings," says Lewis. But that night Lewis has a dream that the peas were feeling bored, angry and upset. Was it a dream? Lewis can't be sure so he eats the peas for breakfast.

We're Very Good Friends, My Brother and I, by P.K. Hallinan. Hambleton-Hill, 1990. What a joy it is to have a brother for a friend.

Just Open a Book, by P.K. Hallinan. Hambleton-Hill, 1998. Here's a book that tells you about the pleasure you get from reading.

Harold and the Purple Crayon, by Crockett Johnson. HarperCollins, 1981. Imagine drawing pictures with a purple crayon — and then stepping magically into the pictures yourself.

The Snowy Day, by Ezra Jack Keats. Viking, 1996. A little boy discovers the joys of his first snowfall in this appealing book that won the Caldecott Medal.

Brave Horace, by Holly Keller. Greenwillow, 1998. Horace is invited to his friend George's monster-movie party, and he's afraid. What kinds of scary things will be at the party? He's reassured by George's big brother that there won't be any really scary things at the party. But when something scary does happen, his friend Fred is so afraid, he's about to cry. That's when Horace finds that he can be brave when he needs to be.

When Spring Comes, by Natalie Kinsey-Warnock. Dutton Children's Books, 1993. A young girl, living on a farm in the early 1900s looks forward to the activities of the coming spring: running barefoot through the fields, gathering wild strawberries for Grandma's biscuits.... She wakes from her reverie to the sound of jingle bells, and joyfully joins her father for a ride through the snow — enjoying the wonder of the present season, as well as the anticipation of spring.

The Carrot Seed, by Ruth Krauss. HarperTrophy, 1989. Everyone tells the little boy in this tale that the carrot seed he planted won't come up. But with the firm belief that carrots grow from carrot seeds, the little boy is rewarded with an enormous carrot.

What Is a Feeling? by David W. Krueger, M.D., *Let's Talk About Feelings Series,* Parenting Press, 1993. The author helps young children find the words to express their many different feelings.

The Grumpy Morning, by Darcia Labrosse. Hyperion, 1998. All the hungry animals on the farm make their own sounds of mooing, neighing, and clucking — grumpy because they haven't been fed yet. But a grumpy morning turns into a happy one when the farmer finally wakes up to give them food and hugs.

Three Brave Women, by C.L.G. Martin. Macmillan, 1991. Caitlin, her Mama and her Grammy don't feel very brave when it comes to spiders. But Caitlin needs her Mama and Grammy to help her prove her courage to Billy Huxley. Otherwise, he will tell everyone she is afraid of spiders. The three brave women enlist in the cause together in this very human story.

Now I Will Never Leave the Dinner Table, by Jane Read Martin and Patricia Marx. HarperTrophy, 1996. A young girl is told by her perfect older sister (and babysitter for the evening) that she must eat her spinach before leaving the dinner table.

Hugs; Kisses, by Alice McLerran. Scholastic Cartwheel, 1993. Two small books filled with love. Toddlers will enjoy the rhyming text, and the joyful pictures of a variety of children giving and receiving hugs and kisses.

Latkes and Applesauce: A Hannuka Story, by F. Manushkin. Scholastic, 1992. A holiday story about the joys of family, food, sharing, and celebration at Hanukkah.

Tom and Pippo and the Bicycle, by Helen Oxenbury. Candlewick Press, 1997. Here is another endearing adventure of Tom and his beloved stuffed monkey, Pippo. The toddler gives Pippo rides on his tricycle, but the monkey often falls off. Tom yearns for a two-wheeled bicycle, like the one his friend Stephanie has. Stephanie helps him problem solve to find a way for Pippo to avoid falling, and assures him that he too will have a big bicycle some day.

The Little Engine That Could, retold by Watty Piper. Platt & Munk, 1984. When the train filled with toys and goodies breaks down, only the little engine will help pull the train over the mountain, repeating the hopeful refrain, "I think I can; I think I can."

Once When I Was Scared, by Helena Clare Pittman. Puffin, 1993. When Grandfather was a boy, one evening his mother asked him to fetch some hot coals from a neighbor just as a storm was brewing. Although he is scared, the boy finds strength by becoming in his imagination like the animals of the forest — thereby conquering his fears.

A Book of Hugs, by Dave Ross. HarperCollins, 1999. With the variety of hugs available, there is no such thing as a bad hug. This book describes them all for you.

A House by the Sea, by Joanne Ryder. Morrow, 1994. A little boy dreams of the wonders of living in a house by the sea, and making friends with all the sea creatures in this cheerful story in rhyme.

And to Think That I Saw It on Mulberry Street, by Dr. Seuss. Random Books, 1997. This book by Dr. Seuss was first published in 1937. It is a joyful example of the author's unlimited imagination.

Laughing All the Way, by George Shannon. Houghton Mifflin, 1992. Duck was having the worst day of his life, and then it got even worse. Bear grabbed him and threatened to pluck out all his feathers. Who would have guessed that laughter would save duck from disaster?

Pete's A Pizza, by William Steig. Michael Di Capua Books, 1998. Pete's in a bad mood. It's raining and he can't go out to play ball with his friends. What can his father do to cheer him up? He can make Pete into a pizza, to the amusement of everyone, including the reader. (The famous author/artist is now over 90 years old.)

I Had a Lot of Wishes, by James Stevenson. Greenwillow, 1995. The well-known author/illustrator tells with humor and understanding about the kinds of wishes he had when he was young: *wishes that something would happen; wishes that something would not happen; wishes that what was happening would stop....* Young children will relate to his wishes about his friends, family, school and camp, and they'll surely think of a few wishes of their own.

Pumpkin Pumpkin, by J. Titherington. Scholastic, 1999. This is a tale about the quiet joy of planting a seed and watching it grow into a wonderful pumpkin.

The Polar Express, by C. Van Allsburg. Houghton Mifflin, 1985. A Christmas story that describes a magical train ride to the North Pole. The illustrations are mysterious and imaginative, and the story about childhood and faith has become a classic.

Alexander and the Terrible, Horrible, No Good, Very Bad Day, by Judith Viorst. Atheneum, 1972. Alexander gets through one of those days which we all have experienced.

Lucky Song, by Vera B. Williams. Greenwillow, 1997. Evie feels so lucky — she wants something new to wear, and on the hook she finds it. She wants something new to play with, and her grandpa makes it for her. When she wants a song, her father sings to her. Lucky Evie!

More More More Said the Baby: Three Love Stories, by Vera B. Williams. Greenwillow, 1990. Three toddlers delight in a loving, playful romp with grownups.

The Monster Bed, by Jeanne Willis. Mulberry, 1999. A little monster named Dennis is frightened. What if humans creep under his bed while he's sleeping? His mama tells him that he shouldn't be afraid. Humans aren't real. But then a little lost human boy wanders into Dennis' cave at night...

Over and Over, by Charlotte Zolotow. HarperCollins, 1995. In this classic story, a mother explains to her little girl about time and the seasons. They look forward together to each special day that will come: Christmas, Valentine's Day, Easter, and through the year to the little girl's birthday. She blows out the candles on her cake and makes a wish. She wishes for it to happen again. *"And of course it did, over and over."*

Section Six

Encouraging Young Children's Positive Views of Family

Section Six
Encouraging Young Children's Positive Views of Family

Introduction

"Remember when we invited cousin Billy to my birthday party and he came on the wrong day?" As this story is retold at a family gathering, it is followed by gales of laughter.

Family stories, told over and over again with laughter or tears, become a part of a child's sense of belonging. Mothers and fathers, brothers and sisters, grandparents, aunts, uncles and cousins — all give young children a feeling of continuity. The items used at family rituals, such as the tablecloth embroidered by an aunt, the spoons grandma brought from the old country, and the songs always sung at family gatherings provide children an understanding of their heritage. Contributors to this section offer insights on family traditions and pride in heritage.

So much has been written about sibling rivalry, it is reassuring to learn from other contributors to this section that siblings can be friends. The authors give sensible advice for encouraging harmony among brothers and sisters.

Other authors point out that males are born with nurturing instincts. Fathers can and should become involved in their children's lives from birth onward.

And there is also a chapter about the family pet, that natural friend of young children. Besides being great fun to play with, having a dog to walk, a cat to feed, or a hamster cage to clean, means that preschoolers have an opportunity to learn responsibility as they become involved in caring for another living thing.

Chapter 21
The Importance of Family Rituals and traditions

Janet Dengel

"Kids find rituals fascinating — artistically, spiritually and emotionally."

Ask any adult what they remember about childhood and they'll recall an event that centered around a family tradition or ritual. The family meal, a holiday gathering or even a nightly bedtime routine are all memorable events in a child's mind.

Although a young child's major objective is to become a separate individual, young children also need to form a strong concept of their place in a larger group — the family. Family rituals can enhance a preschooler's identity, provide continuity during times of stress and connect generations in an enduring bond.

"Children love rituals. Children find a certain security and solace in something that gives a sense of belonging and comfort," explains Dr. Martin V. Cohen, Ph.D., Associate Director of the Marital and Family Therapy Clinic at New York Hospital-Cornell Medical Center. "Kids find rituals fascinating — artistically, spiritually and emotionally."

Rituals Enhance a Preschooler's Self Esteem
Ritual may already be a well-established, set routine in a preschooler's family, handed down through the generations. When you include young children in these important events they will feel that they are an invaluable part of the family group. Preschoolers can be given jobs of honor such as being in charge of turning off the lights at family birthday parties when the cake is brought in, or putting great-grandma's silverware away after it is polished.

Each family can create its own simple rituals that include young children. They can be adapted to fit single-parent or working-parent lifestyles. One two-career couple started a ritual: after work mom, dad and preschooler kicked off their shoes and relaxed on the bed for 15 minutes. Their preschooler felt important telling of her day, receiving hugs or sharing a nursery rhyme while the parents got to put their feet up for a short while. In single-parent families, the preschooler's responsibility to tell a joke at dinner, help plan a Sunday outing, or hold on to the coupons during weekly food shopping will enhance his self-worth by making him feel that he is a very necessary part of the family.

Rituals involving the extended family broaden a preschooler's horizon and introduce him to grandparents, aunts, uncles, and cousins who can all help him feel special. Hearing family stories (including ones about the silly things his parents did as children) will make a youngster feel a sense of belonging.

Rituals provide a Hidden Source of Family Strength
Research done at George Washington University's Family Research Center indicated that children fare better in households where ritual is established

and preserved, even if disruptive problems — such as divorce or alcoholism — are present. A nightly dinner ritual of setting the table together, sitting down as a family, discussing the day's events, or saying grace before the meal can slow down the hectic pace of today's families and provide a sense of meaning and order to the day. When family members are upset with each other, daily rituals can pull them back together and provide the setting for working out problems.

Rituals are also a positive way to help families affirm their beliefs and values. Attending a house of worship, donating groceries to a food bank or recycling together to help the environment can show a preschooler the importance of a family's community involvement.

Rituals Help Young Children and their Families Deal with Stress
"Rituals provide children with something beyond the current stress they are under," says Dr. Cohen. "Rituals are events that happened in the past and will continue in the future no matter what is happening in the present."

Rituals provide a sense of continuity and security that can often help children and their parents work out fears or deal with stress. A nightly ritual of a warm bath, a bedtime story and a prayer can ease children into a restful state. One parent may chase monsters from under the bed or set up a stuffed animal patrol each night to guard the sleeping preschooler until dawn. A daily ritual can often ease the transition to preschool or a stay with a baby-sitter. One mother and her three-year-old devised a secret handshake that included tickling and always guaranteed that their partings were full of laughter, not tears.

Tradition can supply many answers to that famous question, "Why?" It can also help a child learn to cope with disappointment and loss. Even when close relatives die, your preschooler can still feel connected to them in a special way when the family uses aunt Emma's embroidered tablecloth or tells grandpa's favorite joke at a family gathering.

Rituals can reduce a preschooler's feeling of vulnerability and give a sense of control over his world. On his or her birthday, your child will feel like king or queen of the day. Holiday rituals provide a special magic as preschoolers instill "fear" in adults on Halloween by wearing scary costumes or are allowed to fool their parents on April Fool's Day. Even the youngest child will always remember being the one to place the star atop the Christmas tree or to light the candles on the Hanukkah menorah. These symbols of happiness in the home remain in a child's mind forever and can help when facing difficult times.

New twists on Old Traditions

From ceremonial candle lighting to holding an impromptu movie night, rituals can give a preschooler the gifts of family fun and lasting memories. Family traditions don't have to be stuffy or cumbersome. Some family traditions can be serious while others may have a humorous aspect. When you include your child's own ideas, traditions will be enthusiastically embraced by him or her.

Use the five senses to guarantee a lasting memory
• Your youngster will long remember the tunes of family sing-a-longs, the smells of holiday baking, or the feeling of warmth and the sight of dancing flames when the fireplace is lighted after Sunday dinner.
• Make tapes of family stories, history, and songs, and videotape special events so your child can look back fondly on the rituals that were so important in her life.

Adopt some kid-inspired traditions
• Have a sleep-out in the living room once a year with movies, popcorn and flashlights dancing on the ceiling.
• Eat the worst, most sugary, gooey breakfast cereals one Saturday morning a month and watch early morning cartoons.

**Establish constructive rituals that help
solve problems or encourage good habits**
• At dinner, by sharing the best and worst thing that happened to each family member that day you can encourage talking about feelings, problems or accomplishments that may otherwise be overlooked.
• Play "Pass the Book" each night to inspire a love for reading. (Each reader reads a page and passes the book along to the next person.) Children who can't read yet can describe what they see in the pictures or switch from lap to lap as the book is passed.
• Go on a family morning or night walk at least once a week and get in the exercise habit.

Seasonal and holiday rituals have a special magic
• Set up a scavenger hunt to let your child find his birthday present.
• On the first day of spring look at a seed catalog and decide what to plant.
• Put salt in dad's coffee on April Fool's Day.
• Host a watermelon seed-spitting contest each summer.
• Rake leaves and jump in them each fall.
• Have a family snowball fight.
• Turn up the heat in the dead of the winter, put on your bathing suits and have an indoor beach party.
• On Thanksgiving Day hang up your child's artwork depicting things to be thankful for.

Host a family reunion
• Provide young children with many activities and allow them to mix at their own pace.
• Let them pass around a family photo album to use as a conversation starter.
• Tell them some positive family stories beforehand so they will be curious to know "Which one is Uncle Jim who was once on television?"

Take time to teach your children about their ethnic background
• Prepare recipes, read travel books or watch videotapes relating to the countries of their ancestors.

Don't forget the importance of daily rituals
• Your child will never tire of the goodnight kiss, the morning hug or having milk and cookies at snacktime.
• The best family ritual of all is sharing your time together each day.

Some Dos and Don'ts for family rituals
The following were suggested by Dr. Marvin V. Cohen:
• Do keep it fun and relaxed.
• Do establish rituals that ensure family time together.

• Do add symbols that your child will remember and that will promote family identity. A vase that belonged to great grandma can be filled with flowers for Sunday dinners or the homemade decorations your child makes in school can be displayed on holidays.

• Don't bother with empty rituals that have no relation to your family's interest and personality.

• Don't be too formal, making the ritual void of feeling and forced.

• Don't insist on carrying out rituals if they contradict other emotional issues that should be addressed. For example: don't insist on your child sitting on your lap to read if he is upset or angry about something. Discuss what's bothering him first.

Chapter 22
A Preschooler's
Pride in Heritage

Paulette Bochnig Sharkey

*All people are
different __and__ alike.*

My daughter, Jessa, was born in Korea. Her shiny, black hair and almond-shaped eyes make her look different from many other children. When a naturally curious playmate asks me, "Why do Jessa's eyes look like that?" I usually answer, "Jessa is from Korea, and people in Korea have eyes that are a different shape than yours and mine." This information is fascinating to my young visitors, and I know that they go home and talk to their parents about it. I always hope that the parents then take the opportunity to tell their own child about their cultural heritage. And I hope, too, that during those discussions, other parents emphasize that different does not mean bad or wrong — it just means different.

Cultural Heritage and Self-esteem
I take special pleasure in helping my daughter learn about her cultural and ethnic background. We read books about Korea and we experiment with Korean recipes. Or I may simply tell her that I think her hair is beautiful. By helping Jessa see the wonderful ways in which she is unique, I am boosting her self-esteem.

Americans are a multicultural people with a variety of geographic origins, races, religions, languages, and traditions. When you explain to your child about her own personal history, you are helping her develop her own special identity. By encouraging your child to take pride in her heritage, you foster self-confidence and teach her to respect herself. She will recognize later, with your example to follow, that people of other backgrounds also deserve respect.

Ethnic Awareness
My daughter is starting to realize that physical differences exist among people. She is right on schedule — psychologists say that this "ethnic awareness" emerges between the ages of 3 and 5. Children notice differences in skin color first, focusing on eye shape and hair color a little later.

Young children between the ages of 4 and 7 begin to acquire their attitudes about people of different races and ethnic groups. For example, they pick up indirect messages from conversations they overhear, or from watching television or reading books. But children's most important role models are, of course, their parents.

The Role of Parents
Attitudes toward other groups are not inborn; they are learned. Your child will observe how you interact with people of varying ethnic and national backgrounds, picking up your attitudes and making them his own. Learning about people whose ways and lives are different from his own is an important part of your child's social development. Children need a parent's guidance to gain an early appreciation and acceptance of many kinds of people.

My daughter is interested in the fact that some people have light hair, others dark. And we do talk about different customs and traditions and about physical differences among people. But in the end, Jessa is much more concerned about the same burning issues as all other preschoolers — which toys should we play with, and what shall we have for a snack today? This serves as a constant reminder to me that, while the differences among people enrich our lives, it is the deeper similarities that make us all human. All people are different *and* alike.

Helping Children Develop Pride in Heritage

Music and Dance
Young children want to share the music and dance that is part of their heritage, and they enjoy hearing what other cultures have to offer. Sing American folk songs with your child, such as *John Henry, Casey Jones, Home on the Range, I've Been Workin' on the Railroad, He's Got the Whole World in His Hands, She'll Be Comin' Round the Mountain*, and *Hush, Little Baby*.

Songs from around the world include *Frere Jacques* (France), *Kookaburra* (Australia), *Tangalayo* (West Indies), and *A-Hunting We Will Go* (England).

Attend dance programs of various cultures. Encourage your child's preschool to invite parents of different ethnic backgrounds to dance and sing the music of their heritage.

Cultural Exhibits
Watch for exhibits in libraries, museums, and fairs.

Food
A visit to an ethnic restaurant can be exciting for a preschooler. Encourage your child to try a variety of foods. Offer your youngster the opportunity to learn how to use chopsticks.

Television
Watch for the multicultural programs often offered on public television.

Literature
Share literature from other countries with your child. Folk tales and fairy tales are plentiful. When you introduce one, tell your child the country where it originated. For example, "This story is called *The Funny Little Woman* and it is a tale that was first told in Japan."

Young children have not yet developed clear concepts of distance or the meaning of "country." However, telling your child that the story comes from another country introduces the idea that other countries exist, that they have literature, and that stories from many places can be enjoyed. Older preschoolers might like to look at a map of the world or a globe.

Look for children's books that present characters of varying ethnic backgrounds, such as those by Gyo Fujikawa or those recommended by the *Interracial Books for Children Bulletin*. Although overt stereotypes, such as the portrayal of blacks in *Little Black Sambo*, now appear less frequently in children's books than they did in the past, you should be aware that more subtle stereotyping still occurs. For example, books may introduce "foreign" people through stories involving quaint but abandoned customs and ways of life, leaving children with the impression that all Dutch children wear clogs and all Eskimos live in igloos.

Customs and Traditions
Children are the carriers of family tradition. Talk with your child about special holiday celebrations and share photos and stories of important events. Help children to establish a relationship with the older people of your family, so that they may share in the elders' unique life experiences. Teach your preschooler some words in the language of his forbears.

Dolls
Give your child dolls of various ethnic backgrounds.

Travel

Travel is a wonderful way to observe firsthand the customs and traditions of other people. But, when travel is not possible, try issues of *National Geographic* or the travel posters and colorful brochures available from tourist bureaus and travel agents. Children also enjoy maps and globes. Jigsaw puzzles of the United States and other countries are readily available in toy catalogs.

For More Information Contact:
Information Center on Children's Cultures, U. S. Committee for UNICEF, 333 East 38th St., New York, NY 10016, (212) 686-5522. They will send you bibliographies on various countries, information sheets, and teaching units. The U.S. Committee for UNICEF also sells books, games, puzzles and records from around the world.

Chapter 23
A New Baby
in the Family

Michael Searson

Grandma!
It's momma
and the baby!

*There are many ways
to involve children
in the pregnancy.*

The coming of a new baby raises a myriad of feelings for all those involved. In young children, these feelings may include: excitement, anticipation, anxiety, and jealousy, as well as other emotions.

Involving Your Preschooler in the Pregnancy

As with many important events in a preschooler's life, the more she is prepared, the better she will be able to handle the experience. There are many ways to involve children in the pregnancy.

One of the first trips a parent should take after confirmation of the pregnancy is to the library or bookstore to find some of the many excellent books, for adults and children, that deal with childbirth and infancy. (See Resources pages 221-238.)

Many doctors or midwives allow children to be present as mother is examined. Your preschooler may be permitted to watch you being weighed and your blood pressure monitored. (Your child may "get into the act" by having his pressure taken as well.)   Your preschooler may be one of the first to hear the fetal heartbeat through a stethoscope, or observe the fetus on the sonogram screen. At the end of the examination, your doctor or midwife might ask your youngster if he has any questions.

How You Can Answer Your Preschooler's Questions

You can provide your youngster with accurate, honest answers that are appropriate for his age group. However, do not supply children with more information than they request or can handle. The classic story is told of the child who asked, "Where did I come from?" His father went into an elaborate explanation of "The Birds and The Bees." When the father finished, the child said, "But Jack came from Chicago and I want to know where I came from!"

When your child does inquire about reproduction, be sure your terminology is accurate. Avoid describing an embryo as a seed inside of the mother; children can take this quite literally and associate all their knowledge on gardening and plants with human reproduction. Use proper terminology where possible, yet keep in mind the developmental level of the young child. "A baby is growing inside of mommy's belly" is appropriate language for a toddler, while many preschoolers can understand, "The baby is growing in a special place inside mommy, called the uterus."

Helping Your Preschooler Prepare for the New Baby's Arrival

Children may also contribute to the preparation for the new baby's arrival in some concrete ways. They can shop with their parents to purchase baby clothing and diapers. They can also participate in setting up the layette.

Make sure that your youngster understands who will take care of her when you are away at the hospital. If the hospital doesn't allow children to visit, arrange for a telephone in your room so that she may call you daily.

When the new baby is brought home, he will naturally receive an abundance of attention from friends and relatives. Go out of your way to give special attention to your preschooler. Wise is the person who brings a gift for the older child as well as the newborn — perhaps you should have a drawer of small gifts in case the visitors forget!

An Added Bonus
There is an added bonus to preparing your preschooler for the arrival of a new baby. You will become better prepared yourself. Fathers may especially benefit by preparing the older children for the arrival of a newborn. The more they become involved, the more fathers will learn about the pregnancy and birth process themselves. And, like the child, the richer and more rewarding this wonderful experience will be for all involved.

Suggestions to Help Prepare Preschoolers for a New Baby in the Family

During the Pregnancy
•Don't put off telling your child about the pregnancy. He may feel anxious when he hears the whisperings behind his back and knows there's a mystery going on. Give him enough time to get adjusted to the idea.

•Inquire about *sibling preparation classes* at your hospital or maternity center.

•If Mother has been the major caregiver in your child's life, have Father take turns at bathtime and bedtime. Also acquaint your child with the other adults who might care for her, such as a friendly neighbor or babysitter.

•Since your preschooler will be handing down her clothes to the new baby, get her used to the fun of hand-me-downs by having relatives pass some hand-me-downs along to her.

•Major new adjustments for your preschooler, such as starting nursery school or moving to a new bedroom will go more smoothly if you start them well before the birth of the baby.

•Don't oversell the idea of the new baby as a playmate. It will be a long time before they can play Candyland together! Take your preschooler to see your friends' very young babies, so she can get an idea of how babies look and behave.

•Show your firstborn the family album with his own baby pictures in it. Tell him what happened when he was born.

At the Hospital
•If the hospital allows siblings to visit, do let your child come, in spite of the difficulty of parting.

•Say good-by before you leave for the hospital. Don't slip away. If you leave in the middle of the night, you might want to wake your preschooler to say good-by. Be sure she knows beforehand who will be taking care of her.

•Give your child some special chores to do while you're at the hospital, like feeding the cat, or bringing in the newspaper.

•Don't give your first child the choice of a name for the new baby. She may come up with something like "Snoopy." And you'll have a job convincing her otherwise.

•On the day you go home from the hospital, have your preschooler come to accompany you home. Sit with him on the way home. Have Grandma hold the new baby.

After the Baby Comes Home
• Read with your child some of the excellent picture books about a new baby in the family. (See Resources pages 223-238.)

Chapter 24
Building
Sibling Friendships

Harriet Heath

Siblings <u>can</u> be friends.
It's a matter of learning how.

Our tendency is to smile when three-year-old Andy tells us very seriously, "I'm going to ride big wheels with my baby brother when Mom brings him home from the hospital."

If we really stop to listen to what this little guy is telling us, we'd realize he thinks that his newborn sibling will be a carbon copy of his three-year-old self, ready to do with him the things he, Andy, loves to do.

Not knowing what a newborn is like, he has no idea how to relate to the new baby. He enthusiastically gives his new sibling the same kind of bear hug he gives his dad. When the baby cries, he is surprised. He gets bear hugs and loves them. He gives them to his dad who seems to enjoy them. Why does the baby cry when he gives her one?

The typical adult response doesn't clear up Andy's confusion. Usually something is said to the effect, "Don't hurt your baby sister. That's not nice. See, you made her cry." What Andy has learned is that he can make the baby cry and he can get attention by doing so. Neither helps him start to build a friendly relationship with his sibling.

A different approach is to listen to what Andy is telling us. Expecting to ride big wheels with his new sibling shows he really knows little about new babies. The bear hug is just another illustration of his lack of knowledge. A response more useful for Andy would be to help him understand why the bear hug caused his sister to cry. Andy needed to learn how he and his dad are different from the baby, and about ways of touching and loving the baby that the baby would enjoy.

Before the new sibling's arrival
In another family with a three year old named Ken, the parents believed that siblings have to learn about each other. They not only helped Ken relate to his new sister — but prepared him even before her arrival. Several months before Katie's birth, his parents started talking with him about the baby that was coming. They talked about what the baby would be able to do and would not be able to do. They discussed what they would have to do for the new infant. They visited friends with newborns. Ken learned that newborns seemed to do a lot of eating, sleeping and crying and not much else. They couldn't even hold their heads up straight or grasp a toy. They did like looking at things, especially things held at a certain distance from them.

When the new baby is born
Within an hour after Katie's arrival, Ken went to the birthing center with his grandmother. Not only did he get to see Katie but when seated with his

arm well supported he was allowed to hold her. He saw her wobbly head and learned how to cup it in the crook of his arm. He liked the way she stared at him.

At home, as he came and went busy with his own affairs, he continued to learn about Kate and how to interact with her. His mother showed him how to touch her ... hugging her gently or stroking her so she could relax, and when she got older, tickling her gently so she giggled. He heard her cry and learned from his mother that this was Katie's way of saying she needed something. Ken and his mother played guessing games as to what Katie needed: food, diaper change, sleep, position change or something different to look at. Ken became very adept at predicting what Katie needed and at creating diversions for her. His mother pointed out to him how he could tell whether or not Katie liked what he was doing by watching her face. "Babies talk with their faces," she told him.

As the baby grows older

As Kate became older and able to interact more with those around her, Ken responded accordingly. He learned she liked to have a toy similar to the one with which he was playing and would often hand her one. He copied from his parents the games they played with her such as peek-a-boo. They'd both laugh with excitement when he'd reappear. Ken was delighted with the way Kate's face lit up when she saw him. He became aware of the fact that she looked for him. He looked for her too when life was a little boring. His mother learned that often Ken, busy with his cars and trucks, would, unknowingly, entertain Kate, if she were placed within sight of him.

Coping with some difficult times

As with any relationship there were rough times. Kate might have the toy Ken wanted to play with. He had to learn not to grab but that he could get her interested in another toy and then she'd drop the one he wanted. As she grew older and distraction didn't work as well the two children had to learn how to take turns. There were times when his parents would be busy with Kate and he had to wait. This is always hard when one is only three or four. His parents always tried to give Ken time alone with each of them — maybe when Kate was sleeping, busy elsewhere, or with the other parent.

Kate's developing mobility put a major strain on their relationship. One day as she investigated the construction of roads Ken had spent all morning building, she managed to completely demolish it. Ken was devastated and very, very angry. "Keep her in the high chair," he yelled, tears streaming down his face. His mother held him trying to comfort him and to keep him from striking out at Kate. Kate looked on astounded and ready to cry herself but with little understanding of what she had done.

After Kate went down for her nap, Ken with his mother built a new road system. As they worked, they talked about why the road system had been so interesting to Kate, what Kate could understand (that Ken was upset) and not understand (if you wiggle over a hill built with blocks and books it all comes down). They talked about the fact that Kate would be moving around more and more. They talked about Ken's projects — which ones he could do on a table rather than the floor. Kate couldn't get up to the table yet. Ken suggested they could put chairs around his blocks thus barricading them. Mother saw the wisdom of this idea and got out the collapsible children's gate she had bought to use with Ken which he had hated. Now it worked fine with Ken busy inside and Kate able to watch but not disrupt his work. Protecting Ken's projects from Kate was a challenge that took many forms ranging from distracting Kate, interesting her in activities in other parts of the apartment, to eventually locking Ken's door when he was away.

By the time Ken was five and Katie two they had many shared games with cars and trucks. Kate had learned to let Ken build the hills. They both then raced their cars down to see which went faster. Interestingly, more than for many other girls, cars and trucks were an integral part of Katie's play.

As Ken approached six another strain came in the play of the siblings. Ken now wanted the races between the cars to be more structured with starting lines, similar vehicles, the same number of turns and keeping score. Ken would make up the rules and Katie would willingly agree but go on playing as she always had. "She's cheating," Ken would scream. "We agreed that ...." and he'd recite the game plan. All these rules had no meaning to Katie.

It would have been so easy for their parents to assume that their children were now really in a jealous stage and to mourn the good friendship they had had. Instead they recognized that Ken had entered a new level of complexity in his thinking. He was delighting in the rules he could make and could follow. The problem was he expected everyone to do the same. But Katie at three had no understanding of rules.

After listening to Ken's anger and frustration, his parents helped him realize that Kate was not cheating; she simply could not understand. Together they brainstormed his choices such as: playing with Katie without the elaborate rules, playing another game that didn't have rules, and/or playing using the complex rules with his same-aged friends. For a while the two siblings played less with each other. Their parents made sure each saw friends of the appropriate ages. Then with a turn of seasons and trips to the nearby lake, they devised new water games that both enjoyed. They were playing together again.

Encouraging sibling friendships

Parents can encourage friendship to grow between their children as the above description of Ken and Katie illustrates. They do so by providing the relevant information and/or teaching the necessary skills. They are teaching their children to care. To encourage friendship, parents need to believe deeply that siblings have the potential for friendship, as Ken and Katie's parents did. They did not get bogged down in the traditional, culturally accepted interpretation that all sibling interaction is motivated by jealousy, or at least that behavior that causes a sibling to cry is so motivated.

Instead, Ken and Katie's parents focused on facilitating the children's evolving friendship. They saw Ken as curious. He would want to know about newborns, as he wanted to know about everything else in his environment. This included what he could do with this little creature as well as how the little creature functioned. If his behavior was inappropriate, his parents were more apt to check his understanding of the situation than to assume he wanted to hurt his sister. As the relationship between Ken and Katie evolved, their parents recognized, in addition to their children's curiosity about each other, that they wanted to be friends and that they enjoyed each other — a confirmation of the parent's belief that siblings can be friends.

*While living with and guiding their children,
these parents used the answers to five questions
to direct their actions.*

1. What do my children need to know and to be able to do in order to relate to each other? Throughout the above narrative there are many examples. Before Katie had even arrived, the parents, answering this question, realized Ken needed to know what a newborn was like, what a newborn could be expected to do and not do. He needed to know how to relate to this age infant, how to touch and play with her. They were still answering the question when Ken was six and so upset with Katie when she would not follow his rules.

2. What are the needs of the people involved? From the beginning, these parents were aware of the needs of their children. By showing Ken how to touch Katie in appropriate ways, they accomplished two things: Katie's need to he safe and Ken's need to feel competent. Increasing children's sense of competence contributes to building their self-esteem. These parents recognized that Ken's need to have his activities kept safe from his investigating sister was as legitimate as her need to explore. In the last situation when Ken needed to master more complex games that Katie could not follow, Ken even took part in finding ways to meet both sets of needs, his and Katie's.

As all parents know, one of the difficult aspects of parenting is deciding which needs to meet and how and when to do so. Too often the oldest children are expected to wait or even forgo having their needs met. Ken's parents could have told him to build in his room or that having his building knocked down wasn't important as he could easily build another. The parents realized that their role was to balance the needs of all family members, their own included. Too great an imbalance between meeting the needs of the different family members provides a breeding ground for angry and jealous feelings to grow.

3. What is this child really attempting to do? It is essential to look for answers from the child's point-of-view. Katie's mother did this when she saw the devastation her daughter had wrought on her brother's road system. She was aware of her daughter's curiosity and drive to explore, and she saw Katie's surprise and concern about Ken's anger. This made her believe that Katie's actions were not to ruin her brother's road system. This mother did the same kind of analysis as she tried to understand what rules meant to six-year-old Ken.

4. What is age appropriate behavior? Knowing what the average child can be expected to do, provides a check for parents as to what to expect. Parents can refer to the many books in their local library that deal with age-appropriate behavior.

5. Am I in tune with this child? While living with and guiding children, it is so important to have time alone with each, a time when the child chooses the activity. It is during this time that adults can get "in tune" with the child and the child gets the message of being really loved and accepted — something every child needs to feel.

Siblings <u>can</u> be friends. It's a matter of learning how. Parents can be their teachers. The above questions can serve as their guides.

Chapter 25
Encouraging Harmony Among Brothers & Sisters

Janet Dengel

Parents can never totally eliminate jealousy, competition or the inevitable clashes over possessions.

It's been said that when a couple has a child, they become parents; *when they have two or more children, they become referees.* However, parents can find ways to encourage harmony among their children, so that the household does not become overwhelmed by the sound of siblings arguing over toys, territory, and parental attention.

Preschoolers and Younger Siblings

If there is a new baby in the family, a youngster's real feelings about the baby may be ambivalent: he may love the baby, but also resent her as a competitor. Preschoolers should be encouraged to discuss their feelings about their new brother or sister. Your preschooler may feel that it is unfair that the baby seems to get so much more attention than he does. Whatever his emotions, it is important that you listen to him and accept his feelings, letting him know that you care about how he feels and that he *matters* to you.

Spend Time Alone with Your Preschooler. The most valuable thing siblings must have is a share of their parent's love and attention. Find time in your busy day to be alone with your preschooler. Do puzzles together while the baby naps; read a story to your preschooler each night at bedtime. It will show your child that he is special to you.

Encourage Cooperative Behavior. The usual scenario is that, when children are playing nicely together, a mother or father often thinks, "Good, now I can finally get some work finished." They ignore the children unless they misbehave. When parents pay attention only to the fighting, they unknowingly reinforce negative behavior. Saying to your preschooler, "Look at how the baby is smiling. It makes him so happy when you play with him," shows your youngster that she can have a positive effect on her baby brother, and encourages more cooperative conduct. In this way, your preschooler becomes a "partner" in caring for the baby.

Preschoolers and Older Siblings

There is no question that personalities, age and sex differences, and birth order play a large part in determining how siblings will relate to one another. When preschoolers have older brothers or sisters and must compete for their parents' time and attention, the contest may seem to be unequal. Older siblings may seem to have more power and privileges in the family.

Parents can never totally eliminate jealousy, competition or the inevitable clashes over possessions. But, parental guidance can encourage a loving and lasting friendship among siblings .

Don't be a referee. Although parents can make it clear to siblings that fighting in the physical sense will not be tolerated, disagreements are not always bad, and can serve to teach children about compromise, negotiation and open communication.

When there is an argument between siblings, often parents don't know who is "right" or "wrong." It is important not to become a referee, but to let children settle disputes on their own. If the conflict is not resolved, separate the children or remove the toy which is causing the disagreement. Once they're faced with the prospect of missing out on the fun altogether, they may be motivated to work things out by themselves.

Pride of Ownership
While sharing is an important part of family relationships, a preschooler has to have a sense of ownership before sharing is possible. He needs to understand that, "That's *my* teddy bear," before he allows somebody else to play with it.

In addition, each child may have prized possessions that are so special, that he should have control over whether or not to share them. Every family should respect individual differences and rights and establish rules to protect them. If a preschooler has a treasured dinosaur collection, it should be protected from an inquisitive baby brother who shares his room. Preschoolers may eventually be willing to share other toys with siblings if their own valued possessions are respected, .

Taking time to further harmony among siblings at an early age can lead to a healthy family atmosphere in which brothers and sisters reap the priceless gift of gaining a lifelong, trusted friend — *each other.*

Suggestions for
Household Harmony

The following suggestions use a preschooler's natural creativity, openness, and honesty to cultivate good relationships among siblings:

• *Instill pride in family members.* Help your preschooler make her own family album with photographs of her washing the car with her ten-year-old brother, or holding the baby the first day home from the hospital. She can also draw pictures, or include ticket stubs from a basketball game she attended with an older sister, to add to the album.

• *Start a collection of humorous family stories.* Encourage your preschooler and his siblings to tell stories about things that the family experienced together. Not all of them have to have a happily-ever-after ending. "Remember when we went on a picnic and it rained all day?" "Remember when we invited cousin Billy to my birthday party and he came on the wrong day?"

• *Teach siblings to turn to each other for comfort.* When the baby gets a tiny scrape and runs to mommy for a healing kiss, you can tell him that his four-year-old brother also has the magic power to erase the hurt. When you've scolded your preschooler and he is feeling sad, you can ask his older sister to, "Talk to your brother to make him feel better." When parental patience is wearing thin, you can allow siblings to lean on each other for sympathy and understanding.

• *Promote a sense of protectiveness toward family members.* Many a child has been known to say to a playmate, "She's my baby sister and you can't tease her!" Even a four-year-old can valiantly come to the aid of a slightly older sibling who is being bullied. When you discuss the feelings of each family member, children will grow in compassion for each other. If a preschooler knows her older brother feels hurt because friends called him a terrible ballplayer, she might feel more sympathetic toward him, and avoid saying anything unkind.

• *Encourage siblings to help each other.* A five-year-old can "be in charge" of his two-year-old sister in the sandbox while you watch at the window. An older sibling can be encouraged to take his three-year-old brother to the library for story hour or to borrow books. Siblings can also learn that if they help each other clean their rooms, the work gets done faster.

• *Allow siblings to visit their brother's nursery school.* Nothing lifts a preschooler's ego more than bringing a new baby sister in for "Show and Tell." If an older brother or sister can stop by for a short visit, this will also make him feel grown-up and proud.

• *Teach your preschooler how to play with the new baby.* Just as new parents must learn how to feed, bathe and diaper, a three year old also needs to learn finger games like pat-a-cake, songs to sing and the proper handling of a little brother.

• *Invent games which call for cooperation.* Have siblings cooperate in a game where they complete tasks in an allotted amount of time. For example, they will have to run holding hands, then push each other on the swing ten times, next help one another fill a pail with sand and then race back to the finish line.

Smaller siblings can play "Pass the Crayon." They color until you clap your hands, then swap crayons until their pictures are finished.

• *Give each child a space to call his own.* Not everything should be joint property. Where possible, allow for separate shelves, closets and desks.

• *Make sure sharing means that each sibling helps with a fair load of chores.* A three-year-old can use unbreakable items to help to set the table. A four-year-old is capable of clearing the table before he goes out to play. Instill a sense of responsibility by assigning tasks to each child on his level of ability.

• *Use their separate talents and abilities to ensure cooperation.* For example, when baking, an older child can measure, a preschooler can pour, and a toddler can mix. Then when you taste it, you can praise them for their joint effort.

When looking at books, an older child can read and then a preschooler can describe the pictures.

For artwork, preschoolers can glue and trace while an older sibling helps with tricky cutting.

• *Don't push for too much togetherness.* Preschoolers need time away from siblings. They should have time to be by themselves, and have opportunities to play with other children.

Chapter 26
Involved Fatherhood

Kyle D. Pruett

*Males are born
with nurturing instincts.*

"The nurse said I could pick her up. I said, 'Are you kidding? She's only two hours old.' She looked like a little puppy to me. I did pick her up with my hand under her head like they showed me, and then I held her in close — just pulled her in — kind of like a magnet ... She opened her eyes and we just looked at each other. She's the greatest, Doc, and I'm not kidding! I'm going back there later to get some more of that!" (From <u>The Nurturing Father</u> by Kyle D. Pruett, M.D., © 1987)

Fathers who are more than just casually involved in their children's lives profoundly affect the whole family in positive, interesting ways. Intriguing recent research shows that fathers make unique, lasting contributions to the lives of their children, deepen the meaning of their own lives, and enrich the mother's experience of nurturing as well.

During the pregnancy, fathers often find themselves feeling more than they expected to feel. Most pregnant mothers get a lot of attention and support for what is happening to them. Fathers, however, are beginning to feel curiosity, attachment, worry, and excitement but are often reluctant to share these rather surprisingly compelling feelings. Men involve themselves in ways surprising even to them — by gaining weight, feeling jealous, and getting anxious about money and security. "Playing games" with, or singing to the unborn fetus through the mother's abdominal wall — all these some-times funny behaviors, are the father's way of intimately involving himself with his newborn.

Males Are Born with Nurturing Instincts

Fathers begin their own lives as baby boys born with nurturing instincts. Not mothering, but nurturing instincts which may come to fruition in their fatherhood. All we need do is watch the numbers of boys playing happily and expressively in the preschool doll corner.

Any early preparation in the pregnancy helps the father feel he's got some-thing to contribute after his baby leaves the exclusive control of its mother's body. Supporting the mother and helping to pay the room and board are certainly important, but it is a much more fruitful experience if the father takes emotional responsibility for his role in his baby's life.

When fathers involve themselves in the physical care of their babies, intriguing things happen to both. Recent research shows that fathers have the ability to respond to their infants' and newborns' needs in the ways which are so critical to the child's well-being. Despite a usual lack of experience, most men, when given the chance, even without support, are able to figure out the best feeding, diapering, comforting, and bathing approaches for their babies, even though those approaches may differ from those of the mother. Such differences however, do not seem to matter much to the children, as long as they are not wildly different.

Most babies seem to be flexible enough to adapt to the slight differences in style between mother and father in ways that are quite adaptive.

Differences in Style Between Mothers and Fathers
Fathers, for example, tend to handle babies' bodies in less predictable ways, while mothers tend to pick up and handle their babies in rhythmically similar patterns over time. For example, fathers are more likely to playfully manipulate the child's body (tickling or tossing up in the air) before bringing the babies to their bodies. Babies seem to enjoy the difference and may well benefit from it. My own research on fathers who have served as primary caregivers in intact families, has shown that babies seem to problem solve better and have a broader range of social behavior and interaction when fathers are deeply involved.

Mothers' Reactions to Involved Fatherhood
Mothers tend to greatly appreciate involved fatherhood, although most initially struggle with some feelings of competition or jealousy. It can be hard to see your child playing actively with your spouse if you feel stuck with all the less glamorous maintenance tasks. (Fathers do tend to play differently with their children than mothers do, using fewer toys and less predictable responses to routine play.)

Ultimately, mothers feel supported and helped by involved fathers. The mother who attempts to control the access of her husband to her child ("the gatekeeping phenomenon,") has a lot to lose as do her child and spouse.

The bottom line? Children can show fathers how to be good nurturers, every bit as well as they've been showing mothers all these years. When a newborn squirms and wriggles in a father's arms to find a comfortable position, it is teaching the father what it needs, just as it shows the mother. *The rewards to all are permanent.*

How Fathers Can Become Involved

Start early, before delivery
Meet the obstetrician or midwife that you both have chosen. Go to at least one appointment. Pay attention to what's happening to you during your wife's pregnancy. Are you gaining weight? Worrying about money and security, afraid you're about to be replaced as your wife's closest partner? Talk about these issues with your friends, your spouse, or even your own father. They are very important ways in which you are preparing yourself

to meet your child. Lamaze classes, hospital predelivery groups are important — don't miss them. Go, even if your wife can't occasionally. Read about the parental experience and child development if that sort of thing helps you. You are usually behind your wife in experience with children, and information can help.

Be in on things from birth
This is the beginning of your life together with your child. Be at the delivery. Fathers who touch, hold, and physically care for their newborns know them better as people, describe them more richly as people, understand their needs better, feel closer to their children, and get a lot more out of their fathering. Get someone to teach you how to bathe a newborn. Physical care is the way babies get to know you and vice versa. This should start in the newborn period. Some hospitals only allow you to attend a delivery if you have attended classes. It's great to go to such classes; however, if you are unable to go, try to be in on the delivery anyway. Don't get shut out.

Get involved in your baby's routine
Take leave, sick leave, paternity leave, disappear — however you do it, be in your children's life, from the beginning. Hang around for as much time as you can in the first month. Don't give in to the "well he's sleeping or nursing all the time and there's nothing for me to do" trap. Take what you can get, get up at night, do the changing — get _in_ the picture, don't just take them. This is especially true if the baby is a premmie or was born by caesarean section. In both cases, a little extra help is needed, and you can be especially useful. You and the baby will get a lot out of it if you can provide that extra help. Otherwise, this first three months of his life can live up to its sometimes reputation as "the fourth trimester."

Also, when your child is sick, try to take time off from work to be there too. Strong bonds form and are renewed in this nurturing, needy, dependent setting.

Get better at hanging out with your kid
As your child grows older and becomes more interactive and competent, the temptation for fathers especially is to always be *doing something* with or to the son or daughter. There certainly is a place for this, because we know that children respond powerfully and positively to your different style and expectations of them. Playing, teaching, encouraging, and expecting mastery are things that you are particularly good at. However, there is a need to also just *be together.* Let the child set the pace sometimes too. This hanging out is just as important to both of you as your other times.

Make your emotional commitment to your child real

It's one thing to feel profoundly about your child and another to act the way you feel. Don't drift away from the early powerful moments. Take your child by yourself to the pediatrician periodically. It helps you take emotional responsibility for your role in their life. Help to choose daycare or nursery school settings. Interview baby sitters with your wife. Talk to your child's teacher. Help out; go on field trips with them, go in and cook in their classes or group care settings. Bring your kids to your work place. Let them take your life seriously too. It's a powerful message to your employer and colleagues, as well as to your child.

Watch out for competitive feelings

An early complication of involved fatherhood can be feelings of competition between the mother who often feels she must be all things to her newborn, and the father who's trying to elbow his way into foreign territory. Take it easy. There is plenty of work and affection for both. Your baby can also tolerate your different styles as long as they are not wildly disparate. You'll each discover little things that your baby will teach you. Share them, but don't insist that they always be done your way. Babies appreciate variety too. Eventually the competition fades and the partnership returns; don't let it scare you.

Sit back, relax and enjoy. Growing up with your children is the most fascinating journey of your life.

Chapter 27
Fathers and Child Care...
Let Dad Do It His Way

Michael K. Meyerhoff

*...many modern-day fathers
are showing a strong inclination
to get involved.*

My office overlooks a park where the local high school girls' baseball team holds its daily practice. As I observe these adolescent females in action, I'm amazed. Not one of them throws like a girl.

Back in my youth, the expression "throws like a girl" had meaning. In any athletic endeavor, members of the distaff sex generally performed awkwardly and ineffectively, if they participated at all. Consequently, on the few occasions coed sporting activities were undertaken, we boys made sure to keep the girls on the sidelines as much as possible and to step in front of them whenever they did take the field so as to prevent their inevitable blunders.

Maybe we were motivated mainly by self interest. We wanted to win, and we figured the girls would just get in our way. On the other hand, we really didn't want the girls to embarrass themselves. Of course, the girls periodically protested against our boorish behavior. But, never too loudly or for too long. In fact, behind their angry scowls, their eyes betrayed a genuine sense of relief.

What has changed over the last 30 years? Have we somehow bred a generation of New-Age Amazons? No. These girls appear physically identical to the timid and untalented ladies of a generation ago. However, while I'm unable to detect a significant improvement in congenital ability, I can see a dramatic difference in mental attitude. These girls believe they can play baseball. And that's probably because they never believed they couldn't.

Reviewing the Past
Consider the typical scenario of yesteryear. A little girl picks up a bat and tries to hit a ball for the first time. Not only does she miss by a mile, she looks fairly foolish. She thinks to herself, "Enough nonsense...I'm a girl, this is boy stuff, and I'm never going to be able to do it." She then hands the bat over to one of the host of boys itching to take her place.

Meanwhile, a little boy picks up a bat and tries to hit a ball for the first time. Not only does he miss by a mile, he also looks fairly foolish. He thinks to himself, "Wait a minute...I'm a boy, this is boy stuff, and I should be able to do it." He then digs in and tries again. And again and again until he finally makes contact.

Evidently, the girls of today have not been saddled with any erroneous and inhibiting notions about boy stuff. Whether it's medicine, politics, construction, or sports, they have been permitted to picture themselves as inherently competent, and they have been encouraged to stick with the challenges involved until they succeed. As a result, it is not surprising that they play baseball with such ease and proficiency.

As I leave the window, it occurs to me that we have a remarkably similar situation concerning men and young children. When it comes to child care, everyone agrees that "father involvement" is a wonderful idea. Many modern-day mothers are getting caught up in the "superwoman" syndrome, working hard at a job all day long and then performing virtually all of the child care chores when they come home. They sure would appreciate it if their spouses assumed a substantial share of the duties.

Furthermore, many modern-day fathers are showing a strong inclination to get involved. Almost unheard of a generation ago, husband-coached childbirth is commonplace today. And day care centers report that fathers are now taking responsibility for delivering and picking up their children nearly as often as mothers.

But unfortunately, with regard to the day-to-day routines of child care, nice sentiments rarely turn into full-fledged realities. Most new fathers who attempt to participate in the care of their young children discover that they are awkward and ineffective, and they quickly become discouraged. And while most new mothers initially welcome the efforts of their husbands, they soon decide to step in and take over all tasks in order to ensure the well-being of their children and spare their spouses further embarrassment.

Examining the Present
Are modern-day males doomed to failure despite their admirable intentions? Are they fighting against insurmountable biological obstacles? No. Once again, we are merely dealing with mental attitude, not inherent aptitude.

Consider the typical scenario. A first-time father picks up his crying newborn. He rocks and strokes the child, but to no avail. He thinks to himself, "Enough nonsense...I'm a father, this is mother stuff, and I'm never going to be able to do it." He then hands the crying baby over to his wife or any of the several other available females who are rushing toward him with outstretched arms.

Meanwhile, a first-time mother picks up her crying newborn. She rocks and strokes the child, but to no avail. She thinks to herself, "Wait a minute...I'm a mother, this is mother stuff, and I should be able to do it." She then rocks and strokes some more. And some more and some more until she eventually manages to comfort the baby.

Let's face it. With the singular exception of breast-feeding, there is nothing about child care that a mother is innately better qualified to do than a father. Yet we continue to unconsciously perpetuate the myth that men just don't have what it takes to be true partners in the process.

When Mom is out of the house, we say that Dad is baby-sitting. Would we ever say that a mother is "baby-sitting" her own child? And when Dad can't get the diaper on straight, we laugh at him as though he was trying to walk around in high heel shoes. Do we ever assist him by pointing out that all you have to do is lay out the diaper like a baseball diamond, put the kid's butt on the pitcher's mound, bring home plate up, then fasten the tapes at first and third base?

Forging Ahead to the Future

It's time we begin doing for men and young children what we've already done for girls and baseball. A father who will pursue child care tasks with ease and proficiency is simply a father who has never been led to believe he couldn't.

A full and fluid father-child relationship can have an extraordinarily beneficial impact on all aspects of development throughout the preschool years. And every day Dad delays building a strong and healthy foundation for it diminishes the likelihood he will achieve optimal results.

So Mom, lighten up, step back, and give your guy a decent chance. And Dad, dismiss your doubts, ignore the interruptions, and don't let the difficulties get you down. *Just do it.*

Suggestions for Promoting Father Involvement in Child Care

Virtually everyone can be found guilty of contributing to this problem, so it is up to everyone to work toward the solution. The following are some specific suggestions for promoting father involvement in child care.

1. Always Include Dad. Quite often, a father is prevented from participating fully in the care of his young child simply because no one thinks to prepare him for the experience. Maternal nurses, pediatricians, day care personnel, preschool teachers, and others who provide information and instructions tend to focus almost exclusively on the mother. Even if Dad is present, they behave as if he be interested in what they have to say — and if he is, he can get whatever is being offered later on from his wife.

This immediately sets up Dad as a second class citizen, so it should not be a surprise when he merely performs the limited role he has been given. He naturally comes to view everything from bathing the child to administering medication to attending school conferences as chores that are primarily, if not solely, the mother's responsibility.

Consequently, it is critical to make sure that Dad is treated equally right from the start. To the extent that he is considered an active player instead of an idle observer by those around him, he will be inclined to become a full partner in child care rather than only an occasional accessory to the process.

2. Don't Make Dad Feel Different. Sometimes people make a conscious effort to include the father in discussions of child care. However, despite their good intentions, their conscious effort often makes Dad feel extremely self-conscious. Instead of just casually including him in anything and everything, they repeatedly speak about the "special role" of the father. And by thus assigning Dad some illustrious status, they may inadvertently exclude him from many of the routine chores he otherwise would be inclined to pursue, capable of performing, and entitled to enjoy.

For example, in talking about the importance of educational games, some-one might tell the mother about word association, small muscle activities, make-believe sessions, etc., and then turn to the father and say, "Of course, gross motor rough-and-tumble play is very important too." This leaves Dad with the impression that his participation is indeed desirable, but only for certain specific and/or supplementary parts of the job. Therefore, it is necessary to avoid explicitly or implicitly designating any duties as either maternal or paternal — even if it is done with positive overtones.

3. Let Dad Do It His Way. Even when a mother and father start out physically sharing child care chores equally, it is often the case that Mom mentally reserves all of the responsibility. Consequently, in addition to her own activities, she watches everything Dad does and then passes judgment on his performance. This can result in Dad coming to the conclusion that as long as she is standing there and supervising, she may as well go ahead and do it herself.

For example, Dad figures he can take on the task of getting the child dressed in the morning. After selecting various items from the closet and drawers, he notices Mom observing him with a look on her face that says, "Are you really going to let our child go out dressed like that?" After several such episodes, he decides that his efforts are futile and he abandons the whole idea.

The fact of the matter is that if left alone, Dad probably won't make too many mistakes, and those he does make certainly won't be fatal. If Mom can try to develop a mind-set in which she presumes competence, exercises patience, and then supplies only gentle and constructive criticism when absolutely necessary, she can encourage steady improvement without undermining Dad's confidence, enthusiasm, and endurance.

4. Don't Give Dad a Way Out. No matter how enthusiastic a father may be about the idea of full participation in child care, it is easy for him to become intimidated when faced with the realities. While a mother may feel intimidated on occasion as well, she typically assumes she has no choice but to follow through. A father, on the other hand, is often given the opportunity to back out by people who are misguidedly trying to help.

For instance, if Dad announces he is going out-of-town on business for a couple of days, no one thinks twice about Mom having to take care of the kids by herself while he's gone. But if it's Mom who makes such an announcement, everyone from friends and neighbors to grandparents and teachers hurries in to offer assistance with meal preparation, carpooling, play supervision, and any other task they can take off of Dad's hands.

Of course, this is not to say that people should be unsympathetic or refuse to provide assistance when necessary. However, it is essential that a father be treated exactly the same as a mother under these circumstances. Just as Mom must face "sink or swim" situations from time to time, Dad also must learn how to survive — and he'll never be able to do so if well-meaning Samaritans are constantly draining the pool.

5. Watch Your Language. It is true that actions speak louder than words. But it is important to remember that words still have a lot of power. And as long as the language of child care remains as it is, it will continue to at least subliminally reinforce the notion that Dad is a stranger in a strange land.

For example, most hospitals, day care centers, and preschools routinely use terms such as "mother's day out," "memo to mothers," "mother's helper," etc. And in most cases, there is no reason other than outdated tradition why the word "parent" should not be substituted for "mother."

Clearly, promoting full father involvement in child care requires major changes in behavior. However, a few subtle alterations in some common phrases can go a long way toward making these changes easier, more effective, and more permanent.

Chapter 28
Grandparents Give Children Roots

Betty Farber

*Every grandparent has a
personal history to share
with new generations.*

You are the bows from which your children as living arrows are sent forth....
(From *The Prophet* by Kahlil Gibran)

If parents are the <u>bows</u>, using their strength and stability to free their children to go as far as possible, grandparents are the <u>roots</u>, giving children the sense of belonging to something bigger, the sense that they have connections to others — that they are part of a long progression of family history.

Grandparent/Grandchild Relationships
The joy of grandparenting is that as grandparents, you can share your interests, relive your children's youth and your own, give and receive love, and see your own life extended by children who, although unique personalities, are still a part of you.

"Through their experiences with grandparents, children form concepts of what old age is like and attitudes toward it. In playing the role of grand-child, the child learns the grandparent role, in anticipation, and therefore prepares himself for later life..." (*Families* by M.S. & L.S. Smart, Macmillan, 1976.)

Individual Styles of Grandparents
There are many ways grandparents interact with grandchildren. These "styles" are influenced by age, health, cultural background, life experiences, etc. Furthermore, the grandmother and grandfather may react differently to the same grandchild.

Grandparents may consider their role as being instrumental in helping their grandchildren have fun. In this role they may participate in imaginative play or join their grandchildren in active sports. Other grandparents, while showing interest and love for their grandchildren, prefer to confine their interactions to offering special treats and taking care of the children on occasion. Because of distance, some have little contact with their grand-children, while others act as a surrogate parent, caring for the child while the parents work. Still others act as a kindly authority figure and the "reservoir of family wisdom" (*Families* by M.S. & L.S. Smart, Macmillan, 1976.)

Sharing Grandparents' Environment
Over the river and through the wood,
To grandfather's house we'll go...
(From *"Thanksgiving Day"* by Lydia Maria Child)

Whether grandfather's and grandmother's house is located "over the river and through the wood," or in the city... or near the beach... or just around the corner — visiting grandchildren have a new environment to explore. Grandparents who live in a city can take their grandchildren to museums, plays, skyscrapers, and shops — while those who live in more rural areas can share the trees, flowers, animals, and birds. If they live near the seashore, walks along the beach can yield treasures such as shells and smooth, round pebbles. And, you never know where Captain Kidd might have landed!

Sharing Grandparents' Memories
> *How dear to this heart are the scenes of my childhood,*
> *When fond recollection presents them to view....*
> (From *"The Old Oaken Bucket"* by Samuel Woodworth)

Every grandparent has a personal history to share with new generations. Life has changed so much in a few decades that children are amazed to learn of a world without television sets, computers, or microwave ovens. Photographs or slides of how people looked and dressed when grandma and grandpa were young are usually fascinating to children who can gain an understanding of family history, and a sense of roots.

In writing this chapter, I asked several grandparents of preschool children to give me the benefit of their experience as to what <u>has</u> and what <u>has not</u> worked successfully in their relationship with grandchildren. The answers they came up with are loving, inventive and varied.

Grandparenting Suggestions: What Doesn't Work, and What Does

What Doesn't Work
- Don't come on strong — approach a small child gently. Better yet, let the child come to you.
- Never ridicule or laugh at a child. Laughing <u>with</u> a child is great and can make for real communication.
- A young child has a short attention span. Don't dwell on an activity if the child loses interest.
- Be wary of long trips. When unavoidable, think of ways to distract children.
- Don't tire them out by planning too many events on a day's outing.
- Don't overwhelm a young child with too much company.
- Don't ask your grandchild questions about private family matters. This strains a relationship and makes a child uncomfortable.
- Don't demand kisses or make them a condition for giving children money or a toy.
- Don't require a child to rate which grandparent they love best.

What Works

Follow the Child's Lead

• Try to see the world through the child's eyes. Understand his interests regarding the things around him. Operate on his level. (This does not mean using baby talk.)

• Whenever you are together, stop to examine whatever your grandchild is interested in: a flower, a green leaf, the colorful magnets on the refrigerator...

• Be aware of grandchildren's individual preferences.

• Accept your grandchild's feelings when he is afraid . Some children are more cautious of new experiences than others.

• Get down on the floor or on a low chair to play with your grandchild. That way, you can look at things from her level.

• Let them lead the play and then be enthusiastic. "Our grandson plays fireman and rescues us."

• "We make it fun when we play. If it's making a house out of sofa pillows, I'm in there with them."

Have Patience

• Give completely of your time and attention when playing with your grandchild.

• "When we spent the day with our grandchildren we hardly ever said, 'No.' We didn't lose our tempers, even when the kids acted silly. We ignored certain behavior."

Share Your Interests

• Share your day and activities with your grandchild. "I take my grandson with me on errands and we go out to lunch together. He chooses the restaurant from my list."

• "I showed her how to do some simple weaving. We sang songs and played musical instruments. I made a tape of the music and songs, which I treasure."

• "We go for walks around the garden, looking for flowers and bugs."

Have Them to Yourself Sometimes
    • It is important to have them to yourself at times without their mom and dad. You don't feel any constraints, and it brings back a lot of wonderful memories of *your* kid's childhood.
    • Whether they are visiting you, or you are alone with them at their house, ask their parents for a general schedule of the children's home routine. Be aware of what they do for themselves (like brushing their teeth) and what you are expected to do for them.
    • Routines and repetition of familiar activities are comforting. "I like to serve him the same meal each time he comes — and have the same special snack for him."
    • Children love to look at photograph albums and hear stories about when Mommy and Daddy were little.
    • "When my granddaughter visits, her room is next to ours. Almost every morning, she snuggles with us for a few special minutes."

Share Activities
    • Take advantage of places to visit: museums, country fairs, movies, shops, beaches, theaters, etc. (Be flexible and change your plans, if necessary.)
    • Let him choose a book for you to read together.
    • Take walks together and count things: tulips, dogs, tall trees.
    • Participate in their active play, if possible.
    • Play thinking games like Go Fish, Old Maid, Concentration and Candyland.
    • Make a Grandchildren's Scrapbook. "I take lots of pictures when we're together. These are mounted in their special album, along with their cards and letters which they are just beginning to send. They seem to relish this album when they visit."

When More Than One Grandchild Visits
    • "Dispense love equally to each grandchild."
    • "It was great with two children playing with each other, we didn't have to be their playmates, but could concentrate on being their grandparents, which we love."
    • "Don't force two grandchildren to play together — such as when visiting a playground — but allow them to choose the activities they want."

In Summary
    • "We like to give of ourselves, but not expensive toys — that's IMPORTANT."
    • "What worked out well, in a nutshell was that we used love, presents, intelligence, distraction and interesting things to do."
    • "Just enjoy your grandchildren with no strings."

Editor's Note: We want to thank the following persons for their insights on grandparenting: Regina Eggers, Berni and Les Feldman, Ruth and Bill Kitchen, Marilyn and Stuart Knoepfel, Claire and Al Perry, Lois and George Ross, and Barbara and Irving Teicher.

Chapter 29
Children and Pets:
a Natural Combination

Warren & Fay Eckstein

*...the pet is constant,
offering love and physical closeness —
asking for nothing
and demanding nothing in return...*

You just can't beat the combination of children and pets. It's a natural. Youngsters love pets and pets love youngsters. On the surface the reason appears simple enough: young children enjoy a living, breathing play-mate of their own — one that's just about their size and always ready to play.

Pets as Non-demanding Companions

Pets offer children the one luxury they often don't receive, the opportunity to be part of a non-demanding relationship. During a preschooler's developmental years, there are pressures to behave in socially acceptable ways, pressures to learn fundamental skills, and pressures to learn how to relate to adult caregivers and to other children. But the pet is constant, offering love and physical closeness — asking for nothing and demanding nothing in return — no matter how stressful the day. Pets become a good friend that youngsters can count on, can tell their troubles to, share their joys, or invite into their imaginations.

Pets Make Good Teachers

Pets are also an invaluable teaching tool. Pets teach responsibility — that there are obligations when you become involved in caring for another living thing. Children learn that other creatures have needs, feelings, and rights — lessons that many preschoolers carry into their adult lives.

Pets may also teach our children about death. The passing of a pet is often a child's first experience with death and it may help prepare the child for the loss of family members. Parents who take seriously the death of a pet take advantage of an invaluable experience in preparing the young child for the realities of the adult world.

Anticipate Responsibilities Involved in Owning a Pet

Pet behavior problems and concerns should be anticipated in advance and the family must be ready to deal with those problems as they arise. Most new pets will pose a certain number of initial adjustment problems like chewing wood moldings or having "little accidents" on the floor. Adult family members should model a responsible attitude towards dealing with these problems. Parents sometimes give the pet away if the going gets tough. This can be devastating to the child. We want to teach our children about accepting responsibility even when things don't fall into place right away. But, sadly, the so-called "revolving-door pet mentality" is all too commonplace. Therefore, it is critical that the family agree on owning a pet and that the first choice of pet be the right choice.

The Most Important Reason for Preschoolers to Have Pets

The best advantage to owning a pet is the obvious one — youngsters and pets have fun together. In today's world of television violence, nuclear concerns, and fears about personal safety, preschoolers tend to be more sophisticated than their parents were in their more innocent, growing-up years. Pets provide the opportunity for children to be children.

Choosing a Pet

Several scientific studies have confirmed the short and long term benefits that pets provide for children, but not enough have addressed the particulars of the child/pet experience, often leaving parents to fend for themselves.

How to Begin
If there is no family pet, the first step is to determine what pet is best suited for the family. Since a pet becomes a member of the family, it is important that your entire family agrees on the pet selection, including your preschooler. Even young children often have their heart set on a certain type of pet and, when possible, this should be accommodated, particularly when the pet is supposed to establish a bond with the child.

Dog, Cat or Alternative Pet?
Dogs
Dogs are a wonderful choice, offering a variety of sizes and shapes to choose from, and making active playmates for preschoolers. The down side is that if you don't have a fenced yard, or are unwilling to have a paper trained dog, there is the chore of walking in all weather conditions and at varied times, including late at night. Very small breeds of dogs should be avoided as they are often too fragile to take the wear and tear of young children.

On the other hand, large dogs are capable of knocking over preschoolers, although many seem to know to be gentle around the little ones.

Cats
Cats are cheaper to keep than most dogs and don't have to be walked after the 11:00 news; but even so, the litter box will need to be cleaned regularly if the cat is to remain indoors. Some people complain that cats aren't as affectionate as dogs. I have found that each cat or dog is different and sweeping generalizations don't hold true. If a cat interests the family, then, by all means, go ahead with your choice.

Alternative Pets
There are many alternatives to owning a cat or dog. Guinea pigs happen to be one of my favorites. They're easy to care for, cheap, and can be very affectionate. They tend to be a good compromise pet when you don't want the added responsibility of a cat or dog. Hamsters, gerbils and mice are also interesting possibilities, but I find them to be a little too small for the preschooler. The hottest trend in pets at the moment is birds. My feeling is that, as with other small pets, birds can be inadvertently hurt by young children and might be better served with the slightly older child. Rabbits are more common today than many people imagine, and also make good pets for the preschooler who's not too rough. Living in city apartments, rabbits can be trained to use litter boxes and taught to walk on leashes. No more backyard hutches for this pet of the future.

Assess Your Lifestyle
Consider the environment in which you live: rural with lots of room, suburban, or urban with no extra space. The pets should harmonize with the amount of space in which you live. However, big dogs can live in city apartments, provided the family plans to include the dog in a regular exercise program.

Also, latch key pets, like latch key children, need special consideration. Working parents may not have the time to become involved with a pet that requires too much work, and dogs left alone for very long periods of time may not do well when walks are missed. Quality time must be allotted for the pet, no matter how busy the day.

Think about your pocketbook — besides the obvious differences in the cost of feeding between smaller and larger pets, veterinary and kenneling prices vary, and long haired dogs and cats may require professional grooming.

Give Preschoolers Pet Lessons

Don't take chances. Preschoolers should never be left unsupervised with ANY pet. Since young children are just learning appropriate pet handling techniques, mistakes will happen.

It's advisable to give pet lessons with a favorite stuffed animal before the pet arrives. Young children frequently drag their stuffed animal toys around by the tail, squeeze them really tight for a hug, or even throw them across a room. Working with children and their stuffed animals as if they were real will help reduce the risk of your preschooler's mishandling a pet.

What Role Should Your Preschooler Play in the Pet's Upbringing?

Allow your child to do as much as he or she is physically and emotionally ready to do. Obviously, a young child should not walk a dog. However, basic feeding responsibilities can easily be delegated to your older preschooler, and so can chores like rinsing out the water dish and brushing the pet. Teach your youngster to be gentle, and explain why good grooming habits are as important to Rusty and Fluffy as they are for children.

A very common problem is that pets often respond only to adults, while taking advantage of smaller children. Therefore, young children, with supervision, should even be allowed to participate with the pet's training, practicing basic commands like *sit* and *stay*. This will help the pet respect the authority of the child.

Have a Good Time

Be responsible and cautious when necessary, but don't get too involved when the youngsters and pets are playing in their own little world. For example, sometimes you'll find your preschooler sharing his cookies with his animal confidant. It's not a great idea on a regular basis but try to let them be. Youngsters will be youngsters, and that includes both the two-legged human ones and the four-legged animal ones. Just sit back and enjoy the love and happiness that develops from this very special, precious relationship.

Chapter 30
What'll We Do Now?
Activities To Do Together

Betty Farber

Mama & Richie at St. George Island - Richie 1½ yrs.

*The family album is like
an individualized picture book
for your child.*

Activities are sequenced from easy to more difficult.

1. Look through the family album together (ages 1-6).
<u>Materials:</u> Family album or box of family photos.

The family album is like an individualized picture book for your child. In it, children discover information about themselves, family members and the world they live in.

The family album can be used as a reference book — identifying family members who are far away. "This present came from Uncle Jim. Here's his picture in the album." Seeing a photo of Uncle Jim identifies the absent family member more concretely to your young child.

As you "read" the album together, you and your child can talk about the photographs of your relatives, your pets and your children themselves: There's Grandma and Grandpa. They're coming for a visit soon." "That's Spot when he was just a puppy." "That's a picture of you when you were a very little baby." "That's a picture of Mommy when she was a very little baby."

You can discuss the change of seasons, and recall vacations and birthday parties: "Remember when we took a trip to the beach? That's you with your pail and shovel.".... "That was your birthday cake, last year. See the three candles?"

Talk about how people in the photograph seem to be feeling: The baby is crying there. She was feeling sad. But here she's happy. See, she's smiling."

Looking at the album can be an experience that children want to repeat over and over again.

2. Make a Gift Certificate that children can give parents.
Materials: A nicely trimmed piece of paper with the words: **As a Gift to** *(space for the name)* **On the Occasion of** *(space)* **I will** *(space)* **Signed** *(space)*.

Instead of a "store-bought" present, children may wish to *give of themselves* for parents' birthdays or anniversary. A **Gift Certificate** entitles the receiver to some extra effort on the part of the giver. Your child decides what he wishes to give. For example: he may offer to bring your slippers when you return from work, to feed the dog, to serve breakfast, and so on.

The gift certificate may be filled out by an adult, with the child dictating his choice of a gift. Children may sign their name, or draw any symbol for a signature.

(*Note:* The following activities may need more than one session to complete.)

3. Make Greeting Cards for Family Birthdays (ages 2-6).
<u>Materials:</u> Old greeting cards, magazines, photos, ribbon, glue, glitter, round-edged scissors.

Cut pictures from old greeting cards, magazines and duplicate photos — ones you won't miss. Fold construction paper into a greeting card. Make a collage with the materials. Glue the design on the front of the card. Your child may dictate a message for you to write inside the card.

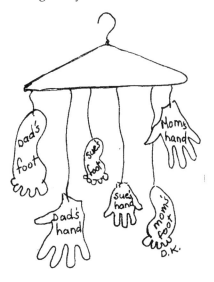

4. Create a Family Hand and Foot Mobile (ages 3-6).
<u>Materials:</u> Construction paper, pencil, hole punch, round-edged scissors, thread, wire hanger.

Trace a hand and foot of each family member using different colored construction paper. Write on each, <u>Daddy's Hand,</u> <u>Daddy's Foot,</u> etc. Cut them out. Punch a hole in each hand and foot, and tie with thread. Vary the lengths of thread. Tie each hand and foot to a wire hanger, so that it is balanced, and hang.

Helpful hints to keep in mind when participating in creative activities with your preschooler:

• **Accept your child's work without criticism.** Each child has different capabilities, and children are easily discouraged if they feel that they can't measure up to expectations.

• **If your child is involved in a creative activity, give help when it is needed, but let the work itself be done by your child.** You may wish to help with the more difficult aspects of the activities, such as cutting out an intricate design. But let the finished work be your child's own creation.

• **When you offer praise about your child's work, make it sincere.** Even if the work is not beautiful by adult standards, you can say: "You worked very hard on that picture." "You used so many bright colors." "You made Daddy's birthday card all by yourself!"

Resources for Section Six: Encouraging Young Children's Positive Views of Family

FOR ADULTS

A Good Enough Parent: A Book on Child Rearing, by Bruno Bettleheim & Anne Freedgood, Random House, 1988. This work explains how simple traditions and rituals can provide security even during stressful conditions.

On Becoming a Family: The Growth of Attachment, by T. Berry Brazelton. Dell, 1982. A supportive book for parents that discusses attachment and how it grows under a variety of circumstances.

Talking with Your Child About Sex: Questions & Answers for Children from Birth to Puberty, by Mary S. Calderone and James W. Ramey. Ballantine, 1984. This helpful volume presents information in response to questions children may raise, on topics including conception and childbirth. Answers are presented according to the child's developmental level.

Enchantment of the World series (94 books) Children's Press. Each volume describes one country and covers topics such as history, geography, customs, family life, school life, sports and games, and folklore.

Fatherhood, by Bill Cosby. Doubleday, 1986. Describing the private joys and sorrows of being a father, this book is wonderfully reassuring.

How to Father, by Fitzhugh Dodson. Signet, 1975. A down-to-earth guide by a professional about how to pay attention to the process of fathering.

Ties that Stress: The New Family Imbalance, by David Elkind. Harvard University Press, 1994. The modern American family is under enormous stress. It is out of balance — failing to meet the needs of children. The renowned child psychologist and author describes what has happened to the American family, and looks at the possibilities of a new balance between the needs of the children and the needs of the parents.

Between Brothers & Sisters: A Celebration of Life's Most Enduring Relationship, by Adele Faber and Elaine Mazlish. Avon Books, 1989. The famous authors of *Siblings without Rivalry* and *How to Talk So Kids Will Listen and Listen So Kids Will Talk,* offer a treasure of black and white photos of siblings of all ages and races. Along with the pictures is the authors' poetic commentary.

Siblings Without Rivalry: How to Help Your Children Live Together So You Can Too, by Adele Faber and Elaine Mazlish. Avon, 1998. Using their knowledge of communication skills, the authors discuss simple, effective techniques to reduce the antagonism between siblings.

Family Wisdom: The 2,000 Most Important Things Ever Said About Parenting, Children, and Family Life, by Susan Ginsberg. Columbia University Press, 1996. Would you like to know what has been said by authors and educators about children's fears, parents' needs, working mothers, or on any other topic that touches family life? Peruse this book's collection of wise, insightful, and humorous quotations.

Pregnant Fathers: Challenges and Discoveries on the Road to Being a Father, by Jack Heinowitz. Andrews & McMeel, 1997. An affectionate look by a psychologist at the paternal side of pregnancy and delivery.

Pregnancy and Childbirth, by Tracey Hotchner. Avon Books, 1997. This is a comprehensive book with a thorough, encyclopedia-type format.

Mothers: Twenty Stories of Contemporary Motherhood, edited and with an introduction by Katrina Kenison & Kathleen Hirsch. North Point Press/Farrar, Straus and Giroux, 1996. The editors came up with the idea for this book when, becoming mothers themselves, they searched for stories that embodied their experience. The reader will discover short stories by Laurie Colwin, Mary Gordon, Barbara Kingsolver, and many other fine writers who share the role of mother and writer.

Getting Men Involved, by James Levine, Dr. Sherrill Wilson, and Dr. Dennis Murphy. Scholastic, 1993. With the authors involved in The Fatherhood Project at The Families and Work Institute in New York City, this book is full of practical suggestions about how to bring fathers and other males into children's lives.

Cultural Awareness for Young Children, rev. ed., by Earldene McNeill, Velma Schmidt, and Judy Allen. Learning Tree, 1981. This helpful volume offers a full spectrum of activities about the cultures and backgrounds of African-Americans, Native Americans, Mexican-Americans, Asian-Americans, Eskimos, and others. It includes art, music, dance, language, and family life.

Fatherhood, by Ross D. Parke. Harvard University Press, 1996. This paperback in *The Developing Child Series* explores what paternal involvement means to families in today's society. Over the past several years, fathers have become more involved partners in parenthood, but in most households they still spend less time with children than mothers. The author shows that men and women are equally competent as caregivers, and both have a profound influence on their children's development.

The Nurturing Father, by Kyle D. Pruett, M.D., Warner Books, 1987. (Out of print — but please check your library.) This is a warm and supportive book, giving a fascinating account of three families in which the father is the primary caregiver. Along the way, the reader learns how all families can benefit from involved fatherhood.

Loving Each One Best, by Nancy Samalin with Catherine Whitney. Bantam, 1996. Written by the author of *Love and Anger: The Parental Dilemma,* and *Loving Your Child Is Not Enough,* this work offers a caring and practical approach to raising siblings. Parents will love the specific scenarios with dialog that they can relate to, and the creative solutions offered.

Sibling Rivalry, by Seymour Reit. Ballantine Books, 1988. A reassuring book with expert advice for parents on what they can do to encourage healthy relationships between siblings.

The Developing Father, by Bryan E. Robinson and Robert L. Barret. Guilford Press, 1986. This work offers a detailed look at the varieties of the fathering experience.

Keeping Family Stories Alive — *A Creative Guide to Taping Your Family Life and Love,* by Vera Rosenbluth, Hartley & Marks, Inc., 1990. The author outlines practical techniques for reviving and keeping family traditions, and tells how children can interview family members.

How to Talk to Your Kids About Really Important Things, (Social & Behavioral Science Series) by Charles Schaefer & Theresa F. DiGeronimo. Jossey-Bass 1994. This useful book includes chapters on "A New Baby in the Family" and "Where Do Babies Come From."

The Father's Almanac, by S. Adams Sullivan. Doubleday, 1992. One of the best ways to involve the father in the pregnancy and childbirth is by having him involved in preparing the older children. This book will help to do the trick.

How to Tape Instant Oral Biographies, 2nd rev. ed. by Bill Zimmerman, Bantam, 1994. Consult with this book if you'd like to know how to interview and preserve on videotape family sayings and anecdotes — including significant settings (heirlooms, ethnic costumes and handicrafts).

FOR CHILDREN

Black is Brown is Tan, by Arnold Adoff. Harper Trophy, 1992. Told in rhyme, with lively rhythm , this is a family story of momma and daddy and children and grandparents who come in all colors and share their love for each other.

The Complete Dog Book for Kids, The official publication of The American Kennel Club, Howell Book, 1996. (There is a new issue every year. Most of the material remains the same; except that new breeds are included.) It gives specific information on the qualities of each breed of dog recognized by The American Kennel Club.

Just like Daddy, by Frank Asch. Simon & Schuster, 1984. A little bear does everything "just like daddy," until the surprise ending.

Here Come the Babies, by Catherine and Laurence Anholt. Candlewick Press, 1993. What do babies look like? What do babies play with? What does a baby do? The answers to these and other important questions about babies appear in this lively book. A joyful, appealing way to introduce a young child to life with a baby.

All in a Day, by Mitsumasa Anno. Putnam, 1986. New Year's Day in eight different countries — Australia, Brazil, China, England, Japan, Kenya, the United States, and Russia — is illustrated by ten artists of international renown.

That Terrible Baby, by Jennifer Armstrong. Tambourine, 1994. The baby crawls at such a fast pace, that siblings Eleanor and Mark are led on a wild chase through the house.

When I Am a Sister, by Robin Ballard. Greenwillow, 1998. A little girl who is staying for the summer with her Papa and her stepmother, wonders if things will be different after their new baby is born. She asks Papa many questions about what will change: will she still have her same room and will they still read a story at bedtime? He answers lovingly and truthfully. So she goes back to stay with her Mama, looking forward to her next visit when she will be a sister.

When We Get Home, by Robin Ballard. Greenwillow, 1999. Driving home with Mama after helping Granny move, a little girl anticipates all the familiar rituals of bedtime with her loving family.

Once Upon a Time and Grandma, by Lenore Blegvad. Margaret K. McElderry Books, 1993. It's hard to think of your grandma as being a little girl once upon a time, even when she shows you a photograph of herself as a child in pigtails. Grandma tells her grandchildren all about what her life was like a long time ago.

The Amazing The Incredible Super Dog, by Crosby Bonsall. HarperCollins, 1986. In this humorous story, a little girl who owns a cat and a dog brags about the tricks her dog can do, and says that her cat is jealous. The illustrations show the girl and her cat doing all the tricks, while the dog looks on; but the little girl never notices that her cat is really the talented one.

If I Were Your Father, by Margaret Park Bridges, Morrow, 1999. A little boy tells his father about all the wonderful things he would do if he were the father. He would take his son fishing on a school day, take him hunting for buried treasure, and let him make all his own decisions. As they sit together at the end of the story, with the father's arm around the boy, the love between father and son is unmistakable in this warm and humorous book.

If I Were Your Mother, by Margaret Park Bridges. Morrow, 1999. A little girl and her mother have a dialog about what the daughter would do if they changed places. "If I were your mother, I'd give you a big canopy bed and bring you breakfast on a silver tray." The little girl imagines a variety of marvelous activities she would carry out, but the conversation ends with her being a daughter again, in her mother's lap.

Lemonade Parade, by Ben Brooks. Albert Whitman, 1992. In this humorous story, Patty and her friends set up a lemonade stand, but there are no customers. Patty's father sees their discouragement, and before long a number of characters arrive one at a time in unusual costumes to buy lemonade: a prospector, a race car driver, an astronaut, and so on. At the end of the day, the children have made a good profit from their business, and Patty's Dad is asleep on the couch, exhausted!

The Runaway Bunny, by Margaret Wise Brown. HarperCollins, 1977. A little bunny tells his mother he will run away and change into something else, but his mother knows how to play that game too.

Grandfather and I, Grandmother and I, by Helen E. Buckley. Lothrop, 1994. The special relationship between children and grandparents is illustrated in these two books.

Where Did Josie Go? by Helen E. Buckley. Lothrop, Lee & Shepard, 1999. All the family is looking for Josie, but where can she be? This story is told in lively rhyme, with warm and loving pictures by Jan Ormerod.

Is That Your Sister? A True Story of Adoption, by Catherine Bunin and Sherry Bunin. Our Child Press, 1992. Illustrated with photographs of her family and narrated by six-year-old Catherine, this book tells her family's adoption story — the building of a transracial family. This book presents questions that children may hear from others.

A Perfect Father's Day, by Eve Bunting. Clarion, 1993. In this funny story, Susie plans a perfect day for her father — consisting of all of <u>her</u> <u>own</u> favorite activities.

Fly Away Home, by Eve Bunting. Clarion, 1993. In another kind of family story, a homeless boy and his father live in an airport and try not to get noticed. They attempt to look at their future with confidence, and when the boy observes a trapped bird that finds its freedom, he sees hope for his father and himself also.

Abby, by Jeannette Franklin Caines. HarperTrophy, 1984. In this picture book, an African-American child adopted when she was an infant likes to look at her baby book and hear the story of her arrival in the family.

Happy Birthday, Biscuit, by Alyssa Satin Capucilli. HarperCollins, 1999. Biscuit's young owner, Daisy, gives her puppy a very special first birthday party.

The Foundling, by Carol Carrick. Clarion, 1986. Christopher keeps remembering his dog, Bodger, who had been killed in an accident. His father takes him to an animal shelter to choose a new dog, but Christopher tells him that he doesn't want a new one. Back home, a puppy that seems to be living next door, keeps following Christopher around. When the boy finds out that it doesn't have a home, he decides that this is the puppy he wants.

Dear Annie, by Judith Caseley. Greenwillow, 1991. When Annie was born, her grandpa wrote a letter to her. And he has kept on writing ever since. Now Annie can write back to grandpa and bring his letters to school for "Show and Tell." All the children in the class want pen pals like Annie's grandpa.

How I Was Adopted, by Joanna Cole. Mulberry Books edition, 1999. A little girl tells the story of her adoption by a loving family. The book begins with a few pages of helpful suggestions, called "A Note to Families."

How You Were Born, by Joanna Cole. Morrow, 1993. A picture book in drawings and photographs, it highlights conception, fetal development, birth, and that new baby. The pictures are of families from a variety of ethnic backgrounds.

The New Baby at Your House, by Joanna Cole. Morrow, 1998. Color photographs by Margaret Miller of a variety of families, illustrate this informative, reassuring book for brothers and sisters. It also includes several pages for parents, along with a list of resources.

My Father, by Judy Collins. Little, Brown, 1997. The songwriter/author shares her father's dreams for his family in this touching book, which includes the music to the song.

Purrrrr, by Pat Cummings. HarperFestival, 1999. This board book tells a simple story in rhyme about a little boy and his sleepy cat. Its cardboard pages are great for toddlers.

Bet You Can't, by Penny Dale. Lippincott, 1988. A sister and her younger brother try to clean up their toys at bedtime. It turns into a challenging game of "Bet you can't!" until the end when they find out, "See. We can."

Feast for 10, by Cathryn Falwell. Clarion, 1996. Count from one to ten as you read about a family who shops, cooks, and serves a delicious feast. A cut-paper technique is used in the appealing illustrations depicting an African-American family.

Cats Sleep Anywhere, by Eleanor Farjeon. HarperTrophy, 1996. Illustrated with gorgeous pictures by renowned cat artist Anne Mortimer, this charming book will be treasured by cat lovers of all ages.

Moja Means One: Swahili Counting Book, by Muriel Feelings. Puffin, 1992. Unique features of African rural life and culture are shown in an unusual counting book.

How My Parents Learned to Eat, by Ina R. Friedman. Houghton Mifflin, 1987. An American sailor and his Japanese bride find that table manners are a cultural difference they can overcome.

Just Like My Dad, by Tricia Gardella. HarperCollins, 1996. This young cowhand wants to be a cowboy, just like his dad. He loves to dress in his cowboy hat, his chaps, and his spurs; he doesn't even mind the work of mending fences because he's with his dad. And he loves when his dad tucks him into bed and says he'll be a great cowhand... just like *his* dad.

William and Boomer, by Lindsay Barrett George. Greenwillow, 1987. In this beautifully illustrated story, William and his parents find an orphaned baby goose by the lake near their home. Boomer, as they name the baby goose, follows William everywhere. The goose is a wonderful swimmer, and the little boy wants to learn too. William practices and soon learns to swim, and he and Boomer swim together the whole summer long.

At Daddy's on Saturdays, by Linda Walvoord Girard. Albert Whitman, 1987. Katie feels angry, sad, and afraid when her parents get divorced, but she finally understands that she can keep a loving relationship with her daddy even though he lives apart from her.

My Little Brother, by Debi Gliori. Candlewick Press, 1992. A young girl thinks her little brother is a pest. He copies everything she does, follows her around like a shadow, and won't let her go to sleep at night. She wishes he would disappear. But one night when his bed is empty, she's really worried. She finally finds him safely asleep, and, decides that while he's still a pest, she wouldn't want him to disappear again.

Did the Sun Shine Before You Were Born? by Sol Gordon and Judith Gordon. Prometheus Books, 1992. Lovely line drawings depict family relationships, conception, fetal development, birth, new baby's arrival, and early infancy.

Nobody's Dog, by Charlotte Graeber. Hyperion, 1998. Nobody in the neighborhood wants the small white dog with one brown ear. He doesn't suit Mr. and Mrs. Fitz — he's too small. Mrs. Applegate doesn't want him — he's too noisy. Everyone has an excuse. What about Miss Pepper? She is worried that the dog will trample on her flowers. But the little dog soon wins her over, and Nobody's Dog is Miss Pepper's dog now.

Daddy Will Be There, by Lois G. Grambling. Greenwillow, 1998. Whether she's playing by herself in her room, or riding her bike, or going home from a birthday party, the little girl in this book is confident that her daddy will be there when she needs him.

Cat and Bear, by Carol Greene. Hyperion, 1997. The cat is the child's favorite playmate, until a new friend turns up in the form of a cheerful stuffed bear. The beautiful lifelike illustrations by Anne Mortimer make you believe you will be stroking fur when you touch them.

Grandaddy's Place, by Helen V. Griffith. Morrow, 1991. A little city girl, Janetta, stands on the porch of her grandaddy's place in the country for the first time and encounters a mean-looking cat, a wasps' nest and a giant mule. She runs inside, saying, "Nothing out there likes me." But grandaddy has patience, imagination and a gentle humor and soon his fantastic stories and unique abilities (such as understanding fish-talk) change Janetta's mind about the country.

Grandaddy's Stars, by Helen V. Griffith. Greenwillow, 1995. Janetta had visited Grandaddy on his farm and now he is coming to Baltimore to visit Janetta. The little girl is so excited, but worried too. She is afraid he will find the city boring. But Grandaddy, a man of humor and wisdom, likes everything she shows him.

Grandaddy and Janetta, by Helen V. Griffith. Mulberry, 1999. Janetta visits Grandaddy on his farm, this time traveling alone, and she's worried that they may not recognize each other. But she doesn't have to worry, because Grandaddy not only looks the same — he has the same straight-faced sense of fun, and tells the same kinds of tall tales that she remembers from her previous visits. A pleasure to read aloud!

Seven Brave Women, by Betsy Hearne. Greenwillow, 1997. A girl tells the inspiring story of her female ancestors, who, without having fought in any wars, were brave and strong and talented.

Baby and I Can Play, and Fun with Toddlers, by Karen Henderickson. Parenting Press, 1990. With many ideas to help big brothers and sisters to play appropriately with their siblings, this is a unique how-to book.

The Purple Coat, by Amy Hest. Simon & Schuster, 1992. Every year Gabrielle's Grandpa makes her a plain navy blue coat in his tailor shop. This year Gabrielle wants something different — a purple coat. Mama says, "Navy blue coats are what you always get." But Grandpa figures out a way to satisfy Gabrielle and Mama.

Spot's Baby Sister, by Eric Hill. Puffin, 1995. The popular puppy is back, delighted with his new sister, in this lift-the-flap book.

Daddy Makes the Best Spaghetti, by Anna Grossnickle Hines. Clarion, 1988. In this story of a loving family, Corey's Daddy doesn't just cook the best spaghetti, he also picks Corey up at daycare, takes him to the supermarket, pretends to be "Bathman" as he gives Corey a bath, and sits with the little boy as Mom reads a story, just before they both tuck him in his bed.

When We Married Gary, by Anna Grossnickle Hines. Greenwillow, 1996. "It used to be just Mama, Beth, and me." Although they had a daddy once, he went away. Then Gary came into their lives. "...I think it's kind of like we're a puzzle — Mama, Beth, and me. Our daddy didn't fit with us, but Gary does." A warm and touching family story.

Fathers, Mothers, Sisters, Brothers: A Collection of Family Poems, by Mary Ann Hoberman. Puffin/Warne, 1993. A collection of wise and witty poems about all kinds of relatives and the funny things that happen in families.

Mommy's Lap, by Ruth Horowitz. Lothrop, Lee & Shepard, 1993. Mommy's lap is the best place for Sophie to be. But when a baby starts growing inside Mommy there's no room for Sophie on her lap. Happily, when baby Sam arrives, there's room for Sophie *and* the baby together on Mommy's lap. And when Sophie holds the baby on her own lap, she even thinks her lap is the best place for Sam to be.

How Many Stars in the Sky? by Lenny Hort. Tambourine, 1991. Mama is away that night and she is the one who knows all about the stars. But when Daddy and his son look for the best place to count them, they find companionship as they sleep under the stars.

When Will Sarah Come? by Elizabeth Fitzgerald Howard. Greenwillow, 1999. Jonathan's big sister, Sarah, started school today. The little boy waits all day with his grandmother for Sarah to come home. As we look at the color photos by Nina Crews, we see Jonathan playing with his toys, and listening to the sounds outdoors, until the wonderful moment when his sister comes home.

Where's the Baby? by Pat Hutchins. Mulberry, 1999. When the monster family tries to find the baby, they go from room to room and discover the terrible mess baby monster has made! (But, as they view the chaos in each room, Grandma always has something positive to say about her baby grandchild.)

Your Dad Was Just Like You, by Dolores Johnson. Macmillan, 1993. Peter and his father don't seem to get along. His father is always telling him to finish what he started, and to be more serious. The boy tells his troubles to his grandfather, who recounts to Peter that his father was very much like Peter when he was a little boy. Amazingly enough, he loved knock knock jokes, and laughed all the time. The reminiscence helps Peter to grow in understanding about his father.

Jam Day, by Barbara M. Joosse. HarperCollins, 1987. Ben and his Mama are going to Grandmam and Grandpap's house for a yearly family get-together of picking berries and making jam. On the way there, Ben wishes he and Mama were part of a big, noisy family, instead of just the two of them. During jam day with his grandparents and numerous relatives, he realizes that he really is part of a big, loving, and sharing family.

Geraldine's Baby Brother, by Holly Keller. Greenwillow, 1994. Geraldine wears earmuffs so that she won't hear her baby brother Willie cry. She is so angry at all the attention he is getting, that she won't even eat dinner. In the middle of the night, she goes into the nursery to tell him, "No more crying." He makes faces at her and gurgles. So Geraldine sits in the rocking chair and reads him stories. In the morning Geraldine wakes up and asks to give Willie his bottle. Then she goes downstairs for her breakfast.

Ganzy Remembers, by Mary Grace Ketner. Atheneum, 1991. A little girl goes with her grandmother to visit her great-grandmother who lives in a nursing home. There the little girl is fascinated by the stories her great-grandmother tells of her childhood on a Texas farm long ago.

Not Yet, Yvette, by Helen Ketteman. Albert Whitman, 1995. "Is it time yet?" asks Yvette. She waits impatiently as her father prepares a birthday party for her mother. But finally it's time!

Just My Dad & Me, by Leah Komaiko. HarperFestival, 1995. A day with just her dad is what she wants, but other people tag along, so this little girl escapes by going underwater all by herself. The fish are fascinating, but she needs sun, air, and her family!

How My Family Lives in America, by Susan Kuklin. Bradbury Press, 1992. In this lively and interesting photo essay, preschoolers can see how an African-American, Hispanic-American, and Asian-American family preserve their traditions while adapting to life in America.

A Baby for Max, by Kathryn Lasky in the words of Maxwell B. Knight. Aladdin, 1987. Using photographs by Christopher Knight, this book tells, in the words of the preschooler, Max, about waiting and preparing for his new sister, seeing her at the hospital, and helping with her care when she comes home.

Grandfather Remembers: Memories for My Grandchild, by Judith Levy, HarperCollins, 1986. This keepsake book includes a family tree, places for photos and pages for grandpa and child to fill out together.

Everything Has A Place, by Patricia Lillie. Greenwillow, 1993. With bright pictures by Nancy Tafuri, and just a few words on each page, this book will appeal to the youngest preschoolers. It has the reassuring words that toddlers love to hear. Everything has a place: a crayon in a box... a baby on a lap, a family in a house.

Why Was I Adopted? by Carole Livingston. L. Stuart/Carol Publishing, 1997. A humorous, brightly-illustrated presentation of the whys and hows of adoption. Emphasizes individual abilities and everyday acceptable behavior and the necessity of parental discipline. Common questions asked by adoptees are included with some suggested down-to-earth answers.

Ollie Knows Everything, by Abby Levine. Albert Whitman & Co., 1994. The O'Hare family is on a trip to New York City, and younger brother Herbert complains that big brother Ollie knows everything. He knows how to put his tray down for eating on the airplane, how to open his eyes underwater in the hotel pool, and even how to get lost on the subway and then found again. But Herbert is glad when his big brother is found, especially when they play together afterward in the pool and Ollie teaches him how to open his eyes underwater.

Watch the Stars Come Out, by Riki Levinson. Puffin, 1995. A little girl listens as her grandmother tells the story of how she and her brother came to America on a boat across the Atlantic as children. The bravery of these youngsters on this long sea voyage makes a wonderful tale in English and also in the Spanish version, ***Mira Cómo Salen Las Estrellas.***

Where's Baby? by Wendy Cheyette Lewison. Scholastic, 1992. A Peek-A-Boo Flap Book. Baby is hiding. Lift the flap on each page and look for the baby, until you find him playing peek-a-boo on the last page. This would be a fun book for a preschooler to "read" to a younger sibling.

Gone Fishing, by Earline R. Long. Sandpiper, 1984. With simple language, this story tells about a wonderful day spent by a little boy and his daddy. The little boy has a little fishing rod; his daddy has a big one, but they each catch one big fish and one little fish to take home to mommy.

Blueberries for Sal, by Robert McCloskey. Puffin, 1993. When picking blueberries, Sal starts to follow a baby bear's mother instead of his own, but it all comes out right in the end.

Boomer's Big Surprise, by Constance W. McGeorge. Chronicle, 1999. There's a new puppy in the house, and Boomer begins to feel that he's no longer top dog. But when the puppy invites him to play, Boomer discovers a new friend right in his own home.

My Father is in the Navy, by Robin McKinley. Greenwillow, 1992. Sara's father is the captain of a big ship, and he's been away so long, Sara doesn't remember him. She says goodnight to his photograph every night, but she doesn't really know him. Now that he's coming home, and Sara and her mother are meeting the ship, will she remember?

Grandfather's Trolley, by Bruce McMillan. Candlewick Press, 1995. The author/photographer uses hand-tinted photographs to capture the days of the early 1900s. In this story a little girl hops aboard a trolley car driven by her grandfather. The tenderness between grandfather and grandchild comes through on these lovely pages.

Mommies at Work, by Eve Merriam. Aladdin, 1996. Mommies may have all sorts of jobs, and this book touches on many of them.

A Birthday Basket for Tía, by Pat Mora. Macmillan, 1992. Cecilia wants to give her great-aunt a special gift for her ninetieth birthday, so she gathers a basket of memories of all the wonderful things she and her tía do together.

Angel to Angel: *A Mother's Gift of Love,* by Walter Dean Myers. HarperCollins, 1998. In this tribute to families, the author of *Brown Angels,* and *Glorious Angels,* presents us with another beautiful book of poetry. The pages are illustrated with unique old photos of African-American families.

Go Away, Dog, by Joan L. Nodset. HarperTrophy, 1997. A big old dog wants to be friendly, but the little boy doesn't like dogs. He wins the boy's heart in this book with simple text and an appealing story.

In My Momma's Kitchen, by Jerdine Nolen. Lothrop, Lee & Shepard, 1999. A little African-American girl tells of many family celebrations that take place in momma's kitchen: like the time her sister Nadene got a letter that told her about her music scholarship, or the day when the aunts gather to make the biggest pot of soup in town, or the stories and songs when they're all sitting together around the kitchen table.

Lulu and the Witch Baby, by Jane O'Connor. HarperCollins, 1986. Lulu, a little girl witch, can't understand why everybody loves her baby sister so much. Lulu uses some magic to make the Witch Baby disappear. Then she worries about bringing Witch Baby back. All is resolved happily.

101 Things to do with a Baby, by Jan Ormerod. Mulberry, 1993. This delightful book is illustrated with wonderful ideas for a sibling to do with a young baby. For example: "say good morning" or "blow on his tummy" or "take him for a slow stroll or a fast roll." It tells you also what to watch out for, such as "hair pulling" "nose grabbing" and "dribbling." And it ends with "give him a cuddle and a kiss goodnight."

Our Puppies Are Growing, by Carolyn Otto. HarperTrophy Let's-Read-And-Find-Out Science, 1998. A little girl's dog is having puppies. This informative book describes their birth and first few weeks of life in simple language so that preschoolers can understand.

Tom and Pippo Read a Story, by Helen Oxenbury. Simon & Schuster, 1998. Pippo is Tom's toy monkey. Tom asks Daddy to read to him, then to read to Pippo. When Daddy can't read any more, Tom reads to Pippo, with the hope that Pippo will learn to read on his own one day.

Scruffy, by Peggy Parish. HarperTrophy, 1990. Todd is promised a cat for his birthday. He and his parents go to the animal shelter to pick out his pet. He finds out important information about caring for pets, and chooses Scruffy for his own.

Any Kind of Dog, by Lynn Reiser. Mulberry, 1994. Richard wants a dog, any kind of dog, but his mother says they are too much trouble. She offers Richard many other kinds of animals, but he only wants a dog, and his persistence brings him just what he wants.

Cherry Pies and Lullabies, by Lynn Reiser. Greenwillow, 1998. This lovely book is about cherry pies, flowers, quilts, and lullabies. It is also about families, love, and how traditions are passed down through generations. Young children will love the repetition of the language, and the author's bright illustrations.

Soon-Hee in America, by Schi-Zhin Rhie. Hollym, 1977. This is the story of the everyday life of a five-year-old Korean girl now living in America. The simple text shows how American customs can become assimilated while maintaining Korean heritage.

Waiting-For-Papa Stories, by Bethany Roberts. HarperCollins, 1990. Papa rabbit is late coming home, and his family is worried. So Mama rabbit entertains the children with stories about papa's past adventures. Finally, he arrives safe and sound, announcing that, "A papa rabbit never misses dinner!"

Hannah's Baby Sister, by Marisabina Russo. Greenwillow, 1998. Hannah's mother is going to have a baby very soon, and Hannah has made up her mind that it will be a girl. She knows her baby sister's name (Patsy), her favorite ice cream (fudge swirl) and her first word (Hannah). What will Hannah do if the baby is a boy? A warm story of a new sibling, illustrated with Russo's colorful, endearing pictures.

Mama Talks Too Much, by Marisabina Russo. Greenwillow, 1999. When Celeste and Mama walk through the neighborhood, running errands, they meet so many neighbors. And each time Mama stops and talks. Celeste wants go quickly to the market, but Mama is still talking. Then they meet a neighbor with a new puppy, and Celeste is the one who wants to stay and talk.

One Hundred Is a Family, by Pam Muñoz Ryan. Hyperion, 1998. A warm-hearted look at groups of families engaged in all sorts of activities, first counting from one to ten, and then by tens to one hundred.

The Relatives Came, by Cynthia Rylant. Bradbury Press, 1985. A charming story about one summer when the relatives came to visit.

Sam, by Ann H. Scott. Paperstar, 1996. Sam is looking for company, but at first nobody in the family seems to be listening to him.

My New Baby and Me, by Dian G. Smith & Staff. The Metropolitan Museum of Art/Charles Scribner's Sons, 1987. A First-Year Record Book for Big Brothers and Sisters. A book that lets you paste in photos, draw pictures, tell about your feelings and keep track of special days. It also gives you a checklist of the things you can do and the things your baby sister or brother can do.

People, by Peter Spier. Doubleday, 1988. A spectacular picture book for all ages, showing the different kinds of eyes, hair, languages, religions, colors, clothes, food, games, holidays, etc. around the world.

Making Babies, by Sara Bonnett Stein. Walker, 1984. An excellent book to promote a discussion on pregnancy and childbirth with young children, presented in a picture book fashion, with many wonderful photographs. Each page has an additional annotated text, providing the adult with information on the appropriate way to handle difficult questions and issues with young children.

The Adopted One: An Open Family Book for Parents and Children Together, by Sara Bonnett Stein. Walker, 1979. A four-year-old adopted boy asks questions about his birthmother. The accompanying text for adults provides clear explanations as to why children may ask certain questions and models helpful ways of responding to these questions.

Baby Says, by John Steptoe. Lothrop, Lee & Shepard, 1988. With just a few words and very descriptive pictures, the author/illustrator shows the interactions between a baby who keeps throwing his teddy bear out of his play pen and his brother who is trying to build on the floor with blocks.

Higher on the Door, by James Stevenson. Greenwillow, 1987. This book begins: "I have a grandson now; that's how old I am. But sometimes I look back and remember..." He remembers about the milkman and the iceman, the things he was afraid of, and the trips his family took into the city — just the kinds of things children want to know, when they ask, "What was it like when you were little?"

Dad's Car Wash, by Harry A. Sutherland. Aladdin, 1994. John had played with his trucks and cars all day and when evening came, he was very dirty and ready for "Dad's Car Wash," his evening bath, described in automotive terms. As dad is pictured giving John his bath, John's toy dinosaur is shown giving John's toy car the same loving wash.

Serefina under the Circumstances, by Phyllis Theroux. Greenwillow, 1999. Serefina's grandmother tells her she's "destined for greatness." Serefina loves that phrase, and is thrilled when grandmother asks her to keep a secret. Tomorrow is Serefina's brother's birthday and there will be a surprise birthday party for him. Will she be able to keep the secret? It is so difficult that, under the circumstances, could she be forgiven for telling? Read and find out.

Me & You: A Mother-Daughter Album, by Lisa Thiesing. Hyperion,1998. Children love to look at photo albums of their parents when they were little. Here's a picture book of photos of a mother as a child comparing her photos with those of her daughter, saying that she loved many of the things her daughter loves now.

A Place for Ben, by Jeanne Titherington. Mulberry, 1999. Ben needs a place of his own now that his brother Ezra's crib was moved into Ben's room. He finds the perfect private place in the corner of the shed. But it's a little lonely. Nobody seems to want to keep him company there. But one person is willing... which is the surprise for the reader.

What Mary Jo Shared, by Janice May Udry. Scholastic, 1991. At Mary Jo's school, they had a Sharing Time, when each child had a turn to share something they had brought. Mary Jo never shared anything. She was shy, and besides, she wanted to share something nobody else had thought of. Then she had an idea, and asked her father to come to school with her the next day. It was *her father* she shared with the class, and Mary Jo felt good; she had shared something nobody else had thought of sharing.

I'll Fix Anthony, by Judith Viorst. Aladdin, 1988. A little brother dreams of attaining the advanced age of six, and thinks of all the ways he will then get revenge on his older brother, Anthony.

Thanksgiving at Our House, by Wendy Watson. Clarion, 1994. A Thanksgiving dinner takes a great deal of preparation. The turkey and trimmings must be bought, the house must be cleaned. The day arrives. The kitchen is full of people. A happy family celebration!

Apple Juice Tea, by Martha Weston. Clarion Books, 1994. Polly doesn't know her grandmother, only gran's picture hanging on the wall. And when gran comes to visit, she seems to be a stranger. Then gran gets Polly to join her in a tea party and they become friends. When her grandmother goes away again, Polly can write to her and get letters back from her "tea party gran."

Max, by Ken Wilson-Max. Hyperion, 1998. With tabs to pull and flaps to lift, toddlers will love this simple story about a little boy, his house, his favorite food, and his pet pig named Max.

Do People Grow on Family Trees? Genealogy for Kids and Other Beginners — The Official Ellis Island Handbook, by Ira Wolfman, Workman Publishing 1991. Your family can play detective together as you solve the puzzle of your past. You can discover how to track down relatives, compile a family tree, and find out where to write for official documents.

All Those Secrets of the World, by Jane Yolen. Little, Brown, 1993. When her father goes off to war, Janie goes with her family to see him leave on a big ship. Later, while playing on the beach, her cousin Michael tells Janie that the little specks they see on the horizon are ships taking soldiers to war. Janie doesn't believe him at first, but Michael explains that one of the secrets of the world is that the ships only look small because they are so far away. When her father comes home a year later, he tells the little girl, "You're so big, Janie." And Janie whispers the secret of the world in her father's ear, in this beautiful and touching story.

Later, Rover, by Harriet Ziefert. Puffin, 1996. Using simple sentences and repetitive words, this appealing story tells of a little boy named Andy who asks the members of his family to play with him. Each one tells him, "Later, Andy." Their dog, Rover, however, is more than willing to play. What happens then, when Andy gets tired?

What Is Father's Day?; What Is Mother's Day? by Harriet Ziefert. HarperCollins, 1992. These two lift-the-flap books tell of a loving mouse family, and how the Little Mouse finds the way to surprise each parent on his or her special day.

Timothy Too! by Charlotte Zolotow. Houghton Mifflin, 1986. Little Timothy follows big brother John around everywhere and John wishes he wouldn't. Then Tim gets a friend of his own, and John misses his little brother's attention.

A Rose, a Bridge, and a Wild Black Horse, by Charlotte Zolotow. Harper, 1987. A small boy describes for his sister all of the things that he will do for her when he is grown up. He will pick the pinkest rose for her to smell, build her the biggest bridge in the world, and even tame a wild, black horse for her to ride. But best of all, they will explore the world together.

Section Seven

Encouraging Young Children's Positive Views of Friends

Section Seven
Encouraging
Young Children's
Positive Views
of Friends

Introduction

More important than toys or equipment, children need other children to play with.

A child may sit sadly alone on a swing, his feet dangling and his head hanging. Suddenly he is smiling and pumping high in the air, welcoming a sudden rush of boys and girls joining him at the swing set.

But, much as they may want to, children don't always know how to make friends. Some youngsters act like sad loners, unable to enter into play, while others may behave aggressively, hitting children or grabbing toys.

The contributors to this section show how the efforts of parents and teachers can help young children learn how to make friends. The authors provide important information about the characteristics of children who make friends easily, offer a myriad of practical suggestions as to how parents and teachers can help youngsters learn social skills, and give examples of enjoyable games and activities to encourage cooperation among young children.

SECTION SEVEN
ENCOURAGING YOUNG CHILDREN'S
POSITIVE VIEWS OF FRIENDS

Chapter 31
Children's
Friendships

Betty Farber

*You can find ways
to help your youngster
learn the positive results
of sharing.*

"Friends are as important to the young child as they are to us."
The Child Under Six James L. Hymes Jr.

Children need other children. They may tell you that they prize their friend because she has a giant toy robot, or because he can run faster than anybody. But the fact is that friendship is an important factor in your child's personal happiness. Friends help children to learn cooperation, negotiation and respect for other people's differences. Friendship helps children to learn to care about others.

Adult Role in Encouraging Friendships
Since friendships are so important, what can you, as a parent, do to encourage your child's interactions with her peers?

Provide opportunities for your preschooler to interact with others: invite a friend home, arrange a special outing with a few friends, or go to the park or playground where other children may be found.

Accept the fact that some children are more outgoing than others. It is best not to push a shy child, but to let her move at her own pace. Shy children may be overwhelmed by large groups. They usually feel more comfortable playing with one friend at a time. On the other hand, if your child seems too aggressive with other youngsters, explain how his behavior is affecting others, and suggest alternatives. For example, you might say, "She feels sad when you grab her toy. Ask her for a turn instead."

Learning to Share
Parents sometimes worry because their child isn't sharing his toys. Learning to cooperate and share is important in getting along with others. But young children will grow in their play development. They usually go from playing alone with their toys to *parallel play* — playing near other children without interacting with them — to *cooperative play* — sharing toys and ideas. Your child may not yet be at the stage of play development where he is ready to share.

One difficult situation that is familiar to parents is when two children want the same toy (such as a tricycle). A technique that aids in the sharing process is to ask the children to take turns with the favored toy. "You can go to the end of the block, and then it's Katie's turn." Or use a time limit. Set a kitchen timer that signals when time is up. "When the bell rings it's Jimmy's turn." If possible have the children set the timer. Don't make the time too long between "turns." Three minutes is about right. (Five minutes can be an eternity to a three year old.)

Help your child to learn to problem solve. When there is a conflict between her and her friends, ask <u>them</u> how they would solve it. For example, if children are building with blocks and one wants to build a house while the other wants a highway, ask <u>them</u> for possible solutions as to how they might solve the problem. You can be the interpreter, but let them decide which is best for them. Children can often come up with unique solutions that adults would not have thought of, but that satisfy the children's needs.

You can find ways to help your youngster learn the positive results of sharing. If your preschooler refuses to share his playthings, you could point out a few similar toys: "Look, here's a dump truck, a pickup truck and a fire truck. *Which one can Jeffrey play with?*" When your child answers, "The dump truck," you can praise him for sharing. With a loving pat you can say, "Thanks, honey. Jeffrey looks so happy because you shared your toy with him."

Chapter 32
Getting Along with Other Children

Anita Gurian & Ruth Formanek

*How do children
make friends?*

Let's watch Andrea as she plays with other children during the course of
one week:
Monday:
The children in the playgroup refuse to play with Andrea because she
pushes and shoves.
Tuesday:
Andrea watches other children but does not approach them.
Wednesday:
Andrea refuses to share her toys when her cousin comes to visit.
Thursday:
Andrea flits from one child to another.
Friday:
Andrea grabs other children's things.
Saturday:
Andrea plays only with the boys.
Sunday:
Andrea joins the other children and waits her turn on the slide.

If we watch 4 1/2-year-old Andrea only on *Monday, Wednesday,* and
Friday, we might be concerned that she's selfish and aggressive. If we watch
Andrea on *Tuesday,* we might be concerned that she's socially isolated. On
Thursday, she's a social butterfly. On *Sunday,* she's cooperative and thought-
ful. And we don't know what next *Monday* will bring.

Most children at some time will act in some or even all of the ways Andrea
did. They can't always be cooperative and social. "That's mine!" is a
frequently heard refrain on playgrounds. Some days a child may want to
share and to play with others; other days she may prefer to be alone in the
sandbox. She needs both experiences.

How do children make friends?
Steven Asher, a University of Illinois psychologist, believes that if we know
what makes some children socially successful, we can help those who aren't.
What are the characteristics of children who make friends easily?

• They get in touch and know how to break the ice.
They offer a greeting:
   "Hi, I'm Jennifer."
They ask for information:
   "What is your name? Where do you live?"
They invite participation:
   "Do you want to play with me? Do you want to come to my house?"

It's not only what they do but how they do it. They wait for children to
answer their questions; they give the message that they're available.

Less socially successful children are apt to be impatient, critical, demanding, or pleading in their strategies. They may just clumsily interrupt, grab things, act bossy, and whine. They may talk too much or not at all. Then, sensing rejection, they don't have the resources or the flexibility to change to another approach and the cycle of rejection perpetuates itself.

"You better be my friend or I'll tell on you!"

"I can so get in your game and I can beat you anytime!"

They stay in touch

Once the ice has been broken, the friendly child maintains the contact, sometimes by what she says, sometimes by what she does. Friendly children express their interest by nodding, looking at the other child, talking, expressing thanks. They express affection by hugging or saying, "I like you," or, "You're my friend."

They offer help or comfort. Again, how they do it seems to be more important than what they do. For example, too much hugging is unpleasant for some children.

They have fights but stay in touch

Socially adept children manage conflict well. They're able to assert their rights without being rejected. Aggressive children — those who, without provocation, initiate fights with others — are less likely to be accepted.

• Socially adept children do the following:

They state a personal right, need, or feeling:

"I'm playing with this right now."

"Stop pushing me. I don't like to be pushed."

They listen to another child and acknowledge the other child's feelings:

"I'm sorry you're crying."

They work out a compromise:

"I'll use it for a little while and then you can have it."

"When the little hand is on the three, you can have a turn."

They stand up against aggression and/or unreasonable demands:

"This is my toy and I won't let you take it away from me."

You can't really sit a child down and teach these skills verbatim, but studies show that they can be taught through imitating parents' behavior (modeling) and pretending to be different people in a social situation (role playing). Parents can also provide opportunities for lots of practice.

What's a Parent to Do?

Provide Varied Types of Social Experiences
Children need lots of active contacts in order to practice social skills. Invite other kids over to play, let your kids visit other kids, and set up supervised play groups when you can. Make sure your child has different types of play experiences: by themselves, with other children, and with parents and other adults.

Arrange for back-and-forth visits that involve the whole family. If you have the choice, try to live in a neighborhood where there are lots of children, adults of different ages, different backgrounds, and lifestyles, and interaction among neighbors.

At the same time, remember the importance of similarity between children who play together. Physically active toddlers seek each other out, as do more quiet children. Both adults and children generally choose friends similar to themselves in intelligence, interests, and values. For children, discovering someone similar serves as validation — it means they're okay.

Although in most cases friends resemble each other, some friendships are built on what looks like an opposite fit. Outgoing children may align themselves with quieter ones. They seem to complement each other.

Encourage friendships with children of the opposite sex. Don't always identify children by gender. Say "Let's invite a friend over," rather than "Let's invite a girl over." Don't divide activities by gender; make all games, activities, and toys available to all. Also encourage friendships with children of different ages.

Don't expect long-term relationships
Bear in mind that children's friendships at this age apt to be short-lived. Listen to Sally, age 4:

> **Sally:** Samara can't play; she's not our friend.
> **Teacher:** You played with her yesterday.
> **Sally:** Well, I hate her today.

Don't force sharing
Remember that adults don't always want to share either. Be sure your child doesn't have to share too much and too often. If you suggest that your child share a toy, see that she gets it back within a reasonable time. If a friend is coming to visit, put away any special toys that you know would be difficult for your child to hand over.

If children are not forced to give up their possessions, they'll discover at their own pace that it's sometimes fun to share. Two children can put blocks in a wagon; one pushes and one pulls. Two can build elaborate structures. You can explain that "Joey is playing at your house and he wants to play with you and your toys. Another time you'll go to Joey's house and you'll play with him and his toys." You'll have to say that many times. Most children have difficulty thinking of another time. It's <u>now</u> that counts. Be patient.

Expect some fighting
A punch or tap may not mean the same thing to your child as it does to you. If a child should strike out, don't punish her. Give her some feedback. "That punch hurt Joey. See, he's rubbing his arm." It's hard when your child is the one who gets punched, or scratched. Before you rush to her defense, however, be sure that your action doesn't prevent her from learning a valuable lesson — that of defending herself. Wait and see if she has a solution of her own before you leap to her defense.

Some techniques to ward off trouble before it begins
* *As a parent you can use verbal reminders, such as:*

   "Remember, if you'd like to play you can ask."

   "Remember, we can <u>talk</u> about how we feel instead of hitting."

   "You can't take that away from Marcy. When she's through you can have it. In the meantime, would you like to play with this?"

• *Put a time limit on a game or set a clock and say,*
"When the clock rings, it will be Jenny's turn."
• *Present toys that both children can use together, like a ball, wagon, or set of doll's dishes.*
• *A story, song, or break for juice are useful diversions when you see conflict brewing.*

When a child needs extra help with aggression

At one time it was believed that if a child expressed his aggressive feelings, "let off steam," the aggression would then be discharged into action and would disappear. This has not proved to be true. In fact, studies show that permission to be aggressive stimulates and increases aggression rather than reducing it. What is helpful is to make it very clear that aggression is simply not allowed. Stop it when it does occur. After a cooling-down period, help the child explore other ways to handle the situation.

When aggressive behavior persists

Despite all your efforts, it often happens that children continue their aggressive and disruptive behavior. At such times a penalty system can be helpful. Here are some points to keep in mind:

• *Help children to avoid punishment by using an early warning system:* "Raisins are not for throwing." If he still continues, you say, "I'll have to take the box of raisins away. They're not for throwing." And be sure to follow through on your warnings.

• *Remember that the punishment should be a logical consequence of the behavior; it should be related to the offense.* If a child is disruptive, removal from the group until he can control himself is a logical action.

• *Don't make the penalty too harsh (go to your room for four hours!).* This makes the child angry and resentful, and he won't make the connection between the crime and the punishment. Some families deprive their children of television as punishment. We know a 7 year old who has accumulated so much deprivation time, she won't see any programs until she's 41.

• *Avoid drawn-out lecturing, scolding or explanation* — which may, in fact, represent the attention the child is seeking. If you decide that attention-seeking is indeed at the root of the trouble, ask yourself why this might be so and try to provide attention in other ways.

Withdrawn, shy, and anxious behavior

A certain amount of reticence is appropriate in all new situations. It shows that the child can distinguish between familiar and strange people and situations. Moreover, Jerome Kagan, a Harvard University psychologist, suggests that shy, inhibited children may later develop some skills that are positive. Their uncertainty and vigilance help them to become intellectually curious. If the child remains anxious or panics, let her know you know she's upset.

• *Some don'ts:*
   Don't push her to interact before she's ready.
   Don't negatively compare her to a more outgoing child.
   Don't laugh at or belittle her social fears.
   Don't label her as shy; this sets up expectations for her behavior and the label may stick.

• *Some dos:*
   You can say, "That's okay, you can talk when you feel like it." Remind her there's no rush, that she has control over what she does or does not do.

   It's also helpful in alleviating fears with some children to remind them of previous successes. "Remember when you went to Jimmy's house? You were a little quiet until you got to know the children better. This is like that time."

   Expose her to other children who will encourage relaxed interaction. Sometimes arranging for her to play with a younger child relieves the pressure. A younger child may offer opportunities to practice new ways of relating that she might be reluctant to try with children her own age.

Tolerate ambivalence
Ambivalence is characteristic of all children. Young children have not yet learned that one can like and dislike the same person. When they argue with a friend, they often decide quickly that they can't ever be friends anymore. You're either a friend or an enemy. Children need to learn that it's all right to feel two ways about one person, that they can be ambivalent.

You can help by saying something like: "It looks like you feel two ways about Adam; you like him but sometimes you feel angry with him and you don't like him. Everybody feels that way sometimes." Saying "Can't you ever make up your mind?" is not helpful and may make the child feel guilty, confused, and less apt to verbalize his feelings at another time.

Children's friendships, similar to those of adults, do not contain only love and affection; there are frequent tempestuous moments. Providing children with a variety of experiences, under the protection of caring adults, enables them to adjust to new people and new situations — and to learn about their world.

Chapter 33
Helping Preschoolers Learn Social Skills

Michael K. Meyerhoff

*...parents need to recognize
that it is during the preschool years
that their child must be taught
how to interact
with his fellow human beings.*

Peter is an extremely bright and apparently happy kindergarten pupil. He will gladly recite all the state capitals and the multiplication table up to "12 times 12." The problem is that he is happiest when he is by himself. Although his teachers and classmates admire him, they don't like him very much. While Peter may be destined to collect honors and awards, he may find himself becoming increasingly isolated and lonely.

Success in life is more than being personally secure and intellectually talented. Because every individual must operate as part of a larger society, it is necessary to be socially skillful as well. The foundation for these interpersonal skills is formed during the preschool years.

Most children emerge from the preschool years armed with considerable abilities for coping with the physical world and how it works. However, far too few have been equipped with superb abilities for dealing with the people who populate that world.

Parents need to teach their children social skills.
Most parents want to help their children grow in every area of development: physical, emotional, intellectual, and social. Mothers and fathers generally recognize that their child must learn to value himself and control himself, and that he must be "socialized" to a certain extent. They pay attention to nurturing emotional security and self-esteem. They use appropriate discipline to guide their child's behavior, and they take time to teach proper eating, dressing, and toileting techniques.

In addition, parents need to recognize that it is during the preschool years that their child must be taught how to interact with his fellow human beings. Because they may assume that social skills will evolve naturally or be picked up casually, they do not necessarily provide their child with relevant lessons.

What kinds of lessons can parents provide?
Fortunately, helping a child develop interpersonal skills is not difficult. However, the lessons need to match the child's degree of readiness. Also the methods used must suit the child's stage of development.

Since babies' first interactions are with adults, it makes sense for parents to focus first on the interactions between children and adults (**adult-oriented abilities**) and then concentrate on interactions between children (**peer-related abilities**).

Adult-Oriented Abilities. Shortly after the first birthday, socially skillful children start to perfect two very valuable interpersonal abilities. One is the ability *to get the attention of other people.* The second is *to use other people as resources.* Obviously, at birth, babies could do both of these things simply by crying. But now, they can do so <u>intentionally</u> rather than <u>reflexively</u> (involuntarily). And more importantly, they can do so in a variety of ways that are infinitely more effective and considerably more "socially acceptable" as well.

Getting other people's attention

Promoting proper attention-getting is simple. As a child approaches the end of the first year, she gradually will begin using the cry not only as a <u>reflexive</u> reaction to physical discomfort, but also as an <u>intentional</u> tool *to alleviate boredom, express frustration,* and a number of other less critical purposes. After a while, alert mothers and fathers can start discerning the difference between "emergency" cries and others. Although they should continue responding immediately to the former, they can gradually start showing a little restraint in responding to the latter. This forces the child to explore other options, such as approaching the adult and tugging on a shirtsleeve, calling out a specific name, waiting patiently until the adult has finished another chore or conversation, etc.

However, parents must be careful not to expect too much too soon. A child who is not yet fully mobile won't be able to approach easily, a child who is not yet speaking won't be able to call out "Mommy," and a child who does not yet have a substantial attention span won't be able to wait patiently for very long. The trick is *to look for slight but steady improvements, and to lavishly praise and generously reward each small increment of progress.*

Using other people as resources

As far as using others as resources is concerned, a child always will need to use his mother and father to fulfill his nurturing needs. But as he approaches and passes the first birthday, he becomes increasingly capable of various "self-help" skills and can start "taking care of himself" to a certain extent. At the same time, however, he develops more numerous and complex needs in other areas. As he becomes capable of getting around on his own, he starts to explore and investigate his environment independently. As a result, from time to time, he will require comfort when he gets hurt, assistance when he gets stuck, etc.

How parents handle their diminishing role in the nurturing area and their growing role in other areas makes a big difference in how well their child learns to use other people as resources in a proper manner. It is necessary for parents to be perceptive and patient, and to try to be careful not to do too much or too little for the child. For example, *a child whose parents do not recognize his growing capacities to use a spoon or to pull on his shirt may not give him ample opportunities to attempt these things himself.* And even if they see his willingness to try, they may be in too much of a hurry and not give him the chance to make a full effort. Consequently, they end up doing every-thing for him, and the child learns to depend on other people to do even those things he may be able to do himself.

On the other hand, a child whose parents do not pay much attention to his explorations and investigations may not be prepared to provide the sort of assistance he genuinely will need on occasion. As a result, the child eventually stops approaching them, even when he really requires their help. In other words, *parents must adjust their behavior so they teach their child to readily use them as resources, but only after first determining that he cannot do something for himself.*

Peer-Related Abilities. Eventually, socially skillful children acquire many sophisticated peer-related abilities, such as how to *share, cooperate, take turns, both lead and follow comfortably, and compete productively.* However, contrary to what might be considered "common sense," a lot of early exposure to other children is not necessary to promote the development of strong social skills such as these. While experience is, indeed, an important element in any learning situation, it will be largely useless if children do not have the capacity to process it in a meaningful way.

Prior to approximately two years of age, although children may be capable of genuine social relations with their parents and other adults, they will generally tend to treat other children like inanimate objects. They may play side-by-side on occasion, but they won't really interact with each other very much.

Between two and three years of age, while they may show an increasing interest in pursuing various activities with agemates, they will only be able to learn about their peers a little bit at a time and in a gradual fashion Consequently, while periodic exposure to other children during infancy and toddlerhood is probably a good idea, extensive exposure should not be regarded as critical or even significantly beneficial.

In fact, it is important to note that infants and toddlers learn social skills almost exclusively through simple trial-and-error and imitation. When surrounded primarily by adults, they will have mostly "civilized" models to copy and ordinarily will receive feedback based upon sensible social rules. On the other hand, when immersed among agemates, they may see a lot of hitting, biting, hair-pulling, and other inappropriate behaviors. And more worrisome, the "success" of certain interpersonal strategies may be determined merely by who is stronger or more aggressive, rather than by who is acting in a more socially acceptable manner. Therefore, mothers and fathers must make sure that any group into which their very young child is placed will be closely and carefully supervised by responsible adults.

In any event, although the sophisticated abilities mentioned above do not blossom fully until well after toddlerhood, they do start to surface gradually during the <u>third year of life.</u> And it is critical to note that *two important mental capacities must be formed before a child can learn such complex social skills.*

First, since some rather complicated instructions are involved, the child must have a reasonably good command of the language. *Second,* since it is necessary to appreciate the perspective of another child, he must emerge from the "egocentrism" that is characteristic of infants and toddlers. In the beginning, a child *sees everything solely from his own point of view,* and it takes time for him to understand that this is not the only way to look at a given situation.

As a child approaches *the third birthday* and his language, memory, and logical capacities improve, parents can begin employing progressively more substantial verbal explanations to teach social skills. As relevant situations arise, they can suggest various interpersonal strategies, provide reasons for using them, and describe a range of possible results as seen from different points of view. At first, it may be rather difficult for the child to grasp some of these explanations in the abstract, so parents should capitalize on his strong inclination to engage in "make believe" activities. By asking him to "act out" a situation or to demonstrate a series of events using dolls, puppets, pictures, or other props, they can make the lessons more concrete and give him the opportunity to play a variety of roles.

By the way, learning to play a variety of roles well is a critical element in social skill development. For instance, many children are excellent leaders, but they fall apart when required to be followers. And many children enjoy engaging in competition when they are sure they can win, but they avoid any contest if there is a chance they may lose. Therefore, mothers and fathers must make a conscious effort to fully explain the joys, challenges, and benefits of all positions in truly satisfying social relations.

Media Influences
It should be noted that while not as powerful as parents, the characters in *books, movies, and television programs* do provide models that a child may tend to imitate as he develops social skills. In addition, he may pick up some lessons through what is called "vicarious learning." It is not always necessary for a child actually to attempt an interpersonal strategy and receive direct feedback himself. If he perceives a character in a book, movie,

or television program to be very much like himself, then what is done by and happens to the character sometimes is personalized by the child. Consequently, for better or worse, books, movies, and television programs may play a significant role in promoting social skill development.

With this in mind, it is definitely a good idea for parents to expose their child to what they consider suitable books, movies, and television programs. On the other hand, they also should recognize that it is practically impossible to shield him completely from less desirable material. The important thing to remember is that the input of his mother and father and what he experiences at home will ultimately be the most influential factors in promoting his social skill development. Therefore, parents should not rely on outside sources to provide positive models and guidance, and they should be prepared to discuss with their child whatever negative models and guidance he inevitably will encounter.

Chapter 34
Learning to
Play Together

Bette Simons

*Children three, four and five years of age
often have wonderful play periods
with each other.*

Parents and teachers hear it often, sometimes with tears, sometimes with anger, "She won't let me play." Another common refrain goes, "They keep chasing me," followed by a flood of tears. Adults know that being left out or being bullied is painful, but what can they do about it? How can adults help children gain ideas for independent action, instead of learning to weep for help?

Children three, four and five years of age often have wonderful play periods with each other. They build ingenious hideouts by turning over a plastic slide, gathering big boxes and tires and covering it all with a blanket. Look inside and you see little faces mysteriously happy with "sand cakes" or a "magic monster machine."

These children have been able to find playmates who agreed as to what they were going to play. Even if the project turned from house to fort to jail before it became a final decision, these children engaged in teamwork. Someone may have been a leader, some arguments might have occurred, but they had a plan and cooperated, however stormily, to finish their project and enjoy it.

Adults who intervene wisely during such play times can help to provide lasting social skills. This begins early in the preschool years.

As two year olds join a preschool, they learn to trust the teacher when mother leaves. Next they must learn to trust other children while they play.

A toddler may go from angrily hitting another child, then running away, to hitting and then hugging apologetically. Adults should know that this is progress. When the child's vocabulary gets larger, adults can then say, "Use your words."

When children of any age interact with each other in preschool settings it is expected there will be some experimentation. There are many ways to acquire a popular toy from another child — from grabbing it to pleading for it. Also a child can enter play in the dress-up area by plunking herself down in the doll bed or carrying the bed off to another location.

Special adult guidance is necessary when children seem to settle on consistent behaviors that don't work well for themselves (like being a sad loner) or don't work well for others, (like being a constant aggressor when others are playing).

Some teachers feel that conflicts involving rejection are important for children as they learn to develop social skills. Other teachers sympathize with the child who seems chronically rejected. They make the rule for all the children: you can't say, "You can't play." These teachers do not want young children to learn to exclude others. They believe that this only sets the stage for biases and prejudices about the ways other people act or look.

To try and help a child who has been excluded from dramatic play with a pretend family, the teacher may suggest, "You could be a letter carrier delivering a package, or the Avon Lady with lipstick samples." While she can't guarantee that these ideas will work, she can make suggestions that the child may not have thought of.

Just as there are children who are born with musical or mathematical abilities, social skills come more easily to some. Children who do well socially often have an attitude of self confidence about their place among their peers. They are flexible if rejected. Such children have been observed to enter groups by playing quietly nearby until they are recognized and accepted.

But every play yard has its little roving warriors, energized by their growing sense of power from riding the trikes so well and so fast. They are ready to whack over a line of sand castles, or take over the already inhabited corrugated refrigerator box.

Those that cry for help, those that make others cry, and those who are naturally adept socially, are all learning something from the way adults understand and guide their attempts to work and play together.

Learning to accept a new player to a group and learning how to be a good player takes time for preschoolers and patience for adults.

Strategies Adults Can Use

Help children to substitute verbal for physical responses: Watch children under three for their growing ability with language.   Express what the child feels in telegraphic form. "Mad. You are mad! Say that. Don't hit."

Use two puppets to act out an argument over a toy. Use the words, "Your turn" and "My turn." Refer to children as friends. "You made your friend happy with your hug." Young children don't hear long paragraphs of explanations about why something is right or wrong. Adults are more effective if they act firmly and with great expression, but talk simply.

Help the left-out child: The child who feels or feigns helplessness about joining a group or having a friend can become exasperating to adults if the child's need for help is overlooked.

When such a child is in a neutral mood, not upset about something, sit and help the child observe how others enter groups. One child may need to see how to state his needs louder and more assertively. Another should notice how using pleasantries is more successful than making demands. When you see the child make efforts towards independence, be sure to reinforce this conduct with praise.

Inviting another child to play at your home is helpful in overcoming your child's feeling of helplessness or the inability to play joyously. Put toys that your child finds hard to share in the closet, so your child's rights are protected, while providing time to gain experience working out problems.

When your child is reluctant to talk about an upsetting situation, describe what is happening, "You are so mad you can't talk. You want the girls to play with you and they won't. It's okay to be quiet and sad about this for a while. You figured out how to do that hard puzzle last night and you can figure this out too." It is always helpful to refer to a child's past successes, to instill confidence in the ability to tackle anything new.

Empower children to solve problems: When problems of play arise, stop the action right away. For example, take a ball that is being grabbed. Then describe what is happening. "Jane is crying so hard her face is red." "Chelsea is so mad she is biting her sweater." Then ask the children, "What shall we do about this?" When adults try this for the first time, children often look angry or blank. Just say, "I see you are too upset to think right now. Let's get a drink of water and then see if you have any ideas." Making it a habit to ask for children's ideas about play conflicts, gets them away from relying on adults to act as King Solomon.

When children say, "He hit me," it's a good rule of thumb to ask, "What happened before that?" There is often a confession, "I hit him," and the children take off, after the adult reminds them to use their words next time. Teachers can use puppets to enact problems during circle time. Parents can use stuffed animals, or sit and play with toy figures. These can have a fight and the parent shows it settled in a way that is good for all.

Expect children to be fickle: Today's best friend may not be willing to play the next day. It's hurtful, but like any crisis, a learning opportunity. How to win back a friend, or be one to someone else challenges thinking skills. It's best for adults not to take sides, but just narrate what happens, or be empathetic.

Don't be afraid to set firm limits: So often, adults supervising children's play need to act swiftly, and according to their feelings. Children should know that adults are astounded at behaviors that are hurtful to others. "Stop! That hurts him. No more shovels for you!" is appropriate if the adult is upset by the child's behavior. However, if the adult can remain calm in this situation, he or she might sound like this: "It looks like you got so mad you couldn't talk — and you hurt her. You need to get stronger about stopping yourself. Yesterday I saw you yell instead of hitting. That was a better thing to do."

Sometimes count to 10: Children in a group often take off like a covey of birds, grabbing a toy or threatening mayhem. Like the birds, they often settle down again, before a teacher can get instructions out of her mouth. Outrageously insulting remarks at the lunch table may send a child into gales of laughter as often as tears. The adult should learn to count to 10 before interfering.

Use books: Good children's literature takes children into other families, other schools and other situations where they can experience through characters, the hurts and happiness that making friends brings.

One of the best resources for adults guiding children's play is a listing of books on different subjects, in order to know exactly which one is needed for a certain child. This source can be the children's librarian, a good bookstore, as well as the Resources on page 269.

Change the environment: Rather than trying to change the child, change the environment. It's obvious that if a crawling baby is knocking down a carefully made block construction, moving the block builder or the baby to a another place puts everyone in a better temper. In preschools, children experiencing difficulty with others might be given a supportive and sympathetic invitation to play in a different room or yard, given a different piece of equipment, or offered a long drink of water. It's natural to need a change of place and pace when learning something as hard as getting along.

Adults are the models for good social relationships: Teachers model good social relationships when they are easygoing about the chores of preschool work and have friendly interactions with other adults. Parents show children they care about neighbors, friends, and family.

Be tolerant: The child who seems to cause a storm over every social encounter may be a nuclear physicist some day. The child who mourns about every rejection may write sensitive poetry in the future. The one who demands the "fast trike" and rides it like a racing car, may turn out to be an outstanding sprinter in high school. It takes empathy, time and skill to help young children grow in their ability to relate to each other.

Chapter 35
Encouraging Cooperation Through Games and Activities

Rae Pica

Competition is not developmentally
appropriate for young children.

The children slowly circle the chairs, listening for the music to stop. When it does they scramble frantically, grabbing and pushing as they compete for a seat, because there is one less chair than there are children! One child, who wasn't quick enough, must leave the game and sit it out watching as the next round begins. As the game continues, more chairs and more children are removed to the sidelines.

This is the traditional version of Musical Chairs. When one chair and one child remain, the game is over. There is one winner — and many losers. And unless you were the most athletic among your peers, you probably recall very well how it felt to be one of the losers — whether in an elimination activity, at the end of an organized game, or when chosen last for a team. It felt terrible!

Consider instead the following scenario. *The children slowly circle the chairs, listening for the music to stop. When it does they scramble, giggling, trying to find a way for everyone to fit on the available chairs. With each round, the goal of getting everyone onto the diminishing number of chairs becomes even more challenging. By the end of the game, the children have erupted into uncontrollable laughter as they all try to crowd onto the one remaining chair.*

This is *Cooperative* Musical Chairs, in which everyone wins — in more ways than one. When children are given opportunities to work together toward a solution or common goal, they know they each contribute to the success of the venture. Every child plays a vital role in the outcome, and each accepts the responsibility involved in fulfilling that role. The children also learn to solve problems in creative and productive ways, to become tolerant of others' ideas, and to accept the similarities and differences of other children. Furthermore, cooperative activities are far less likely to cause the feelings of inferiority that so often result from the comparisons made during competitive situations.

Of course, we've all heard the expressions "It's a dog-eat-dog world," and "It's a jungle out there." The assumption, for years, has been that pitting children against one another is necessary preparation for surviving in such a world. But a little bit of losing goes a long way. And certainly a more important skill is the ability to get along — to live and work — with one another.

For preschoolers, it is unconditional acceptance and an early sense of security that later help them to deal with rejection and face problems head-on. When given a choice, preschoolers will opt for cooperative activities rather than competitive ones. Not only do they find cooperative activities more enjoyable, but research tells us that the motivation to compete is *learned* — and young children simply haven't had time to be indoctrinated into society's competitive ways. Here's what else the research shows.

Competition:
• Is not developmentally appropriate for young children and hurries them into adulthood.
• Causes people to believe they aren't responsible for what happens to them and contributes to the concept of learned helplessness.
• Is detrimental to self-esteem.
• Results in less spontaneity and creativity.
• Significantly increases aggression.
• Invites the use of cheating and other antisocial behaviors in order to win.

Cooperation:
• Gets things done at work and at school more effectively than competition.
• Is more conducive to psychological health.
• Leads to friendlier feelings among participants.
• Promotes a feeling of being in control of one's life.
• Increases self-esteem.
• Results in greater sensitivity and trust toward others.
• Develops patience with peers.
• Enhances feelings of belonging.
• Increases motivation.
• Promotes prosocial behaviors.

The research also shows that America is the most competitive nation in the world. Competition, therefore, is so prevalent in the classroom and on the playing field that parents who try to teach their children to work *with* rather than *against* others will find it's not an easy task. But the evidence can be seen in the research results above: whatever amount of effort it takes, teaching children to cooperate is worth it!

Suggestions for Parents

The experts agree that a child's performance should never be compared with that of someone else's, whether it be a sibling's, a classmate's, a neighbor's, or a parent's. And winning as the only acceptable outcome *must* be de-emphasized. Affection and approval should be granted to children *unconditionally*. If we want to help our children improve certain skills, it is far more effective — and confidence-building — to provide specific feedback, stressing self-comparison. For example, a child learning to perform a forward roll might be told "You tucked your head to your chest much better this time." A child involved in a game situation should hear all the things she or he did well, regardless of who won or lost.

To foster prosocial behavior, parents can choose play materials intended for two or more children (like teeter-totters and board games). Research with preschoolers has shown that such materials foster greater prosocial play behavior than do toys designed for use by a single child. But it is in organized game playing that children are most often confronted with competition. Too often, they are expected to play games that have rules that are intended for adults and are therefore developmentally inappropriate. Parents should ensure that the game fits the child, rather than the other way around.

When given a choice, preschoolers prefer cooperative activities to competitive ones. And, again, studies have shown that cooperative games actually increase the cooperative social interaction among young children. Following are several cooperative activities. Suggest them the next time you host a children's party or any time two or more children get together — or you and your preschooler can do the partner activities yourselves!

Mirror Game: Participants pair off and stand facing each other. One partner performs a series of simple movements (standing in place), which the second partner mirrors. After a while, the partners reverse roles. The object is not to try to trick each other but to resemble a mirror reflection as closely as possible!

Shadow Game: This is similar to the previous activity, but in this game one partner stands with his or her back to the second partner and performs various movements that the latter "shadows." These movements can be performed in place or can move throughout the room. Again, the partners eventually reverse roles so both have a chance to lead.

Footsie Rolls: Participants pair off and lie on their backs with the soles of their feet together. The object in this activity is for partners to roll over without their feet breaking contact. This one takes a lot of cooperation and enough room to move safely and is loads of fun!

Touch and Move: This activity requires partners to connect various body parts, which you assign, and to discover how many ways they can move while remaining connected. You can ask the children to connect one or both hands, elbows, knees, or feet. Backs, bottoms, and tops of heads are also possibilities!

Musical Hoops: This game is another alternative to Musical Chairs. When the music starts, the players walk all around the hula hoops that have been scattered about the room. When the music stops, they are to step inside the hoop closest to them. In one version of the game, you suggest a different motor skill (jumping, hopping, galloping, etc.) each time the music starts. In another, as in Cooperative Musical Chairs, a hoop is removed with each round and the children must share the remaining ones, even when there is just one hoop left! (One solution is for players to each place a foot inside the hoop.)

Bean Bag Freeze: Each player moves throughout the room with a bean bag on her or his head. If the bean bag falls off, that player must remain frozen in place until another player returns the fallen bean bag to the frozen player's head — without losing his or her own!

Group Balance: The players form a circle and place their hands on the shoulders of the players beside them. You then issue challenges for the children: 1) to stand on one foot only, 2) rise onto tiptoe (on both feet), 3) rise onto tiptoe with knees bent, 4) stand on one foot with free foot extended into center of circle, 5) rise onto tiptoe and bend forward at the waist, etc. The object of the activity is to maintain a steady balance through-out all of the challenges! (You might even suggest that the children count aloud the number of seconds they're able to remain steady.)

Let's Slither: Players begin by pairing off and stretching out on their stomachs, one in front of the other. The player in back takes hold of the ankles of the player in front, forming a two-person "snake" that starts to slither across the floor. This two-person snake then connects with another two-person snake, and the process continues until the entire group has formed one big snake!

Resources for Section Seven: Encouraging Young Children's Positive Views of Friends

<u>FOR</u> <u>ADULTS</u>

Howdy Do Me and You: Getting-Along Activities for You and Your Young Child, by Linda Allison and Martha Weston. Little, Brown, 1996. A lively book about getting along with friends, neighbors, and family members, filled with activities that you and your child can do together.

Vaccinate Your Infant Against "The Terrible Twos." This booklet provides a step-by-step behavior management plan for preventing temper tantrums, discipline difficulties, and other serious social problems during toddlerhood and the preschool years. Prepared by Dr. Michael K. Meyerhoff, it may be obtained by sending $3.00 plus a self-addressed, stamped envelope to: The Epicenter Inc., PO Box 6264, Lindenhurst, IL 60046. (Cost for multiple copies available upon request.)

The Big Book of Recipes for Fun, by Carolyn Buhai Haas. CBH Publishing, 1980. If you're looking for lots of imaginative activities to keep your child happily involved, this is the book for you.

Movement Activities for Early Childhood, by Carol Totsky Hammett. Human Kinetics, 1992. This collection of 100-plus child-tested movement activities makes learning new skills fun for preschoolers.

So This Is Normal Too? Teachers & Parents Working Out Developmental Issues in Young Children, by Deborah Hewitt. Redleaf Press, 1995. This paperback was written to help guide parents, teachers, and providers in working out developmental issues in young children, such as separation, toilet training, and socializing. It includes chapters such as: *I Want to Play Too: Joining a Group of Players,* and *It's Mine, Mine, Mine: Turn Taking.*

Pathways to Play: Developing Play Skills in Young Children, by Sandra Heidemann and Deborah Hewitt. Redleaf Press, 1992. This is a resource for teachers who want to support the hard-to-play-with child. It uses a 10-step checklist that pinpoints the skill a child is lacking, helping the teacher to assist the child to find the pathway to successful social skills.

The Child Under Six, by James L. Hymes, Jr. Consortium, RI, 1994. The author was a national authority on early education who taught generations of parents and teachers how to raise and teach young children.

No Contest: The Case Against Competition, by Alfie Kohn. Houghton Mifflin, 1992. This book is described as the first comprehensive book to show why competition is often damaging. It refutes the myths that competition builds character and is an instinctive part of human nature. This book is must reading for every parent!

Raising Good Children, by Thomas Lickona. Bantam, 1994. This work supplies solid guidance for helping a child develop a life-long sense of honesty, decency, and respect for others.

The Cooperative Sports & Games Book: Challenge Without Competition, by Terry Orlick. Pantheon, 1978. This collection of cooperative activities was written by a sports psychologist who has conducted considerable research on cooperation and competition. It book contains over 100 cooperative games.

The Second Cooperative Sports & Games Book, by Terry Orlick. Kendall-Hunt, 1996. This volume consists of 200-plus additional games for players of all ages, including toddlers. The activities emphasize imagination as well as cooperative skills.

You Can't Say You Can't Play, by Vivian Gussin Paley. Harvard University Press, 1992. Filling the pages with vignettes about real children, a creative writer and teacher mixes fantasy and reality as she expresses her philosophy about fairness and rejection.

Experiences in Movement with Music, Activities & Theory, by Rae Pica. Delmar, 1995. This text explores the role of movement in the child's physical, social, emotional, and cognitive development.

Preschoolers Moving & Learning, by Rae Pica, with music by Richard Gardzina. Human Kinetics, 1990. This is a complete movement program featuring 200 movement activities and 5 audiocassettes of original music, all in a three-ring binder.

Everybody Wins: 393 Non-competitive Games for Young Children, by Jeffrey Sobel. Walker Publishing, 1984. The games in this book are designed for children aged 3 to 10 and are intended to promote feelings of self-worth and confidence in children.

The Self-Respecting Child, by Allison Stallibrass. Addison-Wesley, 1989. This work makes a powerful case for the importance of play during the first few years of life; and it emphasizes the numerous physical activities that occupy so much of the time of very young children, particularly as they underlie mental and social development. The author has had extensive experience with "free choice" playgroups for two- to five-year-old children, and she also is an avid student of the child development literature, especially the works of Piaget dealing with play. In her view, the best conditions for the growth of self-respect involve many opportunities to choose activities for oneself while learning to interact with other children.

FOR CHILDREN

Best Friends Together Again, by Aliki. Greenwillow, 1995. A happy reunion takes place when Peter, who had moved away, comes back for a visit with his best friend, Robert. Some small things have changed, but the two boys will always remain friends and will look forward to each other's visits.

Overnight at Mary Bloom's, by Aliki. Greenwillow, 1987. When a little girl spends the night at a grown-up friend's house, they cook, walk the pets, feed the baby, and have a lovely visit together.

The Snow Fairy and the Spaceman, by Catherine Anholt. Delacorte Press, 1991. For her birthday costume party, a little girl is dressed as a snow fairy. The children arrive and are happily playing games, except the little boy dressed as a spaceman. He hides under the table; cries when a balloon pops; creeps out in the backyard, and wishes his mother would come to take him home. But when the spaceman rescues the snow fairy from a fall, they become friends and the spaceman is glad he came.

A Friend for Growl Bear, by Margot Austin. HarperCollins, 1999. Adapted from the 1951 book about Growl Bear, with new illustrations by David McPhail. A little bear wants a friend, but all of the other creatures are afraid of his growl. Only old owl can figure out what the problem is, with happy results.

The Little Red Hen, by Byron Barton. HarperCollins, 1993. With bright, childlike illustrations, the author/illustrator tells the well-known story of the little red hen who asks her friends for help with planting, threshing, and grinding the wheat. "Not I," says each of them. Then it is time to eat the bread she has baked. And her friends reap the consequences of their non-cooperative behavior.

Make Friends, Zachary! by Muriel Blaustein. HarperCollins, 1990. Zachary has fun when he is just with his Mom and Dad, but when he plays with other children, he gets into trouble. To help him make friends, his Mom and Dad invite his cousin Alfie to join them on a camping trip. There is adventure and humor as the two cousins become friends.

Tumble Bumble, by Felicia Bond. Front Street, HarperFestival, 1999. In a spinoff from Goldilocks' tale, this story, told in lively verse, has nine new animal friends end up in a bed in a little boy's house.

Harry and Willy and Carrothead, by Judith Caseley. Greenwillow, 1991. Harry was born with no left hand, but he was fitted for a prosthesis when he was four. At five, he starts school and meets Willy and Carrothead. Carrothead hates that name; his real name is Oscar. These three appealing boys play together, learn about each other's feelings, and become great friends.

Three Wishes, by Lucille Clifton. Doubleday, 1992. "Find a penny on New Year's Day with your birthday year on it, and you can make three wishes on it and the wishes will come true! It happened to me," says Nobie. She's with her friend Victor when she finds the penny. She makes two wishes and when she asks her mother what her third wish should be, her mother's wise words help Nobie understand what is really important in life.

Best Friends, by Miriam Cohen. Simon & Schuster, 1971. Jim was almost sure Paul was his best friend. But that day things happened at nursery school to make them both feel almost like enemies. Then they come to the rescue of some unhatched chicks, and they no longer doubt their friendship.

Will I Have a Friend? by Miriam Cohen. Macmillan, 1967. Jim is concerned about finding a friend when he attends nursery school for the first time.

Cranberry Valentine, by Wende and Harry Devlin. Aladdin, 1992. Mr. Whiskers of Cranberryport admits to Maggie and her grandmother that he has never received a valentine. Mysteriously, he begins to receive fancy valentines without signatures. Who can be sending them?

Metropolitan Cow, written and illustrated by Tim Egan. Houghton Mifflin, 1996. Bennett Gibbons, a dignified little calf, makes friends with Webster, a little pig who is just his age. But Bennett's parents aren't happy with the friendship. What happens next makes some important points (always with a light touch) about compatibility among friends with different backgrounds.

Zinnia and Dot, by Lisa Campbell Ernst. Puffin, 1995. Zinnia and Dot are two boastful hens who are always fighting about whose eggs are lovelier. When a weasel steals all but one of their eggs, they fight over the ownership of the remaining egg. But the weasel returns to claim the last egg, and the two hens, cooperating at last, drive him away.

Two Greedy Bears, Adapted from a Hungarian Folk Tale, by Mirra Ginsburg. Aladdin, 1998, Two bear cubs go out to see the world. But they are always trying to compete with each other: when one is hungry, the other is hungrier; when one has a stomach ache, the other has a bigger one. They see a cheese lying in the road. Because they are so competitive, they are outwitted by a sly fox, who uses their greedy natures to get to eat the cheese himself.

My Friends, by Taro Gomi. Chronicle, 1995. In this story, first published in Japan, a little girl tells how she learned many things from her friends: she learned to jump from her friend the dog, to run from her friend the horse, to read from her friends the books, and to play from her friends at school.

Jamaica and Brianna, by Juanita Havill. Sandpiper, 1996. When Jamaica wears hand-me-down boots, her friend Brianna teases her. Even when Jamaica gets new boots, it doesn't help the situation. She and her friend are angry with each other until they learn to tell each other about their feelings, and repair their friendship.

That Toad Is Mine! by Barbara Shook Hazen. HarperFestival, 1998. In this playful story in rhyme, two friends who share everything can't figure out how to share a toad hopping down the road.

Jessica, by Kevin Henkes. Greenwillow, 1989. Jessica was Ruthie's best friend. She went everywhere Ruthie went . "There is no Jessica," said Ruthie's parents, just because they couldn't see her. On the first day of kindergarten, Ruthie's mother said, "I think Jessica should stay home." But she came anyway. And when Ruthie was standing on line, a little girl asked to be her partner. When she told Ruthie her name — guess what it was!

Spot Sleeps Over, by Eric Hill. Puffin, 1996. Spot, the charming little puppy, goes to sleep at his friend's house and they have a wonderful time playing together. But his mom knows that bedtime in a strange house will be smoother if she brings over his favorite possession. Toddlers will love this simple story with illustrations that include flaps you can lift.

A Bargain for Frances, by Russell Hoban. HarperFestival, 1999. Frances and Thelma are good companions most of the time. But when Thelma sells Frances her old plastic tea set, there's some real friction between the two friends.

A Friend for Little Bear, by Harry Horse. Candlewick Press, 1996. A tiny bear lives on a desert island. He pulls from the sea all different items that float by. But he discovers that the most important thing he ever rescued from the sea is his friend, the wooden horse. A meaningful message about friendship.

It's My Birthday! by Pat Hutchins. Greenwillow, 1999. It's Billy's birthday, and he's invited all his little monster friends to his party. But when he gets new toys for his birthday, he doesn't want to share them with the other little monsters. It is his birthday, and he can have fun playing with the toys all by himself, or can he?

Titch and Daisy, by Pat Hutchins. Greenwillow, 1996. Titch goes to a birthday party, but he doesn't want to join the other children in singing, dancing, or even eating. He just wishes his friend Daisy were there. And then he finds her in an unlikely place! The two of them go on to enjoy the party and to make new friends.

My New Sandbox, by Donna Jakob. Hyperion, 1996. A little boy wants his sandbox all to himself, and chases everyone away. But soon it seems lonely in the sandbox and he decides to share it with some playmates.

Rosata, by Holly Keller. Greenwillow, 1995. Camilla finds a hat decorated with velvet flowers and a small bird made out of real feathers. She names the bird Rosata, and it becomes her friend. For a while, she wears the hat everywhere, even to school. And then Teresa moves next door, and Camilla finds that a neighbor, just her age, makes the perfect friend.

Grandma's Cat, by Helen Ketteman. Houghton Mifflin, 1996. In this story in rhyme, a little girl tries to play with her grandma's cat, but is unsuccessful. When she chases and grabs him, the cat hisses and claws. She learns to use gentleness to win him over so that they can become friends.

When This Box Is Full, by Patricia Lillie. Greenwillow, 1993. The box is empty now, but not for long. Every month of the year another wonderful object will be added, until the box is filled with things to share with a friend.

Emma's Magic Winter, by Jean Little. HarperCollins, 1998. Emma is shy about making new friends and about reading aloud in class. But when Sally, who is just her age, moves in next door, the two little girls decide their boots have magic powers. Those boots even make Emma brave enough to read in a loud, clear voice. The two girls have so much fun that winter, that they discover the magic of friendship, which is the best magic of all.

Frog and Toad are Friends, by Arnold Lobel. HarperCollins, 1970. This wonderful collection of stories uses a simple vocabulary for new readers, and tells about a warm friendship between Frog and Toad. There are several sequels.

Frog and Toad Together, by Arnold Lobel. HarperFestival, 1999. These classic stories of two best friends have been reformatted into picture book size. They are just as much fun to read as they were when they were originally published over 25 years ago.

My Friend Chicken, by Adam McCauley. Chronicle, 1999. The little girl in this story misses her friend so much that if rockets roared by and fish flew through the sky, she wouldn't even notice. Where is her good friend chicken and when is he coming back? This imaginative story is accompanied by whimsical illustrations by the author.

George and Martha Round and Round, by James Marshall. Houghton Mifflin, 1988. There are five little stories about the two hippopotamuses, George and Martha. They may disagree, play little jokes on each other, and even feel angry, temporarily, but they always remain special friends. Other books in the series include: *George and Martha Tons of Fun , George and Martha Back in Town,* and others.

When Dinosaurs Go Visiting, by Linda Martin. Chronicle, 1993. What do dinosaurs do when they go visiting? Why, they do just what people do! They dress in their nicest clothes and bring a gift. When they arrive, they look at photo albums, talk, feast, and dance. And before they know it, it's time to say good-bye. A humorous book about a familiar social activity.

One Zillion Valentines, by Frank Modell. Mulberry, 1987. Two boys who want to send Valentines, but have no money, make their own Valentines of every description.

Teamwork, by Ann Morris. Lothrop, 1999. With vibrant color photographs from all over the world, the author shows how people cooperate by working as a team.

The Car Washing Street, by Denise Lewis Patrick. Tambourine, 1993. Every Saturday morning, all the neighbors on Matthew's block wash their cars. One hot summer day, this neighborhood ritual turns into a way for all the people on the block to have some fun and cool off too!

Margaret and Margarita, Margarita y Margaret, by Lynn Reiser. Greenwillow, 1993. In this delightful bilingual book, a warm friendship develops between two little girls in the park, although Margaret speaks only English and Margarita speaks only Spanish.

The Worst Person in the World, by James Stevenson. Mulberry, 1995. The famous author/illustrator tells about a man who lives by himself in a house surrounded by poison ivy. He meets the ugliest creature in the world who tells him that, "If you've got a pleasing personality that's all that counts." The worst person doesn't believe the creature, about that or anything else. His turnabout at the end is completely believable, and is poignant as well as humorous.

A Book of Friends, by Dave Ross. HarperCollins, 1999. A helpful, positive book about the different kinds of friends you can have, where to find friends, what activities you can participate in with friends, and how to be a good friend.

Let's Be Enemies, by J. Udry. HarperCollins, 1961. There are times when even very best friends don't get along. This time the disagreement is humorously and satisfyingly resolved.

Natalie Spitzer's Turtles, by Gina Willner-Pardo. Albert Whitman, 1992. Friendships become slightly complicated in the second grade classroom, when Jess tries mixing old friends and new friends.

Sand Castle, by Brenda Shannon Yee. Greenwillow, 1999. The beach is the perfect place to make friends. As a little girl builds a sand castle, different children come over to help. The castle grows more and more elaborate as each child adds his or her own ideas. As the day ends, the new friends are reluctant to leave their magnificent castle for fear that someone will wreck it, so they joyfully crush the sand structure together and agree to meet again tomorrow.

Section Eight

Caring
and
Consideration
for Others

Section Eight
Caring and Consideration for Others

Introduction

"What wisdom can you find that is greater than kindness?
Jean Jacques Rousseau in *Emile, or Education*

"Shall we make a new rule of life from tonight: always to try to be a little kinder than is necessary?"
James M. Barrie in *The Little White Bird*

"If children live with kindness and consideration, they learn respect."
Dorothy Law Nolte in *Children Learn What They Live.*

Much has been written about having care and consideration for others. The authors in this section discuss how adults can nurture the values of kindness, caring, and politeness in young children.

Even the youngest children often show an impulse to care. As the author of chapter 36 points out, infants may cry sympathetically when they hear other infants crying; toddlers recognize another child's distress at a scraped knee; preschoolers can plan ahead to make a friend's visit more enjoyable.

Another contributor to this section explains that civility is not a list of outmoded rules, but a way of treating people, making the world more pleasant for others and for yourself. Youngsters who have an understanding of the rules of civility feel more comfortable in social situations, when they know what is expected of them as to what to say and how to act.

And finally, children learn table manners from perfect role models like raccoons, hamsters, snakes, and billy goats, when they read the whimsical poem that ends our book.

Chapter

Chapter 36
How Children
Learn to Care

Harriet Heath

To care is to be concerned for another.
Ben was showing concern
for his unhappy brother.

Ben, who was three, looked at his fussing two-month-old brother. Luke wasn't crying loudly but whimpering with his face all contorted and the corners of his mouth turned down. As Ben gazed, his face grew solemn and his eyes lost their sparkle.

"Luke is unhappy, isn't he?" Ben's mother paused and then continued. "It makes us sad to see him that way."

Ben nodded. "Does he want to play with my tractor?" asked Ben, picking up the small toy and holding it in front of Luke. The tiny plastic tractor was one of Ben's favorite toys. The offer was generous.

As Luke focused on the tractor, his whimpering stopped and his eyes brightened. Ben jumped excitedly, "He likes it!" His mother smiled and nodded, "You did it."

To care is to be concerned for another. Ben was showing concern for his unhappy brother. He was trying to right the situation for Luke as he, Ben, would want it handled. There is a sense of joy when caring is successful.

Caring for another is a complex task.
It requires:
1. A willingness to **be involved.** Ben wanted to make his brother happy. But involvement was not enough.

2. Relevant **information.** Ben had some useful information; he needed more. By empathizing with him, Ben knew Luke was unhappy. He didn't know that the tractor might not be appropriate for Luke.

3. **Useful skills.** Ben needed to be able to use the information he had to devise a plan. He needed to observe whether or not his baby brother was seeing the toy.

From his behavior we can deduce that Ben's thinking may have followed these lines: "When I sound and look like that, I am unhappy; therefore, Luke must be unhappy" (empathy). When I am unhappy, I like to have something fun to play with. I like my tractor. Therefore I will make Luke happy with my tractor" (planning).

Caring involves all three components: an attitude of wanting to **be involved,** **information** about the person and situation, and **skills** for devising and implementing a plan.

Learning to Care is an ongoing process.
Infants demonstrate an early step when they cry sympathetically on hearing other infants crying. Crawling infants show another component — wanting to know about the other baby — when their curiosity drives them to wiggle over to another infant. They explore by looking at, touching, grabbing, and licking that other child to see what this creature is who moves, makes sounds and is small.

Eighteen-month-olds, capable of addressing the distress of another, illustrate a more complex form of caring. When Annemarie's best friend painfully scraped her knee, she ran for her friend's favorite blanket. She recognized the distress — thought: what comforts me will comfort my friend and fetched the desired object. Annemarie *wanted to be involved.* She had *information — my friend is in distress; I know what will comfort her.* She also had *skills,* though very elementary: she could walk and she knew where the blanket was.

Preschool children with the help of an adult can implement the process a step further, as when Sam, anticipating the visit of his friend, saw the rain coming down. "Heck, it's raining and I wanted to ride bikes when Tim came."

"Doesn't look like you'll be able to. It's supposed to rain all day." replied his mother. Sam looked dejected.

"What else could you do?" asked mother. After many seconds passed with Sam making no reply, she continued, "You could get out your train tracks. Tim is a great builder."

"No, that's kids' stuff. Tim wouldn't want to do that." A pause ... "But we could ... " — and Sam was busy listing ideas. As he continued he began to identify ones that Tim would enjoy. "He likes jumping on the trampoline."

After the visit, Sam remarked with a pleased smile, "Tim's coming again tomorrow to play on the trampoline."

"You planned well for your friend," responded his mother.

Becoming a caring person is a lifelong process. Parents and caregivers, as illustrated in the preceding vignettes, have many opportunities to help young children acquire the necessary attitudes, information and skills they need to be caring persons.

Ways to Nurture the Impulse to Care

Be your child's role model.
Recognize that as you care for children, you are modeling for them how to be caring persons. Ben was caring for his brother as he understood his parents to be doing. Children imitate care givers. Ben watched his father give his mother a shoulder massage. Intrigued, he wanted to try. Now he will give one on request. It is so easy to look at his massaging as "cute" rather than as the gift of caring that it is, copied from his Dad.

Keep the impulse to care alive.
• Support children's impulse to sympathize. I observed a two year old rub his arm as he watched another child get a shot. It is too easy to laugh rather than support the child's growing empathy by nodding and saying, "You know it hurts to have a shot."

• Be sensitive to children's motivation. Ben's mother made sure he kept a firm hold on the toy as he worked to make his brother happy. She did not reprove Ben for showing to Luke the tiny toy that a baby might choke on. Often a child's efforts to help or play with younger siblings are clumsy and rough. Crawling infants getting to know another infant are too easily perceived as aggressive. They grab the infant as they grab everything else, whole fisted and not too well coordinated. Similarly the three year old trying to incorporate the immobile younger brother into his play moves the child, one third his weight, as we would move a 40 pound bag, roughly and awkwardly. Look at what the caregiving children are attempting, not just at what they are doing.

Expand the child's ability to care (and protect the other child).
• Help children gain more knowledge about the other youngster. Ask them to, "Watch his face," or, "Listen to her words. How do you think the other child is feeling?" Thus the parent can help the child, who is attempting to care, tell if all is well.

• Give the child more information. "This makes a good toy for Luke; it is soft; it is big enough so that he can't choke on it; he can hold it easily." (Such information needs to be given when it will not undermine the child's efforts. It may be during a period of playing together some time after the inappropriate toy was used.)

• Encourage children's ability to empathize. ("He's fussy: he didn't have a nap. Do you think he's tired?" or, "You knew that Tim would like the trampoline better than the train tracks.")

• Figure out with the children more than one way of caring. "Maybe Luke is tired of sitting up and wants to be laid down or put on his tummy."

• Facilitate the children's ability to carry out their ideas. "This is how you can carry him," or, "This is how you can help Luke hold the toy."

• Teach caring through planning by asking questions, as Sam's mother did, such as, "What are different activities you could do?" or, "What does your friend like to do?"

Verbalize the process.
Talk about all components of the caring process as parents throughout these vignettes have done. Hearing about what is occurring helps children master the language, and gives them a tool for further learning about the caring process as well as emotionally supporting their efforts. For example: verbalizing why a child was holding his arm when another child was receiving a shot is supporting a child's ability to empathize. Telling a child to watch another's face teaches observation skills, a major method of gathering information. Asking questions as Sam's mother did, helped him develop planning skills.

Support children's attempts.
Support your youngster's accomplishments as Ben's and Sam's mothers did with their comments. Review the event with your child who can then acknowledge strengths and feel good about what has been accomplished. Children of four and five can also start to plan what they might do differently if the situation arose a second time.

Recognize the potential for caring in a variety of situations.
All kinds of events can provide opportunities to practice caring. Examples here have focused on younger siblings and friends. A visit with an elderly grandparent provides an opportunity as does the family decision to acquire a pet. In each situation family members will be involved. Much information will be needed. What can the elderly grandparent do? What does she enjoy? How can we help her manage the stairs that are difficult, or how should we speak so she can hear?

The challenge is there. If we, who live and work with infants and young children, want them to grow to be caring adults, we must nurture each child's impulse to care. Fortunately, during children's growing years, we have many opportunities to do so.

Author's Note: Though names have been changed all the examples are true. Purposefully, I have drawn predominantly on examples of boys caring. The assumption is too often made that boys are not drawn to caring. These examples illustrate boys too have the impulse to care. All children, boys and girls, need their impulse to care nurtured.

Chapter 37
Teaching Children Civility: Treating Others with Care and Consideration

Amy Houts

*Learning how to be civil
will help preschoolers in typical
social situations, such as
meeting new people,
eating at a restaurant,
going to a birthday party.*

"Could I please have one of your cookies?"

"May I have a turn on the swing?"

"Thank you!"

Hearing these polite phrases is an unexpected delight, rather than a rule. What is desperately needed today is the idea of treating others with care and consideration. At the very least, we need to teach children civility. Civility, as defined by Webster's dictionary is the "bare minimum" of good manners. Being polite takes civility a step further, implying "polished manners and thoughtfulness."

In today's society, there is a lack of good manners. Often people don't seem to care about how they treat others in what they say or do. Mark Leibovich, in his article *Rude Awakening: Is Politeness a Lost Cause?* (*Utne Reader,* Jan.-Feb. 1993 p. 138) states, "It may seem naive to bemoan rudeness when massive problems [of] crime, disease, famine, war confront the planet." Although most of us cannot have an impact on the massive problems that confront the planet — we can try to better our daily lives by being more civil to each other.

Why Teach Children Civility?

Civility is not a list of outdated rules for people to follow. Civility is a way of treating people. Many children need to learn rules that will help them in their everyday life. There are rules in each household, in school, and in society that people need to live by. Learning how to be civil will help preschoolers in typical social situations, such as meeting new people, eating at a restaurant, going to a birthday party. Learning social manners and rules can help youngsters feel more comfortable in these situations — just as adults feel more comfortable in a situation where they know what to say, what to do and how to act.

When a preschooler asks, "May I have a turn on the swing?" not only will he very likely get a turn, he might also make a new friend. When he asks, "Could I please have one of your cookies?" he is taking a risk. The answer could be, "Yes!" or "No!" Good manners involve risks that are worth taking. When they get a cookie or a turn on the swing and respond with a "Thank you," other children will appreciate their attitude — and learn that politeness has its rewards.

Hopefully, teaching your child good manners will go beyond the superficial act of saying or doing the right thing, and also teach the caring attitude that makes manners come naturally. In many cultures all over the world, there is a saying similar to the Golden Rule: *Do unto others as you would have others do unto you.* This simply means, treat other people as you would want to be treated. This is the basis for civility. Good manners makes life more pleasant for everyone involved.

Different settings, different rules

Being civil relates to so many aspects of everyday life: home and family, meals, parties, introductions, invitations, guests. Your preschooler's world consists of home and community. Your youngster learns that different behaviors may apply in different situations. At home your child can help pick up her toys after she plays. At the grocery store, she might help pick up a box of cereal that has fallen off the shelf. At home your toddler might have a special teddy bear she doesn't want to share with anyone. At daycare, all the toys are for sharing.

When at home, your preschooler might talk about the show you are watching on TV, but at the movie theater, she will have to wait until the movie is over, or whisper quietly, so she does not disturb the other people in the theater. When riding in the car, your child should stay seat-belted in her car seat, but on a train, all the seats might be taken, so you might have to stand, or there might be an elderly person who needs the seat more than you do.

Different settings call for different rules. It's a lot to learn. Before you go to a restaurant with your preschooler, you might tell him what to expect. "We all have to sit quietly while we are waiting for our food." "We all have to wait until we are finished eating before getting up from the table." These expectations are very different from what is expected at home, where the food may be on the table when he sits down for supper, and where he may get up and play when he is finished eating.

How children learn civility

Preschoolers learn to be civil in much the same way they learn to do everything: by listening, watching, and modeling their behavior after parents and caregivers. Youngsters need to be treated with respect and good manners by the adults who take care of them.

Children very much want to please the adults they love. But manners do not come naturally. Manners need to be taught. Preschoolers are egocentric. (That is, they have trouble seeing a situation from an other person's viewpoint, or putting themselves in another person's place.) Sometimes it might not feel good to share, or to say "I'm sorry." It's best not to force your preschooler into being polite, because then, while the outward actions will show correct behavior, the heart will be in the wrong place. If there is a special toy belonging to your preschooler and she really is not ready to share it, ask her to help her friend find one of her other toys to play with. If your preschooler is not ready to say "I'm sorry," don't force her. It will embarrass all the people involved. You can say, "I'm sorry" for her.

Young children are naturally curious. They might ask a question in front of someone that is not polite. For example (pointing to an obese person) he might say loudly, "Why is that man so fat?" This situation can be uncomfortable for you. You can apologize on behalf of your preschooler. Children don't always know when they are being rude. "Our job as parents is to teach children acceptable ways of expressing themselves," point out authors Nancy Samalin and Patricia McCormick in *Your Rude Dude.* (*Parent's Magazine* July 1993 pp. 164-168) Youngsters might also say words you don't want them to say, especially in public.

If you treat your preschooler politely, it is more likely he will treat you and other people politely, also. If you knock on his bedroom door before entering, if you don't scold him in front of his friends, if you show others you care about them, most likely he will reflect your good attitude and good manners.

What Prevents Preschoolers from Having Good Manners?

Several factors can prevent a young child from behaving politely. One is not feeling physically well. If she is tired, hungry, or sick, she might not have the energy or be in the right state of mind to use good manners. If your child is going through the stress of having a new sibling, or starting preschool, or the sadness of a friend moving away, or losing a pet, she might not be able to use her best manners. If an adult is not feeling well or is under stress, he may also say or do something impolite.

Ten social skills preschoolers can learn
1. Use the words "Please" and "Thank you"
2. Don't grab
3. Use a quiet voice indoors
4. Share a toy
5. Take turns
6. Greet with a "Hello"
7. Say "Sorry" if you cause an accident
8. Don't tell secrets in front of others
9. Knock before entering a closed room
10. Help others

Ten table manners preschoolers can learn
1. Come to the table with clean hands
2. Chew with mouth closed
3. Wait until everyone is served before you start to eat
4. Don't talk while chewing
5. Don't interrupt when others are talking
6. Ask someone to pass food rather than reaching for it
7. Don't eat noisily
8. Don't stuff your mouth
9. Use a napkin
10. Ask "May I be excused?" when you want to leave the table

Strategies
Judith Martin, author of the Miss Manners Column, who has written extensively about manners, wrote this in her *Guide to Rearing Perfect Children:* "Children instinctively accept the idea of right behavior and wrong behavior. A good parent owes it to a child to teach manners as an interesting and useful skill."

- When teaching manners, try to state the rule in a positive way.

- If your preschooler doesn't say, "Thank you," or "I'm sorry," then you say it for him.

- If your preschooler grabs a toy, ask him to give it back. Put the timer on for 5 minutes and say, "Let's take turns. When the timer goes off it will be your turn."

- If your youngster won't share a special toy, say, "Let's find another toy for Megan." Explain to Megan that this is a special toy Amanda doesn't want to share.

• If your child says a "bad" word in front of others, apologize for her. Say, "We have other words to use."

• If your preschooler describes someone in an uncomplimentary way, apologize for her, explaining that she didn't understand that she was being rude.

• If your preschooler uses a loud voice (shouts), say, "Please use your indoor (quiet) voice."

• If your youngster licks her fingers, say, "Please use your napkin."

• If your child interrupts, say, "I need to finish my sentence."

Chapter 38
Snakes Never
Slurp Their Soup:
A Time
for
Table Manners

A whimsical poem by
Amy Houts
with illustrations by
Susan Eaddy

Cats come washed and ready to dine.
Squirrels sit straight in their chairs.
Walruses wait before they eat
'Til everyone has his fare.

Boars will boast of a hearty buffet.
Pandas pass family style.
Salmon sit quietly while they are served.
Everyone comes with a smile.

Raccoons remember the "magic word."
Muskrats munch very small bites.
Courteous Gnus don't make noise when they chew
And Peacocks don't pick fights.

Lizards don't leap, they stay in their seat.
Swans don't shovel their food.
A Cow coughs politely, and covers her mouth.
Cheetahs share their good mood.

Cougars converse in prose or in verse.
With mice, soft voices are used.
Sea Gulls don't squawk, so others can talk.
Owls ask to be "excused."

Lions are trained not to fuss with their manes.
Monkeys don't play with their tails.
Hippopotamuses keep their tongues in their mouths
And ponies don't chew on their nails.

Hamsters use handkerchiefs, when they are needed.
Billy goats taste new foods.
'Possums will pick up a fork or a spoon
What about you? Will fingers do?

Snakes never ever slurp their soup.
Turkeys don't gobble their grain.
Grizzlies don't chew with their mouths askew
So their parents will never complain

Children come washed and ready to dine.
They've learned to say "Thank you," and, "Please."
They're so very polite;
They make meals a delight
For they never will fight, shout, or tease.

(That's why they're invited to parties and feasts
More often than snakes or those other nice beasts.)

Resources for Section Eight:
Caring and Consideration
for Others

FOR ADULTS

Letitia Baldrige's Complete Guide to the New Manners for the '90s, by Letitia Baldrige. Simon & Schuster, 1990. This practical and down-to-earth book is just what the title implies, a complete guide. Some situations are new to the '90s. One section is specifically about children.

Kids Can Cooperate, by Elizabeth Crary. Parenting Press, 1984. The well-known author of many excellent parenting books discusses how to help younger children develop problem-solving skills.

How to Talk So Kids Will Listen; and Listen So Kids Will Talk, by A. Faber and E. Maxlish. Avon, 1982. The book summarizes all of the recent recommendations on how to talk with your children, including how to respond to children's feelings.

Miss Manners Guide to Raising Perfect Children, by Judith Martin. Galahad Books, 1993. Judith Martin uses her charming wit and wisdom to guide parents in raising children.

Children Learn What They Live: Parenting to Inspire Values, by Dorothy Law Nolte and Rachel Harris. Workman, 1998. The poem by Dorothy Law Nolte, which begins, "If children live with criticism, they learn to condemn..." has been an inspiration to parents and teachers since it was published in 1954. Each of the 49 couplets of the poem becomes the focus of a chapter in this insightful book.

The Kindness of Children, by Vivian Gussin Paley. Harvard University Press, 1999. Paley, the author of *You Can't Say You Can't Play* (Harvard University Press, 1992) states in this new book, "...I've been watching young children most of my life and they are often more kind to each other than unkind. The early instinct to help someone is powerful." She asks us to reflect on the importance of developing kindness and inclusion for all children.

FOR CHILDREN

Communication, by Aliki. Mulberry, 1999. There are so many ways of communicating, with words and without them. The author/illustrator uses lively illustrations and interesting stories to explain about "telling and listening."

Manners, written & illustrated by Aliki. Mulberry, 1997. Through a variety of situations, on the telephone, at mealtime, etc., this paperback illustrates what constitutes good manners.

Say Please, written & illustrated by Virginia Austin. Candlewick Press, 1996. Every animal in this story says, "please" and "thank you" in its own special way. So a little boy named Tom learns to say "please" and "thank you" in his own way, too.

Mandy, by Barbara D. Booth. Lothrop, Lee & Shepard, 1991. Mandy and her Grandma bake cookies and dance together — although Mandy's hearing aid cannot be turned high enough to hear the sounds of the music. On a walk in the woods, Grandma loses the silver pin that had been a gift from Grandpa. Mandy sees how sad Grandma is, so she secretly goes back into the woods to find it.

Will You Take Care of Me? by Margaret Park Bridges. Morrow, 1999. A little kangaroo wants reassurance from his mother that no matter how big he gets, and no matter how he changes, she will still take care of him.

City Green, by Dyanne DiSalvo-Ryan. Morrow, 1994. Marcy and her neighbors transform a vacant city lot into a beautiful community garden in this upbeat, inspiring story. (Includes information about how you can start a garden in your own community.)

Uncle Willie and the Soup Kitchen, by Dyanne DiSalvo-Ryan. Morrow, 1991. "Sometimes people need help," says Uncle Willie, so he works at the soup kitchen with other volunteers. One day the little boy who tells the story accompanies his uncle to the soup kitchen where he helps to prepare the food for the hungry people who come there.

Beautiful, by Gregg Fowler. Greenwillow, 1998. Uncle George makes magic with his gardens. He teaches his young nephew his secrets so that the boy can have his own garden, while Uncle George goes away to the hospital. When he comes home he is getting sicker. His young nephew can't wait for the flowers to bloom, and as soon as they do, he brings Uncle George the glorious flowers to make him smile.

Mary Had a Little Lamb, by Sarah J. Hale. Scholastic, 1992. Colorful photographs by Bruce McMillan illustrate the nursery rhyme, ending with the lines, "Why does the lamb love Mary so?"/The eager children cry./Why, Mary loves the lamb you know,"/The teacher did reply."

Jamaica's Find, by Juanita Havill. Houghton Mifflin, 1986. A little girl, Jamaica, brings home a stuffed dog she found when playing in the park. As she thinks about the child who lost it, Jamaica decides to bring the dog to the Lost and Found. The next day a little girl in the park is looking for the stuffed dog and Jamaica happily reunites her with her lost toy.

Jamaica Tag-Along, by Juanita Havill. Houghton Mifflin, 1989. Jamaica's big brother Ossie wants to play basketball and doesn't want his little sister tagging along. Sadly, Jamaica goes to the sandlot to build a castle. There a toddler wants to help her build, but she tells him to stay away. The toddler's mother explains, "Big kids don't like to be bothered by little kids." Jamaica realizes how much it hurts <u>her</u> feelings when Ossie says that, and she lets the little one help after all.

Pinky and Rex and the Mean Old Witch, by J. Howe. Atheneum, 1991. Pinky, Rex, and Amanda are playing ball in Rex's yard, when the ball falls by accident onto Mrs. Morgan's property next door. She comes after them with a broom when they try to retrieve it, and they call her a mean old witch. But when Pinky looks through the window and sees her sitting alone in the dark on a sunny day, he feels sorry for her and instead brings her some cookies he had baked.

Lewis & Papa, by Barbara M. Joosse. Chronicle, 1998. Lewis feels like a grownup because Papa wants to take him along on the Santa Fe Trail with a wagon loaded with goods to sell. It is an exciting and difficult trip, and they have many adventures together. They also learn of their love and support for each other. The evocative pictures are by Jon Van Zyle.

What Do You Say, Dear? What Do You Do, Dear? by Sesyle Joslin, illustrated by Maurice Sendak. HarperCollins, 1958. These two longtime favorites send their positive messages about manners with a comical sense of humor.

Love Can Build a Bridge, by Naomi Judd. HarperCollins, 1999. With lovely paintings by Suzanne Duranceau of a variety of children helping and caring about each other, this book offers a philosophy about kindness so needed in today's world. An audiocassette of the song of the same name, performed by the Judds, is included.

Island Baby, by Holly Keller. Mulberry Books edition, 1995. This moving story about growing up and becoming independent is set in the Caribbean. Simon loves taking care of injured birds at Pop's hospital. He has a special friendship for the baby flamingo with a broken leg which he calls Baby. By the end of summer, Baby's leg is healed and Simon hears Pops saying the words that the little boy had been dreading, "I think it's about time to set Baby free." Simon will miss Baby but he lets him go, feeling proud that his Baby will be flying on its own.

Best Friend, by Loretta Krupinski. Hyperion, 1998. Readers will be touched by this tender story of Charlotte, whose family moves west, and her friend, Lily, of the Nez Perce Indian tribe. Charlotte devises a plan to save the tribe from the soldiers, and uses her favorite doll to deliver the message.

The Palace of Stars, by Patricia Lakin. Tambourine Books, 1993. Amanda loves her Saturday outings at the zoo with her Great-uncle Max. To reciprocate, Amanda saves her money and takes Uncle Max to a Saturday matinee at the movies — a magical palace of the stars.

Pookins Gets Her Way, by Helen Lester. Houghton Mifflin, 1987. Pookins wants everything her way, until she learns about cooperation.

Rosie and the Poor Rabbits, by Maryann MacDonald. Atheneum, 1994. Rosie, the little girl rabbit, learns from her mother that some children don't have nice clothing and toys. Her mother suggests that Rosie might give some of her things to a poor family. The little girl rabbit struggles a bit with her feelings but finally she makes positive decisions about parting with some of her clothing and toys.

Who's Going to Take Care of Me? by M. Magorian. HarperCollins, 1990. When Eric went to day care with his big sister Karin, she taught him the words to the songs they sang, and let him sit near her at story time. But now she is going to school and Eric feels small and wonders, "Who's going to take care of me?" At the day care center without Karin, Eric plays with his friends until he notices a new little boy looking scared. So Eric teaches him the words to the songs and lets him sit by him at story time, and finds that he feels big when caring for somebody else.

Lost! by David McPhail. Little, Brown, 1990. A little boy is confident that he can help in this gentle tale of a boy who finds a lost bear, and reassuringly assists him to find his way home.

Tree of Birds, by Susan Meddaugh. Houghton Mifflin, 1990. A boy named Harry rescues a wounded Green Tufted Tropical bird and takes care of her. The tree outside his window is soon filled with Green Tufted Tropicals, friends of the wounded bird, who won't leave without her. With snow on the way, Harry worries that they won't survive the winter. In a surprise ending, he finds a solution.

One Hungry Monster: A Counting Book in Rhyme, by Susan H. O'Keefe. Little, Brown, 1992. One by one, hungry monsters, with atrocious table manners, arrive as uninvited guests to a little boy's house.

Mind Your Manners, by Peggy Parish. Mulberry, 1994. This *Read-Alone book* explains manners with short chapters, in basic language children can understand.

Monster Manners, by Bethany Roberts. Clarion, 1996. It seems that monsters know about good manners, and, while sometimes they forget to use them, at other times they display them beautifully (just like some youngsters you may know).

Lizard's Home, by George Shannon. Greenwillow, 1999. Lizard loves his home on a sun-warmed rock. But snake has moved onto the rock, and won't move. Snake is bigger, but lizard is more clever, and wins back his home in a fair contest! The colorful illustrations by Jose Aruego add to the fun.

What's Polite? by Harriet Ziefert, illustrated by Richard Brown. Puffin, 1995. This lift-the-flap book tells about Scooter's trip to a restaurant, and what manners he should use while he is there.

Big Sister and Little Sister, by Charlotte Zolotow. HarperTrophy, 1990. Big sister always took care of little sister: she held her hand when she crossed the street, kept her from getting lost, and put her arm around her when she cried. But one day little sister gets tired of big sister telling her, "Go there," or, "Do it this way." So she runs off by herself and doesn't answer when big sister calls her, although she's right nearby. Now it's big sister's turn to cry, and little sister's turn to comfort her. "And from that day on, little sister and big sister both took care of each other..."

I Know a Lady, by Charlotte Zolotow. Mulberry, 1992. A little girl tells lovingly about a lady in her neighborhood who bakes cookies for the children, gives them flowers from her garden, and even knows their names.

About the Contributors

Lawrence Balter, Ph.D., is an internationally known child development expert. He is author of three best-selling books on child rearing, and of numerous children's books. Dr. Balter is also a feature reporter on WCBS-TV Television News, and a columnist and contributing editor for *Family Circle* and *Sesame Street Parents.*

Elizabeth Crary is a parent educator, speaker, and author of over twenty-six books, among them: *Without Spanking or Spoiling; Love and Limits;* and *Pick Up Your Socks.*

Janet Dengel is the mother of three children, Linda, John, and Paul. She is a free-lance writer and editor of KIDS Magazine in Westwood NJ.

Pegine Echevarria, M.S.W., is a national motivational expert speaker and author on personal and professional development. She has appeared on MSNBC, CNN, and other TV shows. Her best seller, *For All Our Daughters: How Mentoring Helps Young Women and Girls Master the Art of Growing Up,* has been in the Amazon.com top 100 bestsellers. She makes presentations to corporations, educational groups, and associations.

Susan Eaddy (illustrations) has worked as an art director in book publishing for 8 years and is currently the art director for RCA Records in Nashville. Her portfolio includes illustrations for more than 80 books as well as magazines, CD covers, greeting cards, and newsletters. She has won international awards for her cut paper design and works in a variety of media. She is especially proud that she has been the illustrator for *Parent and preschooler Newsletter* since its inception in 1985.

Warren & Fay Eckstein wrote many books together about pets and animals. Warren has also appeared on national radio and TV, and has been written up in many publications, including *People Magazine, Cosmopolitan,* and *Woman's Day.*

Betty Farber, M.Ed., is President of Preschool Publications, Inc. She was the Editor and Publisher of *Parent and preschooler Newsletter* for 11 years, and edited *The Parents' & Teachers' Guide to Helping Young Children Learn,*(Preschool Publications, Inc., 1997) and *Guiding Young Children's Behavior,* (Preschool Publications, Inc., 1999) . She directed early childhood programs in St. Louis and Memphis and was Instructor and Early Childhood Coordinator at LaGuardia Community College of the City University of NY.

Lester Feldman (cover design) has spent his professional life as an Art Director for a NYC/international advertising agency where he created many ad campaigns during his almost 40 years there. A dozen of his TV commercials are in the Museum of Modern Art collection of "classics," and he's won the gold and the silver medals from the Ad Club of New York.

Ruth Formanek, Ph.D., is Professor Emerita, Hofstra University, and co-author (with Anita Gurian) of *The Socially Competent Child: A Parent's Guide to Social Development — from Infancy to Early Adolescence,* and *WHY? Children's Questions: What They Mean & How to Answer Them.*

Anita Gurian, Ph.D., is Clinical Assistant Professor, Division of Child & Adolescent Psychiatry, New York University School of Medicine. She is also Executive Editor of The Child Study Center website: www. AboutOurKids.org and Associate Editor of the *NYU Child Study Center Letter.*

Fredric C. Hartman, Ph.D., is in full-time private practice in Mineola, NY, specializing in loss and bereavement throughout the life span.

Harriet Heath, Ph.D., Director of the Parent Center, Thorne School • Child Study Institute, Bryn Mawr College, PA, is a licensed developmental psychologist, educator and researcher. She is the author of a parents' manual, *Parents Planning,* a decision-making approach to parenting, and a curriculum for school-aged children, *Learning How to Care: Education for Parenting.* Her newest book is entitled: *Using Your Values to Raise Your Child to Be an Adult You Admire.*

Amy Houts has a background in Library Science and Child Care Administration. She has worked as a preschool teacher and children's librarian, and is currently a reporter for the *Nodaway News Leader* in Nodaway County, Missouri. She wrote the "Preschooler in the Kitchen" column for *Parent and preschooler Newsletter* for over 12 years. She authored a cook book, *Learning Through Cooking Activities* (Preschool Publications, 1993) as well as several picture books. Her latest book is a retelling of *The Princess and the Pea.*

Lee Jackson's background is in home economics. She has written books relating to this field, and a series of cookbooks. Her latest, *Apples, Apples Everywhere: Favorite Recipes from America's Orchards,* Images Unlimited Publishing, 1996

Katrina Katsarelis is a writer and mother of two young children. She writes a column for *Bay Area Parent* and *Valley Parent Magazines* in Northern California.

Elizabeth Kuhlman, M.A., M.S., is an Early Childhood Special Education Consultant.

Stephanie Marston is an educator, speaker, and author of several books including: *The Magic of Encouragement: Nurturing Your Child's Self-esteem,* and *The Divorced Parent: Success Strategies for Raising Happy Children After Separation.*

Michael K. Meyerhoff, Ed.D., a former researcher with the Harvard Preschool Project, is executive director of The Epicenter Inc., "The Education for Parenthood Information Center," a family advisory and advocacy agency located in Lindenhurst, Illinois.

Rae Pica is an adjunct professor with the University of New Hampshire, and is the author of 12 books including the text, *Experiences in Movement,* and the recently-released, *Moving and Learning Across the Curriculum.* She is nationally known for her workshops and presentations, and has shared her expertise with Children's Television Workshop, the Head Start Bureau, Childrens's World Learning Centers, and Nickelodeon's *Blue's Clues.*

Kyle D. Pruett, M.D., Clinical Professor of Psychiatry, Yale University Child Study Center, is the author of *The Nurturing Father.* His latest book is, *Me, Myself and I: How Children Build Their Sense of Self.*

Michael Searson holds a Ph.D. in cognitive psychology from Rutgers University. He is a Professor in the Department of Early Childhood & Family Studies at Kean University in Union, NJ.

Neala S. Schwartzberg has a Ph.D. in Developmental Psychology and has written extensively on children and parenting. Her articles have appeared nationwide and have been reprinted in many anthologies. She is a regular contributor to several publications on health related topics. Dr. Schwartzberg has been the editor of *Parent and preschooler Newsletter* since January, 1997.

Paulette Bochnig Sharkey, M.L.S., has been a freelance writer and librarian, and is currently the Developmental Editor for Ellyn Satter Associates.

Bette Simons, M.S., writes about preschool children and the adults that care for them based on her experiences as a training teacher in the Preschool Laboratory of California State University, at Northridge, as well as in her own child care center, First Step Nursery School in Woodland Hills, CA. She currently edits and writes for her school's web site: www.1stStep.com

Warren Speilberg, Ph.D., is an instructor in the Psychology Department of the New School for Social Research in New York City. He is a co-author of a forthcoming book about the problems of boys.

Louise M. Ward was Associate Professor Emeritus at the University of Memphis. She contributed articles and book chapters in her field, and was the co-author of *Teacher/Parent Communication: Working Toward Better Understanding,* (Preschool Publications, 1992.)

Elizabeth J. Webster, Ph.D., was Professor Emeritus, University of Memphis. Dr. Webster was the author of many books and articles on counseling parents, and the co-author of *Teacher/Parent Communication: Working Toward Better Understanding,* (Preschool Publications, 1992.)

NOTES

NOTES